"If you are looking for a stud[...]nt heroes of the faith for us to [...] be overwhelmed by God's faithful grace in the [...]ges and the difficult personal circumstances of Naomi and Ruth, you will find much to treasure in this book."

—**Iain M. Duguid,** Author, *Esther & Ruth* (Reformed Expository Commentary) and *Is Jesus in the Old Testament?*

"Sarah Ivill has done a masterful job of unpacking the message and meaning of Judges and Ruth. As voices today define freedom as 'every man doing what is right in his own eyes,' Sarah reveals God's words of warning and hope found in these books. Her examination of the text is thorough, and the study questions will deepen your understanding of the Word of God. In examining this dark time in the history of God's people, Sarah maintains a focus on the redemptive story woven through the biblical text. At the end, you, like Sarah, will be overwhelmed with God's grace."

—**Stephen T. Estock,** PCA Committee Coordinator on Christian Education and Publications (CEP)

"Sarah Ivill connects Ruth to Judges, allowing each book to enrich the other, and connects both of those books to the broad scope of redemptive history. She links individual texts to an abundance of scriptural passages and to systematic theology, always pointing to Christ. And she pairs Ancient Near Eastern backgrounds with plenty of contemporary application. A helpful resource for anyone studying Judges or Ruth or leading a study on them."

—**Elizabeth Groves,** Lecturer in Old Testament, Westminster Theological Seminary

"With careful scholarship and sound exegesis, Sarah Ivill takes readers into the difficult realities of the book of Judges and the beautiful redemption of the book of Ruth so that they come away with a deeper understanding of, and a greater longing for, our great Judge and Redeemer, Jesus Christ."

—**Nancy Guthrie,** Author, Seeing Jesus in the Old Testament Bible study series

Judges & Ruth

ALSO IN THE TAPESTRY SERIES

1 & 2 Samuel, Kay Gabrysch

Revelation, Sarah Ivill

Judges & Ruth

THERE IS A REDEEMER

SARAH IVILL

P&R PUBLISHING

P.O. BOX 817 • PHILLIPSBURG • NEW JERSEY 08865-0817

ISBN: 978-1-59638-838-3 (pbk.)
ISBN: 978-1-59638-839-0 (ePub)
ISBN: 978-1-59638-840-6 (Mobi)

Printed in the United States of America

Library of Congress Cataloging-in-Publication Data

Ivill, Sarah.
  Judges & Ruth : there is a redeemer / Sarah Ivill. -- 1st ed.
     pages cm
  Includes bibliographical references.
  ISBN 978-1-59638-838-3 (pbk.)
  1. Bible. Judges--Textbooks. 2. Bible. Ruth--Textbooks. I. Title. II. Title: Judges and Ruth.
  BS1305.55.I95 2013
  222'.306--dc23
                        2013024007

To my kinsman-redeemer, Jesus Christ,
under whose wings I have come to take refuge.
Ruth 2:12

Contents

Foreword   ix

Acknowledgments   xi

A Personal Note from Sarah   xiii

Lesson 1: Introduction to Judges   1

Lesson 2: Judges 1:1–2:5   19

Lesson 3: Judges 2:6–3:6   33

Lesson 4: Judges 3:7–31   45

Lesson 5: Judges 4:1–5:31   61

Lesson 6: Judges 6:1–40   77

Lesson 7: Judges 7:1–8:32   93

Lesson 8: Judges 8:33–9:57   111

Lesson 9: Judges 10:1–12:15   125

Lesson 10: Judges 13–14   145

Lesson 11: Judges 15–16   165

Lesson 12: Judges 17–18   181

Lesson 13: Judges 19–21   199

Lesson 14: Introduction to Ruth   215

Lesson 15: Ruth 1   229

CONTENTS

Lesson 16: Ruth 2   247

Lesson 17: Ruth 3   267

Lesson 18: Ruth 4   281

Question Paradigm for Judges and Ruth   301

Poem: Redeeming Love   303

Bibliography   305

Foreword

EVERYONE HAS A STORY TO TELL, for each life is a story worth telling. All of life is built around stories. We read them in novels. We watch them on the cinema screen. We tell them to one another as a vital part of everyday conversation. We memorize them as part of our cultural DNA.

When a story involves one person, we call it a *biography*. When millions of biographies are meshed together, they tell the story of a people, a nation, or a society. This we call *history*. And the overarching story to both biography and history is the *metanarrative* (a great story) of God himself. It is interesting to note that our word "history" comes from a reference to God, for our history is really *his story*. The Germans call this *Gotts spiel* (God's play or God's story), which became *godspell* in Old English and *gospel* today.

The gospel is God's story that arches over each of our biographies and all our grand histories. The books of Judges and Ruth are great stories, impregnated with the story of God. Sarah Ivill has, once again, brought to life and to light this "God story" in the pages of two rather neglected Old Testament books: Judges and Ruth.

She will call the book of Judges *The Gospel According to Judges* and also *God's Grace According to Judges*. She is correct. I might also humbly add that the book of Ruth is *God's Story in a Young Woman's Life*. Judges is painful history to read. But, as Sarah points out, amidst all its sin, rebellion, human failure, cycles of frustration, and human atrocities—the book can be brutal—the story of God's faithfulness and forgiveness overrides the history of Israel's apostasy. What God does for Israel, the Holy Spirit does for other people, throughout human history.

Ruth is a story. In fact, the literary genre constitutes a short story: a novel about a broken family, a broken old woman, and two broken hearts. But it is also a story about Jesus Christ, for he appears in the form of a noble, humble, and gracious man who becomes a *kinsman redeemer* for two helpless women. Boaz, that noble rescuer, is a type of Christ. What he does for Naomi and Ruth, Jesus does for us.

It is easy (and, I think, very appropriate) to "locate" yourself in the story of Ruth and your people or nation in the history of the judges. Although these people and this one family lived so very long ago, they are truly not so very different from you and me. Ours is a nation in distress. America is a people in decline, and our personal and family lives contain the same vortex of pain that we find in the family of Naomi, Ruth, and Boaz.

Out of these painful stories—Israel's history and Ruth's biographical sketch—comes a most marvelous thing: the Redeemer. For Jesus Christ and his people, his family, and his story are traced through Boaz and Ruth, back through the judges and forward to us and our times.

Sarah Ivill will bring all this to life and light in this delightful and insightful Bible study by the title *There Is a Redeemer.* Sarah's persistent and pervasive focus on Jesus our Redeemer, who is very much a part of Israel's history and Ruth's story, is the refreshing note in this study. As Sarah's pastor and friend, I am happy to commend both this study and this teacher to you. For Sarah Ivill's story is one of the Redeemer and the "God story" he brings to our broken lives.

At the end of this study you will know better and hopefully love more deeply this Redeemer, Jesus Christ. He is the central man of all history; he is our kinsman—a man among humanity; and our Redeemer— the Savior of us all. And he's waiting to change your story with God's story. Enjoy your study, and thanks, Sarah Ivill!

Michael F. Ross
Senior Pastor, Christ Covenant Church
Matthews, North Carolina

Acknowledgments

I WISH TO THANK those in my life who have been a part of this writing process.

Thank you to P&R Publishing's Amanda Martin, Brad Koenig, and Julia Craig for their editorial work. My thanks as well to P&R's Dawn Premako, who designed the cover and typeset this book.

Thank you to Dr. Iain Duguid for his careful reading of the manuscript, his gracious and encouraging response, and his many helpful suggestions to improve the study.

Thank you to the pastors, especially Dr. Ross for writing the foreword, and the women of Christ Covenant Church (PCA), who have been a part of this process and who have encouraged me to keep writing Bible studies for women.

Thank you to the men and women of Dallas Theological Seminary who taught me what it means to be a gracious student of Scripture and who instilled in me the importance of expository teaching and the love of God's Word.

Thank you to Westminster Theological Seminary and the professors who have served there. The many books that have been written and recommended by the professors, as well as the many online class lectures and chapel messages, have been of tremendous benefit to me. They have taught me what it means to see Christ in all Scripture and to understand more deeply the history of redemption and the beautiful truths of Reformed theology.

Thank you to my many dear friends (you know who you are!) who prayed for me and encouraged me to make the dream of writing a reality.

Thank you to my mom and dad, who have always supported me in my love of the Word and encouraged me to do that which the Lord has called me to do. I love you both more than words can express.

Thank you to my husband, Charles, who has always given me his love, support, and encouragement in the writing process and in what the Lord has called me to do.

And thank you to my children, Caleb, Hannah, and Daniel, whose sweet smiles, loving hugs, prayers for "Mom's Bible studies," and patience as I "finish another thought" before tending to one of their many needs are a constant source of encouragement to me as I pray for the next generation of believers to love the Lord and his Word with all their hearts and minds.

Finally, thank you to my heavenly Father, to my Lord and Savior Jesus Christ, and to the Spirit, who helps me in my weakness. To the triune God be the glory for what he has done through me, a broken vessel and a flawed instrument, yet one that is in the grip of his mighty and gracious hand.

A Personal Note from Sarah

WHAT DO YOU THINK OF when you hear the book of Judges mentioned? If you were raised in church, perhaps you remember the stories of Deborah and Barak, Gideon's fleece, and Samson's victory over the Philistines. Maybe the story ended with an exhortation, "Be like Samson!" Or maybe you started the book of Judges and never made it through because it seemed like lots of blood and gore and sexual escapades. Maybe you skip most of the book when you're teaching your children the Word of God because you are not sure the content is appropriate or you are not sure how to explain it. Perhaps the name Judges brings judgment to your mind, and you see the book as one of doom and gloom. Whatever the case may be, I want to propose that Judges is one of the books of the Bible where we see our need for a Savior the most and where we see God's grace shining the brightest. It is a book about needing a true Savior, a true Priest, and a true King. It is a book about the gospel, the gospel according to Judges. And when we are done studying the book, we will have a much deeper knowledge of the depravity of humanity and a much richer appreciation for our Lord and Savior Jesus Christ, who took all our sin and our shame on himself on the cross, having the full wrath of God poured out on him, in our place. He has taken our sin and our shame and given us his righteousness. Martin Luther called it a "wonderful exchange."

> This is that mystery which is rich in divine grace to sinners, wherein by a wonderful exchange our sins are no longer ours but Christ's, and

the righteousness of Christ is not Christ's but ours. He has emptied himself of his righteousness that he might clothe us with it, and fill us with it; and he has taken our evils upon himself that he might deliver us from them.[1]

The book of Ruth shines like a diamond in the rough. Set against the dark ages of the judges, it shines brightly the light of Jesus Christ. It beautifully reminds us that God has not forgotten his promises to Abraham of land, seed, and most importantly, the blessing of all nations of the earth through his chosen family. The book of Ruth is about God's plan of redemption in his Son, Jesus Christ. But it is displayed through the lives of women like you and like me. Women who are wrought with pain, who have needs, who have desires, who struggle with faith and running ahead of God's timing, and yet who teach us what it means to live a life of faith, clinging to the promises of God and embodying his *hesed*, his covenantal lovingkindness. The book of Ruth teaches us that there is a Redeemer, Jesus Christ, who has preserved the name of those who belong to God's family and has bought back our inheritance. Let us give "thanks to the Father, who has qualified [us] to share in the inheritance of the saints in light. He has delivered us from the domain of darkness and transferred us to the kingdom of his beloved Son, in whom we have redemption, the forgiveness of sins" (Col. 1:12–14).

My love for teaching the Word of God was inspired by my own hunger to study it. Longing for the "meat" of God's Word and finding it lacking in so many churches today, I enrolled in Bible Study Fellowship after graduating from high school. It was there that I shared my desire to attend seminary and was influenced and encouraged by a strong, godly woman and mentor in my life to attend Dallas Theological Seminary. During this time I was leading women through in-depth Bible studies and caught a glimpse of how much women desired to be fed the depth of God's Word. This encouraged me even further to receive an educa-

---

1. Martin Luther, *Werke*, ed. J. F. K. Knaake et al., vol. 5, *Psalmenvorlesungen 1519–21 (Ps. 1–22)* (Weimar, 1892), 608; quoted in J. I. Packer, "Sola Fide: The Reformed Doctrine of Justification," *Ligonier Ministries*, accessed June 20, 2013, http://www.ligonier.org/learn/articles/sola-fide-the-reformed-doctrine-of-justification/.

tion that would best prepare me to deliver God's Word to women who hungered for the truth.

On graduating with my Master of Theology, I took a position as assistant director of women's ministry at a large church where I served under a woman who shared my same passion to teach the "meat" of God's Word. Within the year, I had assumed the role of director and delved into teaching the Word of God in an expository and applicable manner. After three years I resigned in order to stay home with my first child, Caleb Joshua. During these years at home the Lord used my experience in seminary and ministry to lead me back to my roots and the full embracing of the Reformed faith. Raised for the first half of my childhood in conservative Presbyterian churches, I had been grounded in the Reformed faith and Reformed catechism from an early age. But from middle school on I was not in Reformed churches. The questions in my twenties then became "Who am I?" and "What do I really believe?"

One of the first steps on my journey was contacting a Reformed seminary and asking them to give me a book list of everything I would have missed by not attending a Reformed seminary. That began my journey of reading some of the most renowned Reformed theologians in the world. It was during those days that the question, "Who am I?" was finally answered, and I began teaching women from the historic Reformed tradition. In fact, that is how my first Bible study came to be published. I had the incredible privilege of teaching my first study to a wonderful group of women for a morning Bible study at our PCA church. And it was from their encouragement and exhortation that I submitted it for publication.

I know it is difficult to pick up a Bible study written by another author and teach or study it. It is for this reason that I offer you the following suggestions as you prepare to teach or study *Judges and Ruth: There Is a Redeemer*. It is my practice that before I ever begin to study a book of the Bible I sit down to read it several times first as if I were reading a letter from a personal friend through for the first time. It is enjoyable reading to get a feel for the "big picture" of the book and how it fits into the rest of the books of Scripture. Then with my own pen, paper, and Bible I divide each chapter (or sometimes half a chapter or two halves from two different chapters) into my own divisions.

Next I try to grasp what the divisions are saying in a nutshell and write that down. From that point I move to writing application questions appropriate for each division, at least one if not several for each division. This gives me "ownership" of the passage. Before going to read what anyone else has to say, I have studied it by myself and allowed the Holy Spirit to speak to my own heart about it. This adds "uniqueness" to your teaching or studying. You don't want to regurgitate what someone else has said. You want to make it your own.

Following this, though, it is important then to study what others have learned from the book. So I try to have at least three good, solid Reformed commentaries for the book I am studying as well as other study tools such as a Bible dictionary, concordance, and an Old Testament or New Testament theology. One of my favorite tools for this study was *Judges: Such a Great Salvation* by Dale Ralph Davis. As I studied the commentaries chapter by chapter, I would highlight what I felt was important for the women to know in this study. Then I would begin writing the lesson notes, using my own outlines and notes, as well as what I had learned from others.

The final step was writing the questions for the women to answer. The study is organized so that the women will read and work on the questions for the passage that will be covered in teaching the following week. This gives the women the opportunity to "own" it for themselves before they ever hear the teaching.

If at any point of the study you grow weary or overwhelmed, I want to encourage you to press on until the very end. As you read, let your heart and mind go where the Word of God takes you, to the depth of sin and judgment and to the heights of grace and salvation. On every page keep your eyes on Jesus, the One to whom all Scripture points, and worship him for the work of salvation that he has accomplished for you through the power of the Holy Spirit, to the glory of God the Father.

Soli Deo Gloria

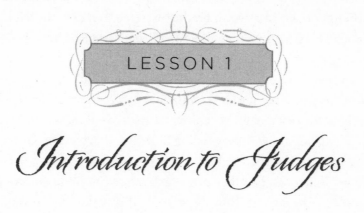

Introduction to Judges

AT THE BEGINNING of every lesson we will identify the aim of the lesson concerning our:

- *Mind*: What do we need to know from this passage in Scripture?
- *Heart*: How does what we learn from this passage affect our internal relationship with the Lord?
- *Hands*: How does what we learn from this passage translate into action for God's kingdom?

INTRODUCTION

Laurie[1] stared down at her hands. Her fingers twitched nervously. She felt sick inside. Her leg bounced up and down from nervous energy. Her whole body felt like it had been run over by a truck. She was seated in a clinic's waiting room to have her follow-up exam from the abortion she had a couple weeks earlier. No one had told her how bad it was going to be. Not one nurse had told her how sick the abortion pill was going to make her. But she had spent days in agonizing physical pain, not to mention the emotional and spiritual pain on top of it. She couldn't bear to look at a mother with her baby. She had once heard a pastor say that

---

1. Laurie represents a number of women who are sitting in our churches today, hurting from the past shame of having an abortion.

women who had abortions were murdering their babies. At the time she had thought that offensive and rather extreme. But now she felt like she had committed a crime that could never be washed away.

Twenty years later . . .

Laurie stared down at her hands again. The Bible study leader was talking about how often women with dark pasts carry that shame around with them for years, never accepting Christ's forgiveness or sacrifice on their behalf, but instead always living in guilt and depression. Tears stung Laurie's eyes as she tried to keep the waterfall from coming before she could get to her car. But they came faster than she could control them. A couple of the women from her small group asked if she wanted to stay after and talk, but Laurie declined. How could she tell these sweet women who seemed to come from such pure backgrounds about her past? She just knew that they would judge her for the abortion, even if they pretended differently. So Laurie left that day without divulging her secret, stuffing it inside for it to erupt another day.

Perhaps you can relate to Laurie. Perhaps you have a dark past and are carrying around shame from years ago, never embracing Jesus' work on the cross for you, always living under guilt and shame. Maybe you remember the night that you lost your virginity to a boyfriend. Perhaps you remember all the times you were bent over a toilet making yourself throw up because you were ensnared in bulimia or the times you starved your body because you were trapped in anorexia. Maybe you remember the smell of the abortion clinic and the physical, emotional, and spiritual pain it brought and still brings. Perhaps you flirted with lesbianism in college and you still carry guilt around about it. Maybe your dad or uncle or brother, men that you thought you could trust, sexually or physically abused you when you were younger and you've never told anyone in order to keep your family's reputation "pure." Perhaps you were addicted to drugs or alcohol in high school and you have faced infertility issues because of it and feel like you've ruined your dreams of motherhood because of poor choices. Maybe your disrespect that you showed your mother in high school and college still forms a breach in your relationship with her today. Perhaps you have "killed" your husband and children with words, looks, or actions that you have done against them. Maybe you are enslaved to gossip or perhaps you are always looking at what other women have and wanting it.

If you can relate to any of the things in the previous paragraph, then you will relate to the tribal leaders[2] in the book of Judges. And if you can relate to the tribal leaders in Israel, which we all can, then you will be overwhelmed with God's grace as you move through the book. Go ahead and read that again. *You will be overwhelmed with God's grace as you move through the book.* That's right. I know the book records many of the faults and failures of the tribal leaders, and it is true that we will see God's judgment of man's sin in the book—we really wouldn't want it any other way. God is a God of justice and that is a good thing. But it is also true that God's grace shines in the book, and I would say that his grace shines far brighter. God loves his people. He is committed to their preservation. He knows we are sinners and have gone astray. His wrath is turned toward us. And he cannot dismiss our sin. But he has poured it out on his Son instead. The gospel is this: God the Father sent his Son into the world to seek and to save the lost. Jesus Christ lived a life of perfect obedience on our behalf. He died on the cross in our place, exchanging our sin for his righteousness. He was raised by the power of God and ascended to the right hand of God the Father where he was crowned with glory and honor and is now our King and High Priest, ruling over the affairs of this world and interceding on our behalf. And he is coming again to save those who are eagerly waiting for him and to make all things new. Now that is good news! And we will see this gospel, although in a less clear way than we see it in the New Testament, in the book of Judges. In fact, we could call this study *The Gospel According to Judges*.

We could also call it *God's Grace According to Judges*. After reading through the book of Judges, make sure you turn to the book of Hebrews and read what God has to say about these men. In one of the greatest chapters on faith in the Bible, some of these weak-willed, idolatrous, personal revenge taking, reluctant to obey God's call, rash

2. The Hebrew words used to describe the judges give us meanings such as "deliverers" or "saviors" or those who "rule, govern, exercise leadership." See Daniel I. Block, *The New American Commentary*, vol. 6, *Judges, Ruth* (Nashville: Broadman & Holman, 1999), 23–24.

vow making, self-serving, sexually immoral tribal leaders are listed as men of faith. And do you know what is written down? Not one of their failures! Instead we read,

> For time would fail me to tell of Gideon, Barak, Samson, Jephthah . . . who through faith conquered kingdoms, enforced justice, obtained promises, stopped the mouths of lions, quenched the power of fire, escaped the edge of the sword, were made strong out of weakness, became mighty in war, put foreign armies to flight. (Heb. 11:32–34)

Now that is what I call grace, God's grace, grace that is greater than all our sin! And don't think that God's record is any different for you. If you know Jesus Christ as your Lord and Savior, there are no marks against you. None of your sins are written down either. The blood of the Lamb has washed them away forever. You stand before the Judge of the universe "not guilty."

AN OVERVIEW OF THE HISTORY OF REDEMPTION AND REVELATION

The history of God's works is never divorced from the history of his Word that interprets those works. It does not take us very long to discover that the Bible does not read as a history textbook, but rather as an account of God's works to redeem his chosen people and God's works to rule his chosen people, often summed up in four words—*creation, fall, redemption,* and *restoration.* Revelation is progressive. As we move through God's Word, we see that God unfolds his plan of redemption over different periods of history. Although some scholars do not begin the history of redemption until Abraham, I think that Genesis 3, the place where we see the curse on the covenant of works/creation[3] simultaneously with the inauguration of the covenant of grace, is the most appropriate

3. The Westminster Confession of Faith uses the phrase "covenant of works," but to avoid confusion I have used both terms together, especially since I am indebted to O. Palmer Robertson's descriptions of the covenants throughout this overview (i.e., the "covenant of preservation" with Noah, the "covenant of promise" with Abraham, the "covenant of law" with Moses, and the "covenant of the kingdom" with David. For a fuller and excellent explanation of these covenants, see

place to start. The gospel is given in seed form, as God states that he will put enmity between the serpent's offspring and the woman's seed, Jesus Christ and his church (Gen. 3:15).

But before we speak of the covenant of grace, there are two other covenants that we need to understand: the covenant of redemption and the covenant of works/creation. The covenant of works took place in eternity past. It was initiated by God the Father with God the Son and God the Holy Spirit. It had the express purpose to save a remnant from sinful humanity to be the people of God for all eternity.

The covenant of works/creation took place in the garden of Eden at the time of creation. It was initiated by God with Adam and Eve and was conditioned upon perfect obedience. The reward was life, and the penalty was immediate death. Since Adam and Eve failed to obey, the penalty of death was applied, not only to Adam and Eve, but also to all mankind, since Adam acted as the representative of all.

The covenant of grace took place after the fall. It was initiated by God with sinful human beings and is conditioned upon faith in Jesus Christ. The reward is spiritual life and the penalty is spiritual death. The covenant of grace includes the covenant with Adam (Gen. 3:15), the covenant with Noah (Gen. 6:17–22; 8:20–22; 9:1–17), the covenant with Abraham (Gen. 12:1–3, 15; 17:1–2), the covenant with Moses (Ex. 19–24), the covenant with David (2 Sam. 7), and the new covenant (Jer. 31:31–34; Ezek. 37:21, 26). The covenant of grace is fulfilled in Jesus Christ. As Paul says in 2 Corinthians 1:20, "All the promises of God find their Yes in [Christ Jesus]."

All through the book of Genesis we see that the author is concerned with the generations of the godly seed. We also have the covenant of preservation with Noah recorded in Genesis 9 and then the tower of Babel in Genesis 11 where God scatters humanity across the face of the earth and confuses their languages so that they will not rise up to be gods (this event is reversed at Pentecost in Acts 2). In Genesis 12 we meet Abraham (at that point still "Abram"). With Abraham, we see

O. Palmer Robertson, *The Christ of the Covenants* (Phillipsburg, NJ: Presbyterian and Reformed Publishing, 1980).

the covenant of promise, which is renewed with Isaac and Jacob in the patriarchal period.

When we come to Exodus, we meet Moses, the mediator of the covenant of law. This is the beginning of the theocratic nation of Israel. God brought them out of slavery in Egypt and into a relationship with him as servants of the Holy God. As such, they were to be a kingdom of priests and a holy nation (Ex. 19:6). We learn in both Leviticus 26 and Deuteronomy 28 that if they were obedient, they would receive blessings (Lev. 26:1–13; Deut. 28:1–14), but if they were disobedient, they would receive curses (Lev. 26:14–46; Deut. 28:15–68). One of these, and the greatest of these curses was exile from the land. But even toward the end of Deuteronomy we see that God made provision for restoration after the exile, which involved the new covenant (Deut. 30:1–10; see also Jer. 31:31–34; Ezek. 37:21, 26).

In fact, Deuteronomy 28–30 is the story of the rest of the Old Testament in miniature form. First, comes blessing, climaxing in the reign of King Solomon (1 Kings 8:24). Then come curses, ultimately resulting in exile from the land (2 Chron. 36:17–21). All the prophets refer to the covenant blessings and curses as they prophesy to Israel and Judah, giving them messages of judgment, as well as holding out hope. They declare that exile is inevitable, yet they also declare God's faithfulness to his covenant, keeping the promise of the new covenant (Deut. 30:1–10; Jer. 31:31–34; Ezek. 37:21, 26) before them.

After Moses died, the Lord raised up Joshua to lead the people into the Promised Land, which was the place where God would dwell with his people in the temple. Up to this point in redemptive history, the garden of Eden and the tabernacle had been the place the Lord had temporarily dwelt with his people. The entire book of Joshua centers around the entry and conquest of the land.

But then we read that Joshua died, and in the book of Judges we see that the people failed to conquer the land as they should have. Instead, they did what was right in their own eyes because there was no king in Israel. The book of Judges anticipates the beginning of the monarchy in Israel with King Saul and King David, the latter of whom God makes a covenant with concerning the kingdom (2 Sam. 7). The period of the monarchy climaxes in King Solomon when we read that the promises have been fulfilled in Solomon's prayer of dedication (1 Kings 8:24). Sadly, it didn't take long (within Solomon's own reign) until the monarchy took a turn for the worse (1 Kings 11). Following Solomon's death, the country actually divided into the northern kingdom, Israel, and the southern kingdom, Judah (1 Kings 12:16–24) in 931 B.C.

Elijah and Elisha preached to the northern kingdom during this time. Although there were a few good kings, the majority of kings in both Israel and Judah did evil in the sight of the Lord and led the people into rebellion as well. In God's grace and mercy, he raised up prophets during this time (known as the preexilic prophets) to prophesy to the people of coming judgment so that they would turn and repent of their wicked ways. Hosea and Amos preached to the northern kingdom, while Isaiah and Micah preached to the southern kingdom. Joel, Obadiah, and Jonah also preached their messages during this time. The northern kingdom, Israel, did not listen and was taken into captivity by the Assyrians in 722 B.C.

A little over one hundred years later the southern kingdom, Judah, followed suit. Jeremiah was prophesying during this time. Judah was taken into captivity by the Babylonians through three deportations in 605, 597, and 586 B.C. The second of these, 597 B.C., took Jehoiachin, the last true Davidic king on the throne, along with the royal family and all the leading classes in Israel, to Babylon. Ezekiel was included among these since he was the son of a priest.

Again, in God's mercy, he raised up both Daniel and Ezekiel to prophesy to the people during the exile. Daniel and Ezekiel spoke messages of both judgment and restoration to the exiles. God would still be faithful to his covenant promise; he would be their God and they would be his people. Both Jeremiah and Ezekiel spoke of the promised new covenant (Jer. 31:31–34; Ezek. 37:21, 26), which would find its ultimate fulfillment in Jesus Christ.

Following the exile, we see the postexilic prophets (Haggai, Zechariah, and Malachi) raised up by God to continue speaking to his people.

7

Though there is a small fulfillment of a restored temple, people, and land under the leadership of Zerubbabel and Nehemiah, the promises of God would not be fulfilled until Jesus Christ came. Jesus came as both the Lord of the covenant (the one who extended grace and mercy to rebellious covenant servants) and as the Servant of the covenant (the true Israel who obediently fulfilled what the nation of Israel could not fulfill, who bore the curse on our behalf, and who rescued us out of slavery to sin into a life of truth, knowledge, and righteousness in him).[4] He came that "all the promises of God [would] find their Yes in him" (2 Cor. 1:20).

After Jesus came to earth as a baby, lived a life of perfect obedience, died for the sins of God's people, was raised as the firstfruits of the resurrection, and ascended to the Father, the Holy Spirit was sent on the Day of Pentecost to renew the church and establish it by his power (Acts 2). The new age was inaugurated through Christ and his church, but it awaits its consummation until Christ returns to bring the old age to a complete end by the final judgment and usher in the new heaven and the new earth. In the meantime, the church is to fulfill the great commission to "go therefore and make disciples of all nations, baptizing them in the name of the Father and of the Son and of the Holy Spirit, teaching them to observe all that [Christ has] commanded [her]. And behold, [he is] with [her] always, to the end of the age" (Matt. 28:19–20; see also Luke 24:47–49).

As we study Judges, it is important for us to keep this overview of the history of redemption and revelation in mind. We must first ask the question, "How does this text relate to the history of redemption?" In other words, where is it placed in progressive, redemptive history? And we must ask, "How does this text relate to the climax of redemptive history: the life, death, resurrection, and ascension of our Lord and Savior Jesus Christ?" The latter question leads us to the next section we need to consider before studying the book of Judges.

4. Dennis E. Johnson, *Him We Proclaim: Preaching Christ from All the Scriptures* (Phillipsburg, NJ: P&R Publishing, 2007), 261.

CHRIST-CENTERED INTERPRETATION OF JUDGES

Evangelical Christians will be the first to heartily agree with 2 Timothy 3:16–17, that

> all Scripture is breathed out by God and profitable for teaching, for reproof, for correction, and for training in righteousness, that the man of God may be complete, equipped for every good work.

But sadly, many seem to have no problem neglecting portions of Scripture that seem difficult in their messages. Judges seems to have been one such book that has been neglected by many Christians. The meanings of the stories of the tribal leaders seem full of blood and gore, sexual immorality and indecency. We too often hurry back to books like the New Testament Epistles that seem less offensive to our minds. But this is a great mistake!

When Jesus appeared to the two disciples on the road to Emmaus,

> he said to them, "O foolish ones, and slow of heart to believe all that the prophets have spoken! Was it not necessary that the Christ should suffer these things and enter into his glory?" And beginning with Moses and all the Prophets, he interpreted to them in all the Scriptures the things concerning himself. (Luke 24:25–27)

In John 5:39 Jesus tells the Jews, "You search the Scriptures because you think that in them you have eternal life; and it is they that bear witness about me."

When Peter spoke in Solomon's portico he said, "But what God foretold by the mouth of all the prophets, that his Christ would suffer, he thus fulfilled" (Acts 3:18). At the very end of Stephen's speech to the Jews, he said, "Which of the prophets did your fathers not persecute? And they killed those who announced beforehand the coming of the Righteous One" (Acts 7:52). And, when the Ethiopian eunuch asked Philip about whom Isaiah 53:7–8 was written, Philip "opened his mouth, and beginning with this Scripture he told him the good news about Jesus"

(Acts 8:26–40). So if we do not understand how Christ relates to all the Scriptures, we have not yet seen the truth of the Scripture.

We have looked at some key texts; now let's look at some key phrases for identifying the continuity between the Old Testament and the New Testament. We might say that we go from Old Testament promise to New Testament fulfillment; or from Old Testament problem (sinners in need of a Savior) to New Testament solution (the Savior comes); or from Old Testament anticipation to New Testament realization, but not just a realization—a far surpassing realization. For example, Jesus Christ is not just a greater Moses, Samson, prophet, priest, or king, but the greatest and final Moses, Samson, prophet, priest, and king. Furthermore, the Lord of history designs historical persons, offices, institutions, and events to foreshadow the full redemption to come. Thus, he foreshadows his great work of redemption in both words and works (events).[5]

The climax of all Scripture is the gospel—the life, death, resurrection, and ascension of Jesus Christ. All the Old Testament writers look toward this climax. All the New Testament writers look both back to this climax and forward to the consummation of the kingdom, Christ's second coming, which was inaugurated at his first coming. The question when we are studying Scripture then is always threefold: (1) "Where are we in the history of redemption in this text?" (2) "How does this text relate to the gospel?" and (3) "How do I apply this text to my life in light of where I am in redemptive history?"

As we study the book of Judges, we will see Christ's work anticipated on every page. Through the failures of God's people, as well as their faith, through the lack of a true king, as well as through the deliverance of those tribal leaders that God raised up to deliver Israel from her oppressors (whether from within or without), we will be pointed to Jesus Christ.

THE AUTHOR AND DATE OF JUDGES

The author of the book of Judges remains unknown. While certain material within the book (ch. 1, 5, 17–21) is said by most commenta-

5. Ibid., 225–26.

tors to have originated closely after the time that the events occurred (1382–1063 B.C.), other material (namely 18:30) suggests that it was put in its final edited form as late as the eighth century B.C. (the exile of the northern kingdom to Assyria) or the sixth century B.C. (the exile of the southern kingdom to Babylon).[6]

THE HISTORICAL BACKGROUND OF JUDGES

We must remember that the book of Judges is part of the progressive revelation that God has given to his people. The book does not stand outside of history; it is given to God's people at a specific time in history for a specific purpose. Yet we must never forget that the message is also for the church today.

The word "judges" is not new to us in the book of Judges. It was used under the Mosaic institution. Moses acted as a judge for the cases brought to him by the people. In fact, you may remember that his father-in-law, Jethro, advised him to appoint other leaders to judge regular cases, and to leave only the most important cases for Moses (Ex. 18). The book of Deuteronomy allows for judges to be appointed and gives specific instruction for doing so (Deut. 1:16; 16:18–19; 24:17; 25:13–16). The priests were also involved with the judges on more difficult cases, so that the people would go to both of them for consultation and a final decision (Deut. 17:8–13). But the meaning of the word takes on a different nuance in the period of the judges. The word means more of a leader in times of battle, a ruler in times of peace, a governor, or a tribal ruler.[7]

The period of the judges is usually reckoned by commentators to have been between 1220 (or 1200) and 1050 (or 1045) B.C., although some date it from 1382 to 1063 B.C.[8] In the book of Deuteronomy we learn that the Israelites were commanded by God to destroy the

6. Barry G. Webb, "Judges," in *New Bible Commentary*, 4th ed., ed. by G. J. Wenham, J. A. Motyer, D. A. Carson, and R. T. France (1994; repr., Downers Grove, IL: IVP Academic, 2008), 263.

7. J. B. Payne, "Judges," in *New Bible Dictionary*, 3rd ed., ed. I. Howard Marshall et al. (Downers Grove, IL: IVP Academic, 1996), 627.

8. Ibid., 631.

Canaanites when they took possession of the land for two main reasons. First, the Lord was using the Israelites to judge the Canaanites for their immorality. And second, the Lord knew that their influence on his people concerning idolatry would be great if they were allowed to remain in the land (Deut. 7). Under Joshua's leadership, Israel had subdued the whole land, but the nature of the conquest was gradual (Ex. 23:28–30; Deut. 7:22), and there were still many Canaanites in the land (Josh. 13:1) that had the potential to lead Israel astray if Israel did not obey the Lord and continue the conquest after Joshua's death. As we will see, this potential became reality because of Israel's failure to drive the Canaanites out of the land.

At the time of the judges, Israel was divided into tribal areas (Josh. 13–21). Nine and a half were located in the area between the Jordan River and the Mediterranean coast. The other two and a half were located in the plateau area east of the Jordan. Conquests by surrounding people, such as the Midianites, Moabites, Ammonites (to the east), and the Philistines (to the west), usually were against one or two tribes, leaving the other areas unaffected.[9]

Since there was no king in Israel yet, the tribes were loosely held together by two main things. First, they shared a common history. Second, they were God's covenant people. But as we will learn, during the period of the judges this common history and place as God's covenant people were not enough to keep intertribal fighting from occurring. Israel needed a king, and not just any king. They needed a king anointed by God. But even a king anointed by God would not prove to be the answer. Ultimately they needed the perfect King, our Lord and Savior Jesus Christ.

During the time of the judges, the Israelites most likely gathered at Shiloh. It was centrally located and the place where the Tent of Meeting had been set up on Israel's arrival in Canaan. They gathered at least one time a year in order to be reminded of their covenant obligations, give thanks, pray, and offer sacrifices.[10]

9. Webb, "Judges," 261.
10. Ibid., 262.

During this period there was no national army organized under a king, so volunteers had to be assembled anytime a threat of war arose. Usually it was the leader with the greatest charisma and strength who was nominated as a leader. Since areas of Canaanites that had yet to be conquered separated tribes from each other, there was little unity and help from other tribes during times of battle. These pockets of Canaanites that separated them also led to Israel's syncretism (worshiping both Yahweh and the pagan gods). However, we must not get the picture that the entire period of the judges was fraught with conflict. As we will learn in the book of Ruth and from the narrator's comments throughout the book of Judges concerning long periods of peace, there were times when a normalcy of life occurred and people could flourish.[11] As we study, it will become clear that the Lord was at work just as much in the times of conflict as in the times of peace, preserving his people and moving the history of redemption forward toward the rise of the monarchy.

As far as the broader historical background with regard to what was going on in the world outside of Israel, it was a period of great ethnic migration in the ancient Near East. It was a time that witnessed the collapse of great cultures such as the Hittites, Minoans, and Myceneans. It was also a period that witnessed the onset of the Iron Age in the ancient Near East, and a time when Crete fell, which led to the Philistines fleeing east to the coastal plains of Palestine.[12]

THE PURPOSE OF JUDGES

At the beginning of the book (1:1–2) the question is asked, "Who shall go up first for us against the Canaanites, to fight against them?" And the answer comes from the Lord, "Judah shall go up; behold, I have given the land into his hand." The same question is asked at the end of the book, except now it does not pertain to their enemies but to their own brothers (20:18), "Who shall go up first for us to fight against the

11. Ibid.
12. Tremper Longman III and Raymond Dillard, *An Introduction to the Old Testament* (Grand Rapids: Zondervan, 2006), 135.

people of Benjamin?" And the answer comes from the Lord, "Judah shall go up first." We must always remember that the Israelites were God's covenant people, and as such had the responsibility to obey him. But the book of Judges informs us that they fell far short of this obedience. From Judah to Dan (1:1–34) and from Othniel of Judah (3:7–11) to Samson of Dan (13–16), Israel sinned and fell short of the glory of God. In this way, the book speaks to all of us. It is the same message that the apostle Paul tells us in Romans 3:23, "all have sinned and fall short of the glory of God."

But we would be wrong to assume that this is the central message of the book. The central message of the book points to God's grace. The downward spiral of Israel and Israel's judges in the book certainly justifies God's wrath against his people. It explains why his promises to the patriarchs to fully possess the land never came true. Israel had disobeyed, and because of their disobedience they were brought under God's curse. Yet he did not leave them alone. Marks of his grace resound throughout the book, as we read of him raising up deliverer after deliverer on his people's behalf despite their sin. He would not let his people go. On behalf of his Son, Jesus Christ, he would preserve his chosen people.

In the climax of redemptive history, the question "Who shall go up first for us to fight against the enemy?" is finally answered. The Lion of Judah, Jesus Christ, went up first for us to fight against the enemy. He went to the cross and conquered death. He took our sin on himself and bore our shame so that we could have his righteousness.

The book of Judges shows us that judges cannot save Israel. And though it prepares us for the time of the monarchy, which climaxes with King Solomon, we learn in 1 and 2 Kings that kings cannot save Israel either. It is only one King, the perfect God-man, Jesus Christ, who can save God's people from their sin. And he has done so victoriously. While the book of Judges may seem dark (and it is), we must not miss the brightness of God's grace that shines through every page, pointing us to our Lord and Savior Jesus Christ.

AN OUTLINE OF JUDGES

While several detailed outlines of Judges can be found in commentaries, I have tried to keep it simple yet thorough for our purposes in this study.

Downward Spiral of Israel's Military (Introduction I in 1:1–2:5)

Downward Spiral of Israel's Spirituality (Introduction II in 2:6–3:6)

Downward Spiral of Israel's Leadership (3:7–16:31)

Othniel (3:7–11)
Ehud (3:12–30)
Shamgar (3:31)
Deborah and Barak (4:1–5:31)
Gideon and Abimelech (6:1–9:57)
Tola (10:1–2)
Jair (10:3–5)
Jephthah (10:6–12:7)
Ibzan (12:8–10)
Elon (12:11–12)
Abdon (12:13–15)
Samson (13:1–16:31)[13]

Downward Spiral of Israel's Religiosity (Conclusion I in 17–18)

Downward Spiral of Israel's Morality (Conclusion II in 19–21)

THE USE OF JUDGES IN THE NEW TESTAMENT

The book of Hebrews contains the best-known reference to the book of Judges in the New Testament.

13. The twelve tribal leaders listed correspond to the twelve tribes of Israel, from Judah to Dan.

> What more shall I say? For time would fail me to tell of Gideon, Barak, Samson, Jephthah, of David and Samuel and the prophets— who through faith conquered kingdoms, enforced justice, obtained promises, stopped the mouths of lions, quenched the power of fire, escaped the edge of the sword, were made strong out of weakness, became mighty in war, put foreign armies to flight. (Heb. 11:32–34)

We will learn at the end of our story how amazing it is that these men were recorded here as men of faith with a seemingly wonderful track record! None of their faults or failures are mentioned, only their faith. This is truly amazing grace!

There are other allusions though in the New Testament. John the Baptist (Luke 1:15) follows in the footsteps of a Nazirite like Samson (Judg. 13:4–5). The angel's visit to Samson's mother (Judg. 13:3) finds a comparison with the angel's visit to Jesus' mother, Mary, in Luke 1:31. The blessing given to Mary by Elizabeth, "Blessed are you among women, and blessed is the fruit of your womb!" (Luke 1:42) finds a comparison with the blessing given to Jael by Deborah (Judg. 5:24). When Paul stood up and addressed the crowd in the synagogue at Antioch in Pisidia, he made mention of the "judges until Samuel the prophet" (Acts 13:20).[14]

However, lest we think that the New Testament only has scattered references to the book of Judges, we must step back and look at the theological themes of Judges and how the New Testament develops these. First, Jesus and the apostles are those to whom the Spirit of God has been given. This is true of the deliverers in the book of Judges as well. Second, the theme of covenant obedience or disobedience, which is so prominent in the book of Judges, is also prominent in the New Testament. For example, 1 John 5:21 says, "Little children, keep yourselves from idols," which essentially means "worship God alone," the summation of covenant obedience. Third, Jesus Christ is not only the final and perfect fulfillment of the office of judge, but is the final and perfect King (the office that the book of Judges anticipates), anointed by the Holy Spirit of God.[15]

14. Block, *Judges, Ruth*, 69–70.
15. C. E. Armerding, "Judges," in *New Dictionary of Biblical Theology*, ed. T. Desmond Alexander et al. (Downers Grove, IL: InterVarsity Press, 2000), 175.

CONCLUSION

You won't find Laurie staring down at her hands and nervously fidgeting today. Instead you will find her working at a Crisis Pregnancy Center, walking with women through the journey of accepting their pregnancies, having their babies, and either keeping them or giving them up for adoption. She is able to share with them her own story and, more importantly, she is able to share the story of redemption through Jesus Christ. Though her past was dark, she knows Paul's words in 1 Corinthians 6:9–11 by heart:

> Or do you not know that the unrighteous will not inherit the king-dom of God? Do not be deceived: neither the sexually immoral, nor idolaters, nor adulterers, nor men who practice homosexuality, nor thieves, nor the greedy, nor drunkards, nor revilers, nor swindlers will inherit the kingdom of God. *And such were some of you. But you were washed, you were sanctified, you were justified in the name of the Lord Jesus Christ and by the Spirit of our God.*

LESSON 2

Judges 1:1–2:5

Please use the question paradigm from pages 301–2 as you work through the following. See the introductory comments there that explain each part of the process below in more detail.

- **Pray.**
- **Ponder the Passage.** Read Judges 1:1–2:5 once a day from different translations for the entire week, looking for its:
  - Point
  - Persons
  - Problem
  - Patterns
  - Persons of the Trinity
  - Puzzling Parts
- **Put It in Perspective.**
  - Place in Scripture. Read Exodus 23:20–33; 34:11–12; Deuteronomy 7:16; 9:4–6; 31:16–18; Joshua 15:13–19; 17:16–18.
  - Passages from Other Parts of Scripture

1. Based on your observations of the text, what is the basic content of this passage? Try to summarize it in your own words, using a sentence or two.

2. According to 1:1, how do the people interact with the Lord after the death of Joshua?

3. Read Genesis 49:8–12 in light of 1:2. Why would the Lord have Judah go up first? How are Simeon and Judah related (see Gen. 29:33, 35 and Josh. 19:1, 9)? How do you see tribal unity displayed in 1:3–4?

4. Why are the people of Israel to fight against the Israelites (see Deut. 7:16; 9:4–6)?

5. What law in Israel do Adoni-bezek's words in 1:7 reflect (see Lev. 24:19)?

6. How does 1:9 set the geographic outline for the verses that follow?

7. Read Joshua 15:13–19 along with 1:10–15. What do you discover? Why is this story important as a testimony of one family in the time of the judges? What values does this family reflect? What strengths do you see in Achsah? What do we know about Othniel from 3:7–11? If you have time, compare this story with the book of Ruth. What similarities do you see between the women?

8. How do you see God's plan to redeem a people from every tribe, tongue, and nation (see Gen. 12:3; Matt. 28:19–20) in this chapter through the persons of Caleb, Achsah, and the Kenites?

9. How does the last phrase of 1:16 inform us about what is occurring between the Israelites and Canaanites in the land?

10. Read Joshua 17:16–18 with 1:19. Are these chariots of iron a valid or invalid excuse to not drive out the Canaanites? How do we see Israel's thinking changed here from the days of Joshua?

11. Compare Joshua 2 with 1:22–26. What differences in the outcome do you observe?

12. Looking back over 1:1–26, what successes do you see and what failures for Judah and Simeon, for the Benjamites, and for the house of Joseph?

20

13. What is the key phrase that is repeatedly used in 1:27–36? Is this "physical geography" or "spiritual geography" being related? How does this passage lay the groundwork for the book as a whole that catalogs Israel's declining spiral into apostasy?

14. Read Genesis 17:7; Exodus 6:2–8 in light of 2:1; and Deuteronomy 7:2; 12:3 in light of 2:2. What do you learn?

15. Read Numbers 33:55; Exodus 23:20–33; 34:11–16; Deuteronomy 7:16; 9:5; 31:16–18 in light of 2:3. What do you observe?

16. What is the people's response to the Lord's words? Is weeping and sacrificing the same as repentance (see Ps. 51:17 and Joel 2:12–13)?

- **Principles and Points of Application.**

1. To whom do you go when you don't know what to do? Do you inquire of the Lord first or do you begin with friends, relatives, counselors, the newspaper column, the Internet, etc.? Take whatever circumstance in which you presently need counsel to the Lord today in prayer and ask him to reveal his will to you through his Word.

2. In Christ, the promises of the land have been fulfilled. God is with us through his Spirit. We have already entered our rest in him. How are you resting in Jesus Christ and the promises that he has already fulfilled today? In what circumstance(s) do you need to rest in him today?

3. What "gods and thorns" are in your life today because of sin? God has given us his Holy Spirit to wage war against these and claim his victory that has already been secured on the cross. Recognize today that your enemies have no hold over you. Take them to Christ and rest in his power to deliver you from them today.

4. Looking back over 1:1–2:5, how do you relate to the compromises of Israel with the Canaanites? How do you feel pulled

21

between the world, the flesh, and the devil, and serving Jesus Christ? Confess any compromise in your life today, and be filled with the Holy Spirit, by whom you were sealed for the day of redemption (Eph. 4:30; 5:18).

NOTES FOR JUDGES 1:1–2:5

Ponder the aim of this lesson concerning our:

Mind: What do we need to know from this passage in Scripture?

> Israel's failure to destroy the Canaanites resulted in God's sure word of the Canaanites' becoming thorns in their sides and their gods a snare in their midst.

Heart: How does what we learn from this passage affect our internal relationship with the Lord?

> It prepares us to be kingdom disciples who embrace the "land of rest" that God has given us in Christ and to recognize that he has given us the Holy Spirit to guard our lives from the thorns and snares of this world.

Hands: How does what we learn from this passage translate into action for God's kingdom?

> It enables us to:

1. Go to the Lord and his Word to inquire of what we need to do in our present life circumstances and decisions.
2. Recognize that Jesus Christ has fulfilled the promise of the land to Israel and is our resting place, and to rest in him today.
3. Claim the Holy Spirit's power to wage war against the "gods" and "thorns" of this world, recognizing that they have no power over us because Christ has won the victory over them on our

behalf, and to fight the battle with the spiritual armor described in Ephesians 6:10–20.

INTRODUCTION

There have been several times in my Christian walk when I have felt a deep tension between following the ways of my flesh, the ways of this world, or the ways of Satan, and following the ways of my Lord and Savior Jesus Christ. Times when I have wanted what I wanted when I wanted it, instead of wanting what God wanted when he wanted it. And during many of those times I knowingly settled with the world, the flesh, or the Devil instead of being filled with the Spirit and submitting to the Word of God. By God's grace I was brought to deep repentance after those times, and despite my sin of compromise the Lord continued to use me in the lives of others to lead them to a deeper knowledge of him. I wish I could say that those times are over, that I never struggle anymore, but the tension remains, and will always remain, on this side of glory.

How are you drawn into the mind-set of our world? How do you compromise with your flesh? When do you listen to the Father of Lies instead of your heavenly Father? Perhaps you are facing an unwanted pregnancy and the compromise of abortion looks like a good option to you. Maybe you are in a difficult marriage and divorce seems right. Perhaps your financial situation is so grim that you are withholding your tithes and offerings. Maybe an innocent relationship with a man who pays more attention to you than your own husband does has turned into an adulterous one. Perhaps the way that you are spending your time in entertainment has subtly taken over all your spare time to serve the Lord and study his Word. Maybe little lies and compromises seem okay in light of "bigger" sins. I pray that by God's grace, through your study of the book of Judges during this season of your life, the Lord is going to reveal the dangers of compromising with the world, the flesh, and the Devil. Even when we fail and are faithless, he remains faithful. Even when we have run to the land of chaos and evil, the Lord still holds out his land of rest.

Judges 1:1–2:5 has much to say about being kingdom disciples who embrace the "land of rest" that God has given us in Christ and recognize that he has given us the Holy Spirit to guard our lives from the thorns and snares of this world.

We can divide the lesson into three sections:

    I. Conquest of Canaan Continued (1:1–26)
   II. Conquest of Canaan Uncompleted (1:27–36)
  III. Covenant Curses Instituted (2:1–5)

The author of the book of Judges intentionally organizes 1:1–2:5 as he does for several reasons. First, the first two verses (1:1–2), which affirm the Lord's guidance and promise, stand in contrast to the last five verses (2:1–5), which state the Lord's accusation and curse. Second, the accomplishments of Judah in 1:3–21 stand in contrast to the failures of the northern tribes in 1:22–36. Third, the failures in the north steadily progress in each succeeding verse (1:22–36). Fourth, 1:9 introduces 1:10–15 pertaining to the hill country, 1:16–17 pertaining to the Negeb, and 1:18 pertaining to the lowland and beyond. Finally, the phrase "to go up" is repeated at the beginning of each main division (1:4, 22; 2:1) and is also seen in 1:1, 2, 3.[1]

It has also been noted by commentators that 1:1–2:5 forms the first of two introductions to the book (also 2:6–3:6) that parallel two conclusions (17:1–18:31; 19:1–21:25). This first introduction gives the Israelites' point of view, while the second introduction gives the Lord's.[2] The structure of 1:1–2:5 also states a point; Israel spirals downward into more and more apostasy, which some commentators have labeled "the Canaanizing of Israel."[3]

I. Conquest of Canaan Continued (1:1–26)

Joshua, the great leader of the people and Moses' successor, has died, and the people are left to continue the second stage of the con-

---

1. Dale Ralph Davis, *Judges: Such a Great Salvation* (Fearn, Great Britain: Christian Focus, 2000), 17–18.

2. K. Lawson Younger Jr., *Judges/Ruth*, The NIV Application Commentary (Grand Rapids: Zondervan, 2002), 61.

3. Daniel I. Block, *The New American Commentary*, vol. 6, *Judges, Ruth* (Nashville: Broadman & Holman, 1999), 76.

quest of the land without him—the settlement of the land. This is not the first time one of God's great leaders has died. The book of Exodus begins with Joseph's death. The book of Joshua begins with Moses' death. The book of Judges begins with Joshua's death. The book of 1 Kings begins with David's death. But God's kingdom is not dependent on God's servants. Even when he takes his greatest servants home, he ensures that the history of redemption continues. God's people are always dependent on him alone.[4] Joshua had prepared them well to continue the work without him, but would they choose to do so? They seem to get off to the right start by inquiring of the Lord concerning who should go up first (chronologically) against the Canaanites to fight against them.

Who are these Canaanites whom they are fighting against? Are they innocent people who are in the wrong place at the wrong time? No, they are a wicked people, and the Lord is using Israel to judge their wickedness by destroying them (Deut. 9:4–6). The Lord's answer to Israel's question was Judah, for he had already given the land into Judah's hand. We immediately see that Judah invited his brother Simeon to go with him. Some commentators see this as unity among the tribes that will stand in stark contrast to the disunity that we see by the time we reach the end of the book. Other commentators see this as an act of compromise of God's desire for each individual tribe to trust him in the process of settling in the land.[5] Regardless, the Lord was gracious to give the Canaanites and Perizzites into their hand at Bezek. God's faithfulness does not depend on our faithfulness, but his. This is good news! Let us pause for a moment and ask ourselves to whom we go when we don't know what to do. Do we inquire of the Lord first and look to his Word for instruction, or do we inquire of our own hearts, our friends, our counselor, etc.? While godly counsel from others can prove beneficial, the Lord is the one with whom we should always begin, seeking his Word above all others.

4. Davis, *Judges*, 20.
5. Davis sees it as unity, while Younger views it as distrust. Davis, *Judges*, 20; and Younger, *Judges/Ruth*, 65.

The note about Adoni-bezek will prove to be ironic as we move through the book of Judges. Adoni-bezek is most likely a title (instead of a personal name) for the king meaning "Lord of Bezek," and referring to the governor or mayor of the city.[6] Here is a pagan king who acknowledges God's hand in his loss as repayment for what he has done in the past to enemy kings. This law of an "eye for an eye" was clearly stated in God's law to Israel (see Lev. 24:17–23), but we will soon find that this pagan king knows God's law better than God's own people do. God's people should not have just mutilated his thumbs and big toes; they should have put him to death in response to God's instruction (Deut. 7:1–2; 20:16–17).[7] Instead God executes the sentence that they failed to when Adoni-bezek dies in Jerusalem (1:7). Furthermore, this pagan king who deserved and received God's judgment stands in sharp contrast to Israel, who also deserved God's judgment but over and over again throughout the book receives his grace.[8]

Judah captured Jerusalem by the sword and fire and then continued toward the hill country, in the Negeb, and in the lowland to fight against the Canaanites there. Then they went against the Canaanites who lived in Hebron, then went against the inhabitants of Debir (1:8–15). These verses are also found in Joshua 15:13–19. Caleb gave the men an incentive to attack and capture Debir; whoever did so would receive his daughter Achsah as a wife.

Othniel, who will be the first deliverer that the Lord raises up for Israel in the book (Judg. 3:7–11), captured Debir and received Achsah as his reward. Achsah acted as a wise woman when she urged Othniel to ask her father for a field. She was concerned about their future and their well-being. When her father, Caleb, asked her what she wanted, she boldly asked for a blessing. It wasn't a purposeless blessing though; she was concerned that they have springs of water in a land that did not produce fresh water. So Caleb answered her boldness with a blessing, and she secured land of worth because she secured a water source along with

6. Block, *Judges, Ruth*, 90.
7. Ibid., 91.
8. Younger, *Judges/Ruth*, 66.

it. This was not just any land; this was God's land that he had given to his people. There is "spiritual" geography intertwined with "physical" geography. Achsah will serve as the first in a line of several women in the books of Judges and Ruth who are held in high esteem, while the men (excluding Boaz) are portrayed as inadequate leaders.

Achsah's family lived as an Israelite family should have lived. Her father secured a good husband for her, and she wisely had their future as an interest and boldly asked for springs of water to be added to her place of living to make it useful. Her father gladly blessed her, and we are left with the impression that this is a family that has one another's best interests at heart. Achsah is also a woman who displays strength and is rewarded for it. In a day and age when women in the church seem confused as to whether to be strong or weak, this should encourage us that strength and boldness used for the advancement of the kingdom are rewarded by the Lord (see also the book of Ruth). However, as we move through the book, we will find that this is extremely rare in Israel during the time of the judges. It will be more common for people to use their strength and boldness for their own personal gain.

Significantly, the Kenites (descendants of Moses' father-in-law and thus non-Israelites) went up with the people from Jericho (the city of palms) and settled with the people. This latter point is significant. It is easy to read right over it in the text, but we need to pause and reflect on how easily this decision seems to have been made. *They settled with the people.* They were not supposed to do this! They were not supposed to comfortably settle with this wicked people; they were supposed to drive them out! They were supposed to be agents of God's judgment. But instead, they live right in the midst of them and *settle.* It seems to be intentional. But before we shake our heads and point our fingers, let us consider how easily we too move right into the midst of compromise and settle in it. How often we turn away from the Lord's clear commands and tolerate that which his Word so clearly says is wrong.

Again, Judah went along with Simeon to capture Zephath, which they renamed Hormah. They also captured Gaza, Ashkelon, Ekron, and their territories. And we read that the Lord is with Judah at this point, blessing his obedience to try to de-Canaanize the land, and giving him the hill country. However, we also read that Judah could not defeat all the Canaanites because they had chariots of iron. This is an important historical marker in the book as it dates Judges to the beginning of the Iron Age in Palestine (1200 B.C.).[9] But more importantly, this is a theological note, as not even iron chariots were to keep Israel from conquering the Canaanites (see Josh. 17:16–18).[10] When God gives us commands, he also gives us everything that we need to accomplish them. But Israel was deterred far too easily by the strength of the world and forgot the strength of the Lord.

Hebron was given to Caleb, as Moses had said (Num. 14:24; Deut. 1:36), which is important because it verifies Moses as a true prophet of God. His prophecy had been fulfilled. While Caleb was having success and driving out the three sons of Anak, we read that Benjamin did not drive out the Jebusites who lived in Jerusalem, but instead co-inhabited with them. This note concerning the Benjamites will prove to be important as we move through the book to the final chapters and see the deep corruption of this tribe.

The Lord was also with Joseph's house as they went against Bethel. Reminiscent of the story of Rahab in Joshua 2, the spies from the house of Joseph asked a man coming out of the city to show them the entrance while holding out the reward of kindness toward him and his family if he complied. However, unlike Rahab's response of faith in Joshua 2, there is no evidence in this account of this man having faith.[11] The man did comply and was rewarded with deliverance, which was followed by his founding a city in the land of the Hittites called Luz. This land, according to Joshua 1:4, was supposed to be the territory of Israel. But instead the tribe of Joseph enabled the founding of another Canaanite city.[12]

Let us pause here for a moment and reflect on the fact that Caleb, Othniel, Achsah, and the Kenites were not Israelites, yet God's grace

9. Block, *Judges, Ruth*, 99.
10. Ibid., 100.
11. Ibid., 103.
12. Younger, *Judges/Ruth*, 70.

rested on them.[13] Missions does not begin in the New Testament. Even in the Old Testament we see that God is calling out a people from every tribe, tongue, and nation to serve him. How are we joining together as the church to fulfill the Great Commission by the power of the Holy Spirit?

II. Conquest of Canaan Uncompleted (1:27–36)

We have already seen some of Israel's failures to destroy the Canaanites in the land in the previous verses with the tribes of Judah and Benjamin (1:19, 21), but here we see that six more tribes failed. Though it may sound monotonous to our ears, the phrase "did not drive out" occurs seven times in verses 27–33. Remember that the number seven in Scripture symbolizes completeness. This is not about geography but theology.[14] Manasseh failed to drive them out because they persisted in dwelling in their land. While the Israelites did grow strong (an important historical note) and were even able to subject the Canaanites to forced labor, this was disobedience to God's command to drive out the Canaanites completely. If they were strong enough to subject them to forced labor, they were strong enough to drive them out of the land. As we will later see, this failure is the root cause of Israel's apostasy that is recorded all through the book. All the "ites" (Canaanites, Perizzites, etc.) were going to be seen as "yikes" for Israel's spiritual health! It is important for us to recognize that spiritual disaster didn't happen in a day. As the Israelites intermingled with the Canaanites and tolerated their existence in the land, they were subtly moving into spiritual decay. Isn't this how it always is? We rarely set out for spiritual decay; it is usually a subtle moving away from the Lord and his Word. It is one compromise at a time that leads us further away from the Lord's will for our lives.

Ephraim also failed and co-inhabited with the Canaanites. Zebulun too failed and, like Ephraim, subjected the Canaanites to forced labor. Asher also failed and co-inhabited with them. Naphtali too failed and,

13. "They are Kenizzite proselytes, who have been so thoroughly integrated into the faith and culture of the nation that Caleb could represent the tribe of Judah in reconnaissance missions, and all model the life of Yahwistic faith in the face of the Canaanite territory." See Genesis 15:19; 36:11, 15, 42; Numbers 32:12; Joshua 14:6, 14; Judges 1:13. Block, *Judges, Ruth*, 97.

14. Davis calls it "theological geography"; *Judges*, 23.

like Ephraim and Zebulun, subjected the Canaanites to forced labor. Dan also failed to conquer the Amorites and was forced out of their allotted land back into the hill country. However, the house of Joseph subjected the Amorites to forced labor as well. So we see here a very disturbing picture. In Joshua 1, God clearly commands Israel to inherit the land that he has given them. In Deuteronomy 7, the Lord commands his people to devote the Canaanites to complete destruction, for the Israelites are a chosen people holy to him. Their failure to drive out the Canaanites is a failure to keep the covenant with the Lord and a failure to be holy to him. Obviously strength was not the issue, since they were able to subject the Canaanites to forced labor.[15] The issue was that the Israelites did not drive them out because they were willing to comingle with them.

At a breach of the covenant, the reader may well expect the covenant curses to fall on Israel throughout the book. However, what we will find is that here in the Old Testament, in the book of Judges, in the midst of the apostasy of God's chosen people, God pours out his grace and his mercy on an undeserving people. And he does so in order to point us to the great Deliverer who was yet to come for those in the days of the judges, but who has already come in our day, our Lord and Savior Jesus Christ. Even in Judges, as in all the Old Testament, the gospel of Jesus Christ shines forth through the symbolic office of deliverer. Though every deliverer that God will raise up in the book of Judges will fail to heal the land from apostasy (indeed many make it worse), there is one who has been raised up to heal the apostate hearts of God's people, and it is to this Deliverer, Jesus Christ, that we bow our knee in worship and adoration, in thanksgiving and in praise.

III. Covenant Curses Instituted (2:1–5)

Now the Lord himself, in the form of an angel, speaks to Israel at Bochim. First, he reminds them of his past faithfulness and covenant with them. He was the one who brought them up from Egypt and into

---

15. Younger, *Judges/Ruth*, 72.

the Promised Land. The promise of the land had been a focal point of the Abrahamic covenant but had been included in the Mosaic covenant as well. The Lord was the one who had made an unconditional covenant with them and commanded them to break down the altars of the Canaanites. This reveals the real issue in the book. It is not political or social wrongdoing but religious apostasy that is being addressed. It is a breach of the covenant that is being brought into account. It is disobedience to the covenant command. The question "What is this you have done?" (2:2) sets the responsibility squarely on the people's shoulders. They are the ones who have breached the covenant. They are the ones who have failed to keep the command of the Lord. So the faithful God is true to his word. The Canaanites will become thorns in their sides, and their gods will be a snare to them (Deut. 31:16–18). He had warned them of this in Exodus 23:32–33:

> You shall make no covenant with them and their gods. They shall not dwell in your land, lest they make you sin against me; for if you serve their gods, it will surely be a snare to you.

In Exodus 34:12 the Lord says, "Take care, lest you make a covenant with the inhabitants of the land to which you go, lest it become a snare in your midst." Deuteronomy 7:16 says, "And you shall consume all the peoples that the LORD your God will give over to you. Your eye shall not pity them, neither shall you serve their gods, for that would be a snare to you." What was the response of the people? They lifted up their voices and wept, naming the place Bochim ("weepers"), and sacrificed to the Lord. However, this response was not the same as repentance, as we will see as we move further into the book.

It is our Deliverer, Jesus Christ, who has truly broken the thorns and snares in our lives and called us to come to him to enter into rest. He is the one in whom the promise of the land has been fulfilled. His presence is with us as he indwells our hearts through his Spirit. Are we resting in him today? Are we fighting against the thorns and snares with the spiritual armor that he has provided (Eph. 6:10–20)?

CONCLUSION

My husband and I just came through a situation in which we were encouraged to compromise. We were encouraged to think like the world instead of in light of God's Word. We were offered "permission" by another Christian to embrace the mind-set of deceit in order to gain an advantage for ourselves financially. But by God's grace we stood firm and chose to remain true to the living Word. By God's grace we did not grieve the Holy Spirit of God, by whom we have been sealed for the day of redemption (Eph. 4:30). By God's grace we were filled with the Spirit (Eph. 5:18) and submitted to Jesus Christ rather than the gods of this world. And by God's grace you too can embrace the "land of rest" that God has given us in Christ and recognize that he has given us the Holy Spirit to guard our lives from the thorns and snares of this world.

Judges 2:6–3:6

PLEASE USE THE QUESTION paradigm from pages 301–2 as you work through the following. See the introductory comments there that explain each part of the process below in more detail.

- **Pray.**
- **Ponder the Passage.** Read Judges 2:6–3:6 once a day from different translations for the entire week, looking for its:
  - Point
  - Persons
  - Problem
  - Patterns
  - Persons of the Trinity
  - Puzzling Parts
- **Put It in Perspective.**
  - Place in Scripture. If you have not done so, read Deuteronomy 7; 28:15–68; Joshua 24:1–28.
  - Passages from Other Parts of Scripture

1. Based on your observations of the text, what is the basic content of this passage? Try to summarize it in your own words, using a sentence or two.

2. Compare and contrast the first introduction (1:1–2:5) with the second introduction (2:6–3:6). What do you see?

3. Read 2:6–9 alongside Joshua 24:29–31. What do you learn? What new information do we learn in 2:10? Why is this significant for the book of Judges?

4. Compare the phrase "did not know the LORD" in 2:10 with the same phrase in 1 Samuel 2:12. What is the context in 1 Samuel 2:12? What does this imply that "did not know the LORD" means in Judges?

5. How does 2:11–15 expand on 2:10?

6. Using a Bible dictionary, look up the words "Baal" and "Ashtaroth." What do you learn?

7. Where in the Bible did the Lord warn Israel and swear to them concerning covenant curses? How does 2:15 display his faithfulness to his word?

8. What do we learn in 2:16 that challenges the formula "obedience brings blessings and disobedience brings curses"? Why is this important to see in the Old Testament, which is sometimes wrongly pitted against the New Testament as law versus grace?

9. Judges 2:16–19 gives a paradigm for the major section of the book in 3:7–16:31. Although we haven't studied those chapters yet, what do these verses tell us will happen?

10. Compare 2:17 with Exodus 34:15–16. What do you see?

11. How is 2:18 key for the interpretation of the entire book? Who is doing the delivering? Who always does the delivering? When and by whom was this most clearly manifested in the history of redemption?

12. Compare the word "groaning" in 2:18b with the same word in Exodus 2:24; 6:5. What do you learn?

13. How does the Lord test Israel's commitment to him and why (2:22–3:2)?

14. Compare the "test" that God gave Abraham in Genesis 22:1–2 with the test God gives the Israelites in 2:22–3:2. Contrast the outcomes.

15. Compare 3:3 with Joshua 13:2–6. If you have a map, try to place the names mentioned in 3:3. What do you observe concerning the geography represented?

16. Read Deuteronomy 7:3–5 along with 3:6. What do you find? Contrast 3:6 with 2:7. What has happened within one generation of time? Why?

- **Principles and Points of Application.**

1. We cannot give salvation to the next generation; God alone can save our children and grandchildren. No matter how much we teach them or model the faith for them, we must cry out to God to save them from their sin. How are you doing this today? The passage this week has also reminded us to keep the Lord's Word and work constantly before us by hearing the preaching of the Word, by partaking of the Lord's Supper, and by remaining in fellowship with his church. How are you actively pursuing these things in the power of the Holy Spirit?

2. How do you recognize God's jealous love for you? Zephaniah 3:17 says, "The Lord your God is in your midst, a mighty one who will save; he will rejoice over you with gladness; he will quiet you by his love; he will exult over you with loud singing." Do you rejoice over this love of God? Do you recognize it as love that he has for you? How do you respond to him in thankful service because of it?

3. To whom or what do we attribute deliverance and salvation in our lives? How do we respond to God's grace and deliverance in our lives? Do we cry out for relief from the Lord only to return to our old ways after he graciously delivers us? Or do we cry out in true repentance, turning from our sin to worship him?

4. We cannot ride on the coattails of the faithful who have gone before us. Every individual is responsible to give an account before God. For those of us who are hidden in Christ, our account of judgment is cleared and we have the words "forgiven,

35

loved, and my daughter" stamped across our names in the Book of Life. Are you hidden in Christ today? If not, seriously consider placing your faith in Jesus Christ today. If so, thank the Lord today for clearing your guilt and rendering you righteous before the Holy God.

5. God has every right to judge his people. They are totally undeserving of his grace and mercy. He could have wiped them out and been totally justified. Yet instead, he displays his grace and mercy on his people. What a beautiful picture that finds its climax in the Father sending his Son, Jesus Christ, to die for those who stand guilty and worthy of eternal judgment. Rather than treating us as we deserve, he makes us sons and daughters through Christ. What wondrous love is this! That the Father would send his only Son and that this Son would willingly obey so that we might be sons and daughters of God! Praise him and thank him for such wonderful love today through writing him a poem, journaling a prayer of thanksgiving, singing him a song of praise, or listing how he has displayed his love in your life this week.

6. The danger of compromise with the world still stands true for the church today when she refuses to maintain any distinction with contemporary culture. But distinction from the culture does not mean departing from the culture. We must encourage Christians to pursue their callings to be teachers in the public schools, writers for the local newspaper, politicians, nurses and doctors in the hospitals, musicians and artists, and scientists and mathematicians. If we believe that God is Lord over all, then we should be actively involved in all that he is over. How are you actively pursuing the calling that God has given you and impacting our culture for Christ while recognizing that you are not to blend with the culture?

7. Sin is a power that ensnares you. It is difficult to escape its tyranny. That is why it is good news that Jesus Christ broke the powers of darkness on the cross for you and for me. We are no

longer slaves to sin but are free in Jesus Christ to be servants of righteousness. What sin is ensnaring you today? Cry out to God to deliver you from the snares of Satan, from the futility of the flesh, and from the wiles of this world.

NOTES FOR JUDGES 2:6-3:6

Ponder the aim of this lesson concerning our:

Mind: What do we need to know from this passage in Scripture?

It is the Lord, in his grace and mercy, who raises up deliverers for his people throughout the history of redemption, climaxing in the perfect and final Deliverer, Jesus Christ.

Heart: How does what we learn from this passage affect our internal relationship with the Lord?

It prepares us to be kingdom disciples who embrace Jesus Christ as our Deliverer and Savior, entering into his promised rest and serving him out of thankfulness for the work of deliverance that he accomplished on the cross.

Hands: How does what we learn from this passage translate into action for God's kingdom?

It enables us to:

1. Learn about the Lord and the work that he has done for his people from those generations that have gone before us, while also teaching those generations that will come after us.
2. Recognize that it is the Lord who works through the offices of his chosen instruments in order to deliver his people.
3. Rest in God's Word and the power of the Holy Spirit as we endure times of testing in our lives.

4. Choose not to be yoked to unbelievers in marriage (if we are single) and to pray that the Lord would save our spouses (if we are married to unbelievers).

INTRODUCTION

When I was in high school, I bought into the terrible lie that if I didn't perform well for my coaches, I didn't deserve to eat. If I wasn't as thin as the models on the billboards and magazines, I wasn't lovely. Over the years this lie became deeply ingrained in my heart and my mind until I was a slave to it. I cannot explain the power that it had over me, but although I was a child of God, I served the god of anorexia alongside him. I remember the well-meaning counsel of family, friends, and counselors as if they had given it yesterday. Their advice seemed to assume that I could just return to eating normally by one simple mental switch and one bite at a time. What they didn't realize was how strong and powerful the god of anorexia was. Why? Because behind the god of anorexia stood (1) the Father of Lies, wanting to gain a foothold in my life to devour me, (2) my own flesh that wanted to satisfy the desires of my own heart to be beautiful and accepted in the world's eyes, and (3) the world that constantly shouted that I had to be "this" or look like "that" in order to be loved. I was enslaved to my sin, and I was loyal to my master. It was not until my Lord and Savior Jesus Christ delivered me from the tyranny of anorexia through the work of his Spirit in my heart and mind that freedom came.

Judges 2:6–3:6 has much to say about being kingdom disciples whose only hope and freedom from sin is to embrace Jesus Christ as our Deliverer and Savior, entering into his promised rest and serving him out of thankfulness for the work of deliverance that he accomplished on the cross.

We can divide the lesson today into four sections:

  I. The Generation of Joshua Serves the Lord (2:6–10)
 II. The Generation after Joshua Disobeys the Lord (2:11–15)
III. The Lord Raises Up Judges (2:16–19)
IV. The Lord Tests Israel (2:20–3:6)

I. The Generation of Joshua Serves the Lord (2:6–10)

The second part of the double introduction is in 2:6–3:6. Remember that the first introduction is from the perspective of Israel and gives the literary and moral movements of the book, while the second is from the perspective of the Lord and gives the pattern of a downward cycle in the book. Both should always be read together.[1] Judges 2:6–9 is a summary of the book of Joshua, which could be labeled "the possession of the land." It is the same summary that the book of Joshua has in 24:29–31. Joshua faithfully led the people in the possession of the land, and he died at the age of 110 years old. He was buried within the Promised Land in the portion of his inheritance (Josh. 19:50). But Judges 2:10 is new information. First, all the rest of Joshua's generation died too. Second, "there arose another generation after them who did not know the LORD or the work that he had done for Israel." The latter gives us one of the themes of Judges, "the Canaanization of Israel." The phrase "they did not know the LORD" is also found in 1 Samuel 2:12 concerning the two sons of Eli, who were priests in the sanctuary but were pagans at heart.[2] This is important, because they knew about the Lord but did not honor him as Lord. This serves as a reminder to those of us who are mothers and grandmothers. We cannot give salvation to the next generation; God alone can save our children and grandchildren. No matter how much we teach them or model the faith for them, we must cry out to God to save them from their sin. But it also serves as a reminder to keep the Lord's Word and work constantly before us by hearing the preaching of the Word, by partaking of the Lord's Supper, and by remaining in fellowship with his church.

II. The Generation after Joshua Disobeys the Lord (2:11–15)

These verses expand on 2:10 and give the result of the people's not knowing the Lord or the work that he had done for Israel. They did evil

1. K. Lawson Younger Jr., *Judges/Ruth*, The NIV Application Commentary (Grand Rapids: Zondervan, 2002), 84.
2. Dale Ralph Davis, *Judges: Such a Great Salvation* (Fearn, Great Britain: Christian Focus, 2000), 35.

in the Lord's sight (a statement that will be repeated in every developed judge cycle in the book[3]) and served the Baals. They abandoned the Lord who had redeemed them from Egypt. They actively sought other gods from the peoples around them and worshiped their gods. We know from Deuteronomy 7 that this was in direct contradiction to the Lord's will for them as a holy people to him. What was the result?

The Lord was angry because they had abandoned their covenant to him and bowed down to serve the Baals and Ashtaroth. Baal was the god of the storm and fertility (along with his female counterpart, Ashtaroth, otherwise known as Astarte, the goddess of love and war[4]). The people, instead of placing their trust in Baal to act as the great god of nature and bring the blessings of rain and grain, of wine and oil, had to help him to do so. They did this by acting out on earth what they hoped he would do with his female goddess in heaven—have sexual intercourse. So Baal worship consisted of cult prostitution where the men would lie with the women, as they hoped Baal would lie with Ashtaroth in order to bring fertile crops to the land.[5] Because of their sin, God gave them over to plunderers and sold them into the hand of their enemies so that they could not withstand them. The Lord was faithful to his covenant curses and was against the Israelites for harm, which caused them great distress. He was not arbitrary in his judgment but was faithful to fulfill the covenant curses that he had had the Levites recite in the hearing of all the men of Israel on Mount Ebal (Deut. 27:9–26; 28:15–68). God's anger displays how great his love is for his people. As the Covenant Lord, he is jealous for his wife (his people) and is jealous for her love of him (Ex. 34:14).

How do you recognize God's jealous love for you? Zephaniah 3:17 says, "The LORD your God is in your midst, a mighty one who will save; he will rejoice over you with gladness; he will quiet you by his love; he will exult over you with loud singing." Do you rejoice over this love of God? Do you recognize it as love that he has for you? How do you respond to him in thankful service because of it?

3. Younger, *Judges/Ruth*, 88.

4. Daniel I. Block, *The New American Commentary*, vol. 6, *Judges, Ruth* (Nashville: Broadman & Holman, 1999), 125.

5. Davis, *Judges*, 32.

III. The Lord Raises Up Judges (2:16–19)

Although the Lord was faithful to his covenant curses and had every right to judge his people, in his grace and mercy he raised up deliverers for Israel to save them from their distress and the plunderers. Thus we will learn in the book of Judges that God often does not act according to the formula "obedience brings blessings while disobedience brings curses." Instead he often operates on the principle of grace.[6] These verses give a summary of the cycle of the judges in 3:7–16:31. We must be careful to clarify the "cycle," though, as one that gets progressively worse as the Israelites spiral downward into more and more apostasy.[7] Verse 17 recalls Exodus 34:15–16, which is found in the broader context of Israel worshiping the golden calf (Ex. 32). The same metaphor is used in that passage as here: "for they whored after other gods and bowed down to them."[8] And 2:18 is key to the interpretation of the whole book. It was the Lord who saved Israel from her enemies all the days of the judges. Why? Because the Lord was moved to pity by their groaning. The word for "groaning" here is the same word that is used in Exodus 2:24 and 6:5 in the context of the exodus from Egypt. By this word we are meant to reflect on God's faithful character in the exodus, which is still the same in the days of the judges.[9] And by doing so, we have great hope that the Lord who brought Israel out of her groaning in Egypt will again bring his people out of her groaning in the days of the judges.

As we study the book of Judges, we will learn that the judges God raised up are not men to model our lives after. The focus is on what God does through the deliverers. Salvation is of the Lord. While he works through the judges that he raises up, it is the Lord who delivers Israel. But Israel did not listen to the deliverers that the Lord raised up; instead the Israelites went after other gods and worshiped them. In contrast to Joshua's generation, they did not obey the Lord. Although each deliverer

6. Block, *Judges, Ruth*, 128.
7. Ibid., 132.
8. Ibid., 128.
9. Davis, *Judges*, 40.

would bring some relief and leadership for the present, after the judge died Israel would return to her old ways of idolatry.

To whom or what do we attribute deliverance and salvation in our lives? How do we respond to God's grace and deliverance in our lives? Do we cry out for relief from the Lord only to return to our old ways after he graciously delivers us? Or do we cry out in true repentance, turning from our sin to worship him?

IV. The Lord Tests Israel (2:20–3:6)

Because the people disregarded their covenant with the Lord, he tested Israel's commitment to walk in his ways by not driving out the nations before them that Joshua had left when he died. Instead they were to drive out the nations, displaying obedience to God's Word (see Deut. 7; 9:1–12). We cannot ride on the coattails of the faithful who have gone before us. Every individual is responsible to give an account before God. For those of us who are hidden in Christ, our account of judgment is cleared and we have the words "forgiven, loved, and my daughter" stamped across our names in the Book of Life.

The word for "test" in 2:22 is the same word used in Genesis 22:1 when the Lord tests Abraham with the sacrifice of Isaac.[10] However, we will see that the outcomes will stand in stark contrast to one another. Abraham was faithful, while Israel was not. Those who were tested had not experienced all the "wars in Canaan" (Judg. 3:1), another term for Israel's holy war in Joshua's day, and they needed to learn war. It is not that the Israelites needed to learn how to physically fight, but that they needed to learn the spiritual significance of this holy war.[11] The nations that the Lord left (see Josh. 13:2–6 for a more complete list) were the five lords of the Philistines (southwest), the Canaanites (southeast), the Sidonians (northwest), and the Hivites (northeast). This list encompasses the entire territory of the nation, and thus emphasizes that not one piece of land is untouched from spiritual apostasy.[12] We will see that every act

10. Block, *Judges, Ruth*, 133.
11. Ibid., 136.
12. Ibid., 139.

of war in the book revolves around throwing off the tyranny of oppression rather than conquering territory.[13]

The author doesn't make us wait to learn what the outcome of the test will be. We are told in 3:6 that Israel failed the test by intermarrying with people of other nations and by serving their gods. Why? Because they failed to separate from their ways and so became engaged in their ways. This failure is important for us to keep in mind as we move through the book of Judges. God has every right to judge his people. They are totally undeserving of his grace and mercy. He could have wiped them out and been totally justified. Yet instead he displays his grace and mercy for his people. What a beautiful picture that finds its climax in the Father's sending his Son, Jesus Christ, to die for those who stand guilty and worthy of eternal judgment. Rather than treating us as we deserve, he makes us sons and daughters through Christ. What wondrous love is this! That the Father would send his only Son and that this Son would willingly obey so that we might be daughters of God!

The danger of compromise with the world still stands true for the church today when she refuses to maintain any distinction from contemporary culture. But distinction from the culture does not mean departing from the culture. We must encourage Christians to pursue their callings to be teachers in the public schools, writers for the local newspaper, politicians, nurses and doctors in the hospitals, musicians and artists, and scientists and mathematicians. If we believe that God is Lord over all, then we should be actively involved in all that he is over for his name's sake.

The concluding verse concerning intermarriage with pagans and idolatry (see Deut. 7:3–5) stands in stark contrast with 2:7, "and the people served the LORD." Sin is a power that ensnares you. It is difficult to escape its tyranny. That is why it is good news that Jesus Christ broke the powers of darkness on the cross for you and for me. We are no longer slaves to sin but are free in Jesus Christ to be servants of righteousness.

13. Ibid., 133.

CONCLUSION

Sometimes our lives don't look very different from the Israelites' in the days of the judges. Enslaved by sin, we give the triune God syncretistic worship. This was true of me when I loyally served both the true God and the god of anorexia. But the Lord Jesus Christ did not leave me in the darkness of my sin. He heard my cry for deliverance, and in his mercy and grace he pulled me up out of the miry pit and delivered me. I was helpless to do it alone, and so was Israel. But by God's grace, which is manifested most fully in Jesus Christ, he raised up deliverers for Israel, he delivered me from the god of anorexia, and he has the power to deliver you from the sin in your life. May it be said of us that we served the Lord "all of our days" instead of turning to other gods.

LESSON 4

Judges 3:7–31

PLEASE USE THE QUESTION paradigm from pages 301–2 as you work through the following. See the introductory comments there that explain each part of the process below in more detail.

- **Pray.**
- **Ponder the Passage.** Read Judges 3:7–31 once a day from different translations for the entire week, looking for its:
  - Point
  - Persons
  - Problem
  - Patterns
  - Persons of the Trinity
  - Puzzling Parts
- **Put It in Perspective.**
  - Place in Scripture. Read Deuteronomy 7; 28:15–63.
  - Passages from Other Parts of Scripture. Read Judges 2:11–15.

1. Based on your observations of the text, what is the basic content of this passage? Try to summarize it in your own words, using a sentence or two.

2. Compare 3:7–11 with 2:11–15. How does the story of Othniel function as a paradigm for the time of the judges?

3. Who sells Israel into the hand of the king of Mesopotamia, Cushan-rishathaim (3:8)? Why? Did God have a right to be angry? See Deuteronomy 28:15–63. How many years does Israel serve this foreign king?

4. What do the people do in response? Is this a true cry of repentance or simply a cry of distress? Read 10:14 before you answer.

5. What is the Lord's response? In light of Israel's cry, why is this response especially gracious? Did the Lord owe Israel a deliverer? Was he obligated to save them? Does the Lord owe anyone a deliverer or is he obligated to save anyone? Where in Scripture do you see the Lord's greatest act of deliverance and whom does God raise up as the greatest Savior?

6. What is the name of the deliverer that the Lord raises up on behalf of Israel in 3:9? Where have we already seen this deliverer in the book? How was he characterized? This characterization is both important and intentional, as we will see reading through the other stories of the judges. This is the beginning of a downward spiral that will be seen both in the lives of Israel and in the lives of the deliverers. Is Othniel a true Israelite or a proselyte (one who was recognized as an Israelite because of his faith)? How does this display God's promise to Abraham in Genesis 12:3?

7. Who is on Othniel when he judges Israel (3:10)? Why is this significant? How does this fact, along with the fact that the Lord raised him up, guarantee Othniel's success?

8. Compare "he went out to war" (3:10) with 3:2. What does this imply about Othniel?

9. How long does the land have rest under Othniel's leadership? Compare this with how long they were enslaved to the king of Mesopotamia (3:8). How do you see God's grace?

10. What is the last phrase of the story (3:11)? Compare this with 2:8–9; 8:32; 10:2, 5; 12:7, 8, 11, 15; 16:30–31; Hebrews 7:22–25.

Whom do all these deliverers anticipate? Who is the only deliverer who will never die? From what has he delivered us?

11. How does 3:12–30 follow the paradigm of the story of Othniel? Who brought Eglon king of Moab against them? Using a concordance, what is Israel's history with Moab? Of what did Eglon take possession (this is another name for Jericho)? Compare this with Joshua 6:26. How long do the people of Israel serve Eglon?

12. What is the people's response to servitude? Again, is this repentance or a cry of distress (see 10:14)? What is God's gracious response?

13. How does the story in 3:15–29 ring of irony and satire? How does Ehud deceive? What does the phrase "he passed beyond the idols" in 3:26 imply about the land during this period? To whom does Ehud give credit for handing the enemy into their hands (3:28)? How does the totality of destruction (3:29) display God's power and glory?

14. Compare how many years the land had rest under Ehud (3:30) with how many years they served the king of Moab (3:14). How does this display God's grace?

15. Who is the third of the twelve deliverers the book of Judges records? How can we use the paradigm of Othniel's story in 3:7–11 to fill in the missing details? Using a study Bible or other reference tool, is Shamgar an Israelite? To what does "son of Anath" (3:31) refer? What does this tell us about God's choice of deliverers? Even though Shamgar does not receive much space in the text, how do we know that he was known in Israel (see 5:6)?

16. Whom does Shamgar kill and with what? What is the most significant note of the story? Who is the primary "he" behind saving Israel?

- **Principles and Points of Application.**

1. In what ways have you seen the Lord display grace in your life this week even when you had not yet repented of a sinful attitude

or action? Have you thanked him for this and repented of that sin? Spend time doing so today.

2. Meditate on Romans 2:4. What kindness has the Lord poured out on you today? Has he given you rest today from the chronic pain that often overtakes your body? Has he given you rest from financial distress? Has he given you rest in a country that does not persecute Christians? Has he given you rest by ample provision? Has he given you rest from rebellious children? Has he given you rest from conflict with your spouse or other loved ones? Has he given you rest from a habitual sin that often rears its ugly head in your life? Spend time today praising him and thanking him for giving you rest today.

3. Can you relate to Israel? Perhaps you have done something today that you know deserves God's just condemnation. Maybe you dare not even hope that he will draw near to you in grace and mercy again. Perhaps it's not the first time that you have made this same mistake and you don't possibly think that the Lord could extend grace again. But he does! He hears your cry before that cry is even a repentant one, and he draws near to you in his grace. Do you believe that? You have a Savior who comes down to you. He doesn't wait until you clean yourself up. He comes into your muck and mire. He is not afraid to rub shoulders with the unclean. He wraps you in his own clean robes of righteousness. He picks you up by his gracious hand and plants your feet on solid ground again. But he doesn't leave you there to walk alone. He gives you his Spirit so that you can walk in his ways and bring glory to him. Take refuge in his wings, repent of your sin, and praise him today!

4. How does the fact that the deliverers in the book of Judges always die, and more have to be raised up to deal with the people's sin, anticipate the need for a perfect and final Deliverer? Who is this final and perfect Deliverer who has come? Spend time in prayer and thanksgiving today for our Lord and Savior Jesus Christ.

NOTES FOR JUDGES 3:7–31

Ponder the aim of this lesson concerning our:

Mind: What do we need to know from this passage in Scripture?

> The Lord displays his grace through Othniel, Ehud, and Shamgar, and each one anticipates the need for the final and perfect Deliverer, Jesus Christ.

Heart: How does what we learn from this passage affect our internal relationship with the Lord?

> It prepares us to be kingdom disciples who respond in thanksgiving to Christ's deliverance from the power of sin and death.

Hands: How does what we learn from this passage translate into action for God's kingdom?

> It enables us to:

1. Spend time today praising the Lord and thanking him for giving us rest.
2. Recognize that the downward spiral of apostasy ends when we come to the Lord and place our trust in him, and recognize that the Holy Spirit enables us to be righteous, for we are new creatures in Christ.
3. Confess any unrighteousness and sin in our life, placing our hope and trust in Christ's righteousness, taking refuge in his wings, and praising him today!
4. Point our children or grandchildren or those who sit under our teaching to the perfect and final Savior, Jesus Christ, who has been and is and will be "all" for them.
5. Give thanks that we are in Christ, the true Israel, and are accepted before the Father on his merit, not ours, and give praise this

week that we are hidden in our perfect Deliverer, the One who has saved us from our sin.

INTRODUCTION

Mary[1] was hesitant to walk down the aisle when the pastor offered a time of prayer at the altar. She felt dirty inside and couldn't bear the thought of taking her sin before the Lord again. How many times she had gone before him, promising to never commit this sin again, and yet she always seemed to fail. How could the Holy God of the universe even bear to have someone like her in his presence, much less commune with her? She wanted to scrub herself clean first. Surely next week she would look better. Perhaps she could go a whole week without sinning and come into his presence next week feeling a little less dirty. As Mary walked out of the church that day, though, she placed little hope in the fact that she would be any better next week. Habitual sin seemed to be the story of her life. She thought she would never be good enough to come into the Lord's presence.

We have all been in Mary's shoes, haven't we? Because we can relate to Mary, we will be grateful that the Lord has included the stories he has from the book of Judges in the Bible. Perhaps some of them would receive an R rating, but then wouldn't the story of all our lives? Don't we oftentimes live in the muck and mire of sin, if we are honest? Aren't we messy people, covered with the filth of sin and unable to get clean? Don't we try to clean ourselves up before approaching the Lord? Haven't there been times when we have not gone before him in prayer because we don't feel worthy to do so? Aren't there times when we have wanted to call a substitute for our ministry position because we have messed up too badly that week to serve? Aren't we all legalists at heart, wanting to punish ourselves for our sin and clean ourselves up before entering into the presence of the almighty God?

The book of Judges gives us the clear answer that we will never be able to do that. We will never be good enough for God on our own. All

---

1. Mary represents many women whom I have counseled over the years.

of us left to ourselves will spiral downward into sin and apostasy. We need a Savior, and not just a temporary one or just a human one. We need God himself to come down to us and meet us where we are in the muck and mire of our sin. We need God to clean the dirt off us and make us acceptable to approach the throne of grace. The good news is that he has. Jesus Christ left his perfect home of glory and came down to our world of sinful people in order to clean us up and save us from the filth of our souls. We do not have to reach up to him; he came down to us. And he is the one who makes us holy, pure, spotless, acceptable, beautiful, and worthy to be in our Father's presence. Whatever that "one sin" is that keeps you from prayer is one of all the sins that Jesus bore on the cross. You are beautiful before your heavenly Father because you are robed in the righteousness of Christ. You don't have to get clean before you repent. Christ has already made you clean. He has delivered you from the power of sin and of death and wants you to commune with him today. Judges 3:7–31 has much to say about being kingdom disciples who respond in thanksgiving to Christ's deliverance from the power of sin and death.

We can divide the lesson into three sections:

   I. The Lord Displays His Grace through Othniel (3:7–11)
  II. The Lord Displays His Grace through Ehud (3:12–30)
 III. The Lord Displays His Grace through Shamgar (3:31)

I. The Lord Displays His Grace through Othniel (3:7–11)

Israel's unfaithfulness that was described in 2:11–14 is described again in almost the exact same language in 3:7–8. The Israelites did evil in the Lord's eyes by forgetting him and serving the Baals and Asheroth. Here it is Asherah, the fertility goddess represented most often by an upright wooden pole, that is in view.[2] God's righteous anger was kindled, and he was faithful to his covenant promises by selling the Israelites into the hand of an enemy. This time, instead of being given

2. K. Lawson Younger Jr., *Judges/Ruth*, The NIV Application Commentary (Grand Rapids: Zondervan, 2002), 101.

over to plunderers, they are sold into the hand of Cushan-rishathaim for eight years. The meaning of this ruler's name in the Hebrew is "Cushan-double wickedness," which is probably a name coined by the oppressed Israelites for him.[3] The Lord who had delivered his people from slavery in Egypt puts them back under slavery in the Promised Land because they had abandoned their covenant with him. Yet even in this we see God's grace, for it is often during slavery that the Lord turns our hearts away from the idols so prevalent in and around us and toward the true God. The Covenant Lord is always pursuing, never apologizing for using hardship to awaken dead and rebellious souls.[4]

The distressed Israelites cried out to the Lord. What does this verb mean in the Hebrew? It means crying out for help because of distress or anguish, often directed toward the Lord, but sometimes to anyone who will listen. In other words, this verb does not convey true repentance.[5] This is further confirmed by the Lord's response to their cry in 10:14 when he tells them, "Go and cry out to the gods whom you have chosen; let them save you in the time of your distress."[6] Yet despite their unrepentant hearts and because of his marvelous grace, the Lord raised up a deliverer for them who saved them. The phrase "who saved them" (3:9) takes the emphasis in this story, as there are exactly eight lines before and after it in the Hebrew.[7] The Lord was not obligated to do this. This was not part of the covenant curses. He would have been just in ignoring their cry for help and punishing them for their disobedience. But instead, here in the book of Judges in the Old Testament, the Lord displays his grace of salvation in a mighty way. He raises up Othniel the son of Kenaz, Caleb's younger brother.

We have already met Othniel in the book in 1:13. He was the one who took Caleb's challenge to attack and capture Kiriath-sepher for the reward of Caleb's daughter Achsah as wife. He is associated with the

---

3. Dale Ralph Davis, *Judges: Such a Great Salvation* (Fearn, Great Britain: Christian Focus, 2000), 51.

4. Ibid., 49.

5. Ibid., 49–50.

6. Younger, *Judges/Ruth*, 102.

7. Ibid., 104.

first story in the book of Judges that seemed to paint a good and normal family. He is also a proselyte; he is included in the tribe of Judah along with Achsah and Caleb (Kenizzites) because of their faith in the Lord.[8] So here we see that one of the promises of the Abrahamic covenant is being fulfilled ("in you all the families of the earth shall be blessed"; Gen. 12:3). Nothing negative is said about him in these verses. We read that the Spirit of the Lord was on him and that he judged Israel. This is the key to Othniel's power. It was not that Othniel was powerful or great in and of himself, but that he was deliverer of Israel because the Spirit of the Lord was on him. Salvation is always and only from the Lord.

He went out to war (so he knew war, unlike those described in 3:2) and thus passed God's test (2:22–3:2). So the Lord gave Cushan-rishathaim, the king of Mesopotamia, the instrument that God had previously used to judge Israel, into his hand and allowed his hand to prevail against this enemy king. This, by the way, will not be the last time we see this pattern in Scripture. The Lord often raises up his people's enemies to be an instrument of judgment against them (i.e., Assyria and Babylon), but in the end destroys them.

The land of Israel had rest for forty years while Othniel was alive. Let us not pass over this time of rest too quickly, for it is another testimony of God's grace. Remember that the length of time the Israelites were oppressed by Cushan-rishathaim was only eight years in comparison to forty years of rest! Not exactly equal lengths of time! God graciously poured out on his undeserving people more rest than he had judgment. Often it is the kindness of God that leads us to repentance (Rom. 2:4).[9] What kindness has the Lord poured out on you today? Has he given you rest today from the chronic pain that often overtakes your body? Has he given you rest from financial distress? Has he given you rest in a country that does not persecute Christians? Has he given you rest by ample provision? Has he given you rest from rebellious children? Has he given you rest from conflict with your spouse or other loved ones? Has he given you rest from a habitual sin that often rears

8. Ibid., 106.
9. Davis, *Judges*, 53.

its ugly head in your life? Spend time today praising him and thanking him for giving you rest today.

"Then Othniel the son of Kenaz died" (3:11). Like a resounding gong this phrase will be heard over and over again in the book. We have already seen it in 1:1 and 2:8 concerning Joshua and in 2:10 concerning Joshua's generation. Here we see it concerning the first deliverer. Though it may seem redundant and insignificant, it is deeply significant, for it continually points us to the fact that there is no lasting deliverer or savior for Israel. Except One. And that One has now come in the Lord and Savior Jesus Christ. God had to come as both Lord and servant. He came as the true Israel to fulfill the law that Israel failed to fulfill, and he came to save God's people from sin and to be exalted as King. He will never die, but reigns eternally as our King and our High Priest. Glory be to his name!

Unfortunately the other eleven of the twelve deliverers will not continue Othniel's pattern, although the story itself reads like a paradigm for life in the time of the judges.[10] Instead the book of Judges reads like a downward spiral into apostasy with each successive story of the judges. Right away that should signal to us that the book of Judges is not about the judges of Israel, but about the grace of God. The same is true for our own stories that the Lord is writing with our lives. Our stories are not about us, but about the grace and glory of God that is written across them every moment of every day. It is the Lord who raises up deliverance for his people through the office of judge in order to bring glory to his name and to display grace to his people.

Each of the twelve stories points to the greatest event in the greatest story ever told, the story of redemption in the Bible. Each deliverer whom God raises up points us forward to the need for the true and final Deliverer, Jesus Christ. For not one of the deliverers in Israel that God raised up could solve the problem of Israel's apostasy. Indeed many of the judges themselves were a large part of the problem. This is not a book about heroes of the faith. It is a book about the one and only hero of the faith, Jesus Christ. It is a book about man's inherent sin and the

10. Ibid., 48.

need for the Spirit of God to awaken the unrighteous from their spiritually dead state and enable us to believe in the Lord. It is a book that points us to the land that has rest for eternity, because the true Deliverer, Jesus Christ, never dies. The downward spiral of apostasy ends when we come to him and place our trust in him. The Holy Spirit enables us to be righteous, for we are new creatures in Christ.

II. The Lord Displays His Grace through Ehud (3:12–30)

Again we read that Israel did what was evil in the sight of the Lord, and so the Lord handed Israel over to Eglon the king of Moab (along with the Ammonites and Amalekites), who took Jericho (the city of palms, the first and greatest Israelite victory by the power of God recorded in Joshua 6, and the city that Joshua had cursed; 6:26) and placed Israel under servitude for eighteen years. The Moabites had tried to defeat Israel earlier in their history by hiring Balaam to curse Israel (Num. 22–24), but God had his way with this false prophet and brought glory to his name by having Balaam bless Israel instead.

Again, in his grace and mercy, the Lord raised up a deliverer, Ehud (3:15). This is the key of the entire story. This is a story about God's deliverance. And it is not deserved deliverance. God would have been fully justified in leaving Israel in their sin and shame, but instead he pursued them in his love, responded to their cries for help even though they did not bear a note of repentance, and delivered them from what they had done to themselves and fully deserved. This is the God of grace that we serve.

Can you relate to Israel? Perhaps you have done something today that you know deserves God's just condemnation. Maybe you dare not even hope that he will draw near to you in grace and mercy again. Perhaps it's not the first time that you have made this same mistake and you don't think that the Lord could possibly extend grace again. But he does! He hears your cry before that cry is even a repentant one, and he draws near to you in his grace. Do you believe that? You have a Savior who comes down to you. He doesn't wait until you clean yourself up. He comes into your muck and mire. He is not afraid to rub shoulders with the unclean. He wraps you in his own clean robes of righteousness. He picks you up by his gracious hand and plants your feet on solid ground again. But he doesn't leave you there to walk alone. He gives you his Spirit so that you can walk in his ways and bring glory to him. Take refuge in his wings and praise him today!

Ehud was the son of Gera and was a Benjamite who was left-handed. While at first glance his left-handedness seems insignificant, it becomes extremely significant in the story, so stay tuned! It is interesting that the men of Israel sent tribute by him to Eglon the king of Moab. Was this Ehud's strategy at work to try to gain favor in the eyes of this oppressive king? Ehud made a two-edged sword and bound it to his right thigh under his clothes. Why is this significant? Remember the note on his being left-handed? Well, most people would be expecting a right-handed man, whose sword would be placed on his left thigh under his clothes. So Ehud already had the advantage over his enemy. He presented the tribute to the fat king of Moab, strategically sent away the people who had carried the tribute, and turned back at the significant point of the idols near Gilgal. He commanded silence as he stated that he had a secret message for the king. Ehud said it was secret in order to move the attendants out of his presence so that it was just Eglon and Ehud together in the room. While the fat man sat in his cool roof chamber, Ehud came to tell him that he had a message from God for him. At this word Eglon rose from his seat. It was at this moment that Ehud reached with his left hand, took the sword from his right thigh, and thrust it into Eglon's fat belly. Thus the one who brought the tribute to the king (Ehud) now makes the king himself the sacrifice, and rightly so. This greedy king had gotten fat off extortions from Israel.[11] The sword penetrated so deep and so low that Eglon's dung came out of his body, thus stinking up the room. Ehud left by way of the porch, closing and locking the doors behind him. The enemy was killed before the battle had even begun![12]

11. Younger, *Judges/Ruth*, 115–17.
12. Ibid., 121.

A while later Eglon's servants came and thought that the locked doors meant that Eglon was in the bathroom. Of course, the smell of dung coming from inside must have contributed to their thinking this! So they waited until he was done. But it was taking so long that even the servants grew embarrassed on behalf of the fat king! When he still did not unlock the doors, they finally did, and there he lay on the floor dead.

Ehud escaped while Eglon's servants were thinking that they were waiting for the king to finish in the bathroom, appropriately passing by the idols that obviously could not help the fat king, and escaped to Seirah. The fact that Ehud so easily passed the idols by and the narrator says nothing at all about them signifies that they had become common fare to the Israelites.[13] When he arrived at Seirah he sounded the trumpet in the hill country of Ephraim to announce his victory. The people of Israel willingly followed him as their leader who told them that the Lord had given the Moabites into their hand. They seized the fords of the Jordan against the Moabites and did not allow anyone to pass over. Not one of the ten thousand strong, able-bodied Moabites escaped. The Lord delivered them from their oppressors through Ehud the deceptive deliverer, and the land had rest for eighty years. Again, do not pass over this note of grace too quickly! The land had rest for eighty years in comparison to the eighteen years of oppression. What a merciful Lord we serve!

Was Ehud successful? The story ends on a note of rest. But we have only to read 4:1 to learn that the rest Ehud brought to the land was short-lived, for "Israel again did what was evil in the sight of the LORD." Again, the text points us to the need for a different kind of deliverer. God himself must come. And he has. Jesus Christ stepped down from his perfect world into our imperfect one, rubbed shoulders with and healed the unclean, cast out demons, reached out and gave respect to the socially ostracized, lived a life of perfect obedience on our behalf, and died a criminal's death in our place so that we might enter the courts of heaven with praise, having been

13. Daniel I. Block, *The New American Commentary*, vol. 6, *Judges, Ruth* (Nashville: Broadman & Holman, 1999), 165.

reconciled to our Father through the death of his Son, Jesus Christ. Now that's amazing grace!

III. The Lord Displays His Grace through Shamgar (3:31)

While Shamgar only receives one sentence in the text, it is an important one for several reasons. First, he is the third of twelve deliverers that the author of Judges records. While we know almost nothing of his roots, most commentators agree that he was most likely not an Israelite.[14] In fact, his name most likely means that "Shamgar was devoted to the service of Anath," who was the consort of Baal and Canaanite goddess of war.[15] This further confirms that the deliverers are not to be used as examples to imitate. We do not teach our children or grandchildren or those who sit under our teaching to be like the judges, but instead must point them to the perfect and final Savior, Jesus Christ, who has been and is and will be "all" for them. There is nothing left to do for God. He has done it all through his Son, Jesus Christ. It is the Lord who saves, and it is the Lord who sanctifies. We live and move and have our being in him (Acts 17:28).

This is not the only time in Scripture that we see the Lord raise up those from other nations to deliver Israel (e.g., Cyrus; see Isa. 45:1–7). We also know little of Shamgar in general, but this does not mean that he was not well known in Israel's day. In fact, he is spoken of in Judges 5:6, implying that he was a significant and well-known deliverer.[16] Second, he was raised up after Ehud (a chronological note), so God's grace continued to be seen. Third, he killed six hundred of the Philistines, an enemy of Israel that we will encounter later in the book as well (see the story of Samson). Fourth, he did it with an oxgoad, which by its very nature attributed glory to God. An oxgoad "might be eight feet long and up to six inches in circumference at the larger end. The smaller end was armed with a

14. Davis, *Judges*, 66.
15. Block, *Judges, Ruth*, 173.
16. Davis, *Judges*, 66.

sharp prick for driving the oxen, the other end with a small spade or iron paddle for cleaning out the plow."[17] In other words, this could cause some damage to people when used as a weapon! Fifth and most importantly, he saved Israel.

Again the Lord displays his grace. Apparently after the previous eighty years of rest, the Israelites had again done evil in the eyes of the Lord and had been delivered over to the hand of the Philistines. They had likely cried out again (not in repentance, but in distress), and the Lord had graciously responded by raising up Shamgar. In order to display his glory and display that he alone saves, he used an oxgoad to kill the Philistines at the hand of Shamgar. The fact that Shamgar saved Israel, but not for long, pointed to the need for a greater Deliverer who could save God's people for good. And this Deliverer has come. Jesus Christ came to save and to seek the lost. He came to subdue the enemy of God and deliver God's people from oppression by the enemy. He came as the perfect and final Savior. But he also came as the perfect Israel. What Israel could not do—obey God's commands and keep covenant with him—Jesus Christ did perfectly. And all of us who are in Christ, the true Israel, are accepted before the Father on his merit, not ours. We are hidden in our perfect Deliverer, the one who has saved us from our sin.

CONCLUSION

Are you waiting until you get all cleaned up before coming to the Lord and Savior Jesus Christ? Perhaps you need to come for the first time and place your trust in him alone. Perhaps you have been away for a long time like the Prodigal Son and need to come home today and find acceptance in the arms of your Father opened to embrace you. Maybe you have messed up this week and need to quickly repent and draw near to him again. Your Deliverer has already accomplished your deliverance and stands with arms wide open to welcome you into communion again. Won't you run to

17. Ibid.

the shelter of his almighty wings today? He is not a deliverer who is human and dies, he is not a deliverer who deceives and lies, he is not a deliverer who is outside the people of God. Jesus Christ is the perfect God-man who lives to intercede eternally for you. He lived a life of perfect righteousness and died a criminal's death to bear God's wrath in your place. He is the perfect Son of God, the Elder Brother of all God's children, and he delights to sing over you with his love. Now this is amazing grace!

LESSON 5

Judges 4:1–5:31

Please use the question paradigm from pages 301–2 as you work through the following. See the introductory comments there that explain each part of the process below in more detail.

- **Pray.**
- **Ponder the Passage.** Read Judges 4:1–5:31 once a day from different translations for the entire week, looking for its:
  - Point
  - Persons
  - Problem
  - Patterns
  - Persons of the Trinity
  - Puzzling Parts
- **Put It in Perspective.**
  - Place in Scripture. Read Deuteronomy 28:15–68.
  - Passages from Other Parts of Scripture. Read Exodus 14–15; Revelation 19:11–16.

1. Based on your observations of the text, what is the basic content of this passage? Try to summarize it in your own words, using a sentence or two.

2. In light of 3:31, what name would we expect in 4:1 in place of Ehud?

3. Is Israel's cry one of repentance or distress in 4:3 (see 10:14)?

4. Are the people of Israel supposed to fear the chariots of iron (4:3)? See Joshua 17:18.

5. How many years does the king of Canaan oppress the Israelites?

6. How is Deborah introduced in 4:4? How does this differ from the way the other deliverers have been introduced? Look up the word "prophetess" in a concordance. Who else in Scripture is named this? What else do you learn about this role?

7. How does Deborah represent the voice of God in Barak's life? How does Barak act like the other judges that the Lord has called to be military leaders in the book? Read Hebrews 11:32. Who is named from this story? In light of Barak's resistance to God's call, how does this display God's grace?

8. What two tribes is Barak to take with him into battle (4:6)? How does Deborah speak of them in 5:18?

9. What is the prophecy given in 4:9? How is this fulfilled in 4:21?

10. How does 4:11 prepare us and connect us with 4:17? What does it reveal about God's providence?

11. How is 4:14a the key to the entire passage? Whose battle is this, and yet whom does he call to fight on his behalf? How does this battle anticipate the final battle (see Rev. 19:11–16)?

12. What does the note in 4:11 and 4:17 reveal about Israel during this time?

13. How does Jael use hospitality to trap Sisera? Does the author commend or condemn her actions? What does this reveal about the Lord's ways?

14. How does Barak's pursuit of Sisera betray his lack of trust in God's prophetic word and his desire to receive his own glory?

15. Who is blessed in Deborah's song (5:2)?

16. What are the three different contrasts in 5:2–11c, 11d–23, 24–30?

17. Note which tribes are faithful and which are unfaithful to join in the Lord's battle (5:14–18).

18. Describe the battle in 5:19–22. Compare this with the exodus (Ex. 14–15). How do these verses anticipate the second exodus (Rev. 21)?

19. Who do the inhabitants of Meroz (5:23) represent in a broader context, and how does this reflect the covenant curses in Deuteronomy 28:15–63?

20. Contrast Deborah, Jael, and Sisera's mother.

21. How does Deborah's prayer in 5:31 anticipate the Lord's Prayer in Matthew 6:9–13?

22. How do the years of rest (5:31) in comparison to the years of oppression (4:3) display God's grace?

- **Principles and Points of Application.**

  1. Let us ponder the phrase "the road on which you are going will not lead to your glory, for the LORD . . ." (4:9). This is one of those verses we would do well to memorize for our lives. The road on which we are going will not lead to our glory, but to the Lord's. What is our goal in life? Is it to be a successful career woman? Is it to get married and have a family? Is it to build a dynamic women's ministry? Is it to have financial security? Is it to have successful children or a successful husband? Spend time today memorizing this phrase, confessing any glory that you are seeking for yourself, and committing to run the road that will lead to the Lord's glory.

  2. Reflect on 4:11, 17 in light of God's providence in our lives. He always has the right people in the right place at the right time (a theme that we will see in the book of Ruth as well!). In what area of your life do you need to trust God's providence today?

  3. How do you show bold justice and righteousness in your spheres of influence today? Are you willing to do the right thing even if it costs you? Spend time committing your situation to the Lord today, recognizing that the Holy Spirit will give you just the right words to say and actions to take.

  4. We do not serve a God who is afraid to move on behalf of his people. All through history, the Lord reveals himself as the active

63

God of the universe, fighting on behalf of his people. In what situation in your present life do you need to recognize this? Do so today, and rest in him as your Warrior.

5. How do you offer yourself willingly for the kingdom of God? How do you repeat the triumphs of the Lord? How do you come to the side of the Lord in his battle? Would others know that you are in the Lord's army? Spend time today offering yourself to the Lord, recognizing that his Spirit will give you all that you need to accomplish your service for him.

6. Can we identify with the unfaithful tribes of Israel (5:15–18)? Has the Lord called us to do something, and we give it deep consideration, weigh the pros and cons, and decide against it because it would bring us more harm than good, even though in the long run our disobedience to the Lord's call brings us more harm? Or what about Dan? He seems to stay behind with the ships in order to not miss out on wealth from trade. Have we ever put wealth before the Lord? Confess any unfaithfulness to the Lord today, turning toward faithfulness by the power of the Holy Spirit.

7. Have we ever sat idly by while others are speaking or acting against our Lord and not come to his defense? The blessing and praise that Deborah gives to Jael will stand in stark contrast to this curse. It is a serious thing to oppose the will of God. His children are to be his helpers. His enemies are to be our enemies. Though our warfare is different on this side of the cross (see Eph. 6:10–20), we are still called to be in the Lord's army and fight with him against the spiritual rulers of this world.

8. Deborah, as a woman of God, serves him with the gifts that he has bestowed on her. As such, she serves as a wonderful testimony of God's faithfulness to use his daughters in the history of redemption to declare his glory. Perhaps your roles as a woman in the church has brought confusion to you, or maybe you recognize that the Lord has given us different roles from men and delights to use us in his service. Spend time in prayer

today, asking him to lead you and guide you in the service that he wants you to be involved with for his kingdom.

9. The Lord's friends are those who love him with all their heart, mind, and soul. This was Israel's greatest responsibility, and it still remains the greatest responsibility for the people of God. Do we love him? Do we really love him with all our heart, soul, and mind? Or are we more taken with the gods of this world than we are with him? Spend time in worship and confession today.

NOTES FOR JUDGES 4:1–5:31

Ponder the aim of this lesson concerning our:

Mind: What do we need to know from this passage in Scripture?

The Lord alone delivers his people by whatever means he chooses, bringing glory to his name.

Heart: How does what we learn from this passage affect our internal relationship with the Lord?

It prepares us to be kingdom disciples who are bold in the Lord's battle as we fight against the spiritual enemies of this world, recognizing that the Lord has already won and singing a song of praise and glory to him.

Hands: How does what we learn from this passage translate into action for God's kingdom?

It enables us to:

1. Be encouraged as women by the Lord's choice of Deborah to speak his word and Jael to fulfill his word, recognizing that while we are not to usurp the authority distinctively given to men,

we as women do have a significant, though different, design to fulfill for the kingdom of God.

2. Recognize, confess, and repent of any road that we might be traveling for our own glory, committing that road to the glory of the Lord.

3. Exemplify bold justice and righteousness in our spheres of life today, being willing to do the right thing even if it is costly, while relying on the power of the Holy Spirit.

4. Offer ourselves willingly for service in the kingdom of God, to repeat the righteous triumphs of the Lord, to come to the Lord's help in the spiritual battle of this present world, and to display our commitment to our Warrior by being warriors for him through the enablement of the Holy Spirit.

5. Love our enemies and do good to those who persecute us, while telling them the gospel and warning them of the final day of judgment.

INTRODUCTION

There seems to be a great deal of confusion today within the church concerning the role of women in ministry. This should not be. Not only has it done a great deal of harm to women, it has also done a great deal of harm to men, and thus the church has suffered as a witness in this world to display the beautiful truth that the Lord made a helper for man because the Lord did not think that it was good that man should be alone. We are to be our brothers' helpers. While recognizing that the Lord has given us different designs, we are to recognize that the Lord has also called his daughters to serve him and glorify him in mighty and strategic ways in the body of Christ.

Has the Lord given us any such examples in his Word? Yes, he has. While the time of the judges was a dark time, Deborah the prophetess stood out as one of a few lone voices that brought glory to God by singing of his word and his works. She was used by God to speak truth and to encourage Barak to pursue the Lord's call on his life. She did not usurp the position that was not hers, but graciously and boldly fulfilled the role that the Lord gave her in salvation history. As such, she serves as a reminder that the Lord delights in using his daughters in the service of his kingdom and will do so with all those who are faithful to turn their eyes toward him, committed to fulfill the roles that he has given us. As we do, we join together with all kingdom disciples who are bold in the Lord's battle as we fight against the spiritual enemies of this world, recognizing that the Lord has already won and singing a song of praise and glory to him.

We can divide the lesson into two sections:

I. The Lord Raises Up Deborah, Barak, and Jael to Defeat the Canaanites (4:1–24)

II. The Lord Raises Up a Song of Praise by Deborah (5:1–31)

I. The Lord Raises Up Deborah, Barak, and Jael to Defeat the Canaanites (4:1–24)

Before we begin reading chapter 4, it is helpful for us to note its carefully crafted literary structure, for this speaks of the meaning of the text itself and helps us see the climax of the story.

> The king of Canaan oppresses Israel (4:1–3)
>> Deborah the prophetess summons Barak (4:4–9)
>>> Barak calls out his troops and Sisera calls out his (4:10–13)
>>>> The Lord goes before Barak to win the victory (4:14a)
>>> Barak goes down to attack and Sisera goes down to flee (4:14b–16)
>> Jael meets Sisera to kill him and meets Barak to speak of victory (4:17–22)
> God delivers Israel from the king of Canaan (4:23–24)[1]

We again read that Israel did evil in the sight of the Lord. Interestingly, the text says, "after Ehud died" (4:1), where we would expect

---

1. Dale Ralph Davis has a similar outline in his commentary; *Judges: Such a Great Salvation* (Fearn, Great Britain: Christian Focus, 2000), 71.

"after Shamgar died." The Lord sold them into the hand of Jabin king of Canaan, whose commander of his army was Sisera, who lived in Harosheth-hagoyim, most likely meaning "cultivated field of the Gentiles."[2] The people cried out to the Lord for help, which again does not convey repentance but a cry of distress. They were afraid because Sisera had nine hundred chariots of iron. This has been noted as a problem in the book before. In 1:19 we read that Judah took possession of the hill country but could not take possession of the plain because the inhabitants had chariots of iron. However, we saw in Joshua that even the chariots of iron were not to keep them from possessing the land (Josh. 17:18). The Lord was stronger than both chariots of iron and the Canaanites. Israel lived under the oppression of the Canaanites for twenty years.

In the first three accounts of judges in Israel, we read that the Lord raised them up and they went out in a military victory. But here we read that Deborah was a prophetess who was already judging Israel at the time of Israel's servitude to Canaan. This serves to confirm the failure of the priesthood in Israel at the time of the judges, for the Israelites should have sought the word of the Lord from the priests.[3] The fact that Deborah receives the title "prophetess" links her to the other prophetesses in Scripture in the line of Moses,[4] and should encourage us that the Lord still uses Deborah to speak to the church today through his word in her song (ch. 5). The people of Israel sought her out for judgment. It was Deborah the prophetess who sent and summoned Barak, the one whom the Lord had commanded to be the military leader (as he had raised up Othniel, Ehud, and Shamgar). Interestingly, in Hebrews 11:32 we read of Barak, not Deborah. Deborah was to communicate the Lord's response to the people's cry, but it was Barak who led forth the battle in the pathway of the Lord.[5] Barak was to take ten thousand from the tribe of Naphtali and Zebulun and gather at Mount Tabor, for the Lord would draw out Sisera and his troops to meet him at the river

2. Daniel I. Block, *The New American Commentary*, vol. 6, *Judges, Ruth* (Nashville: Broadman & Holman, 1999), 190.

3. Ibid., 197.

4. Ibid., 192.

5. Ibid., 195.

Kishon where the Lord would give him into Barak's hand. The Lord is portrayed as the mighty warrior who fights on behalf of his people. The same is true today. Our King, Jesus Christ, is coming a second time as the mighty warrior who comes to judge and gather his own from every tribe, tongue, and nation to take his bride home.

Barak's reply further confirms Deborah as a prophetess, for he responds to her as if he is responding to the Lord. Barak will not go unless the voice of the Lord goes with him. Or another way of looking at it is that Barak will not go unless a woman goes with him, which was shameful in those days.[6] However, his answer also betrays his resistance to God's call.[7] This is ironic since his name means "lightning." Barak is anything but quick to act and early to arrive. The Lord displays his grace through Deborah who immediately agrees, but she does tell Barak that the road on which he is going will not lead to his glory, for the Lord would give Sisera into the hand of a woman. At this point in the story, it is easy to think that it will be Deborah who will defeat Sisera. But we are in for a surprise! This is also a note of prophecy, and when it is fulfilled there can be no doubt that it was the Lord's doing.[8] So both Deborah and Barak go to Kedesh where ten thousand from the tribe of Zebulun and Naphtali went up to battle.

Before leaving these words, let us ponder the phrase "the road on which you are going will not lead to your glory, for the LORD . . ." (4:9). This is one of those verses we would do well to memorize for our lives. The road on which we are going will not lead to our glory, but to the Lord's. What is your goal in life? Is it to be a successful career woman? Is it to get married and have a family? Is it to build a dynamic women's ministry? Is it to have financial security? Is it to have successful children or a successful husband? The Lord is not interested in bringing us glory. Man's chief end is to glorify God and to enjoy him forever (Westminster Shorter Catechism, A1). The road that we are on will not lead to our glory, but to our good (Rom. 8:28). It is

6. I am indebted to Dr. Iain Duguid for this thought.
7. Block, *Judges, Ruth*, 199.
8. Davis, *Judges*, 75.

the Lord's glory road that we are on, and the sooner we learn that, the more fully we can enjoy the journey.

We come to an interesting note in 4:11. Heber the Kenite had separated from the Kenites, the descendants of the father-in-law of Moses. So even in one of the godliest families in Israel, separation unto ungodliness is occurring. Heber had pitched his tent as far away as the oak in Zaanannim near Kedesh. Keep this in mind because it's going to connect to a later part of the story, and it confirms to us the glorious truth of God's providence in our lives. He always has the right people in the right place at the right time (a theme that we will see in the book of Ruth as well!).

Sisera found out that Barak had gone up to Mount Tabor, so he called out his chariots and men. Deborah, being a prophetess, knew it was time for Barak to get up and go down to fight. She assured him that it was the day that the Lord had given Sisera into his hand and that the Lord was before him. This is the key to both chapter 4 and chapter 5. The battle is the Lord's! And yet he calls and expects his people to fight on his behalf. It was the Lord who routed Sisera and *all his chariots* and *all his army* before Barak by the sword. While Sisera got down from his chariot and fled away on foot, Barak pursued the army, and *all of them* fell by the sword.

However, there was one man, the commander of the army, Sisera, who had fled by foot to the tent of Jael, who we now learn is the wife of Heber the Kenite who was introduced in 4:11. We also learn that there was peace between them, which means that one in Moses' family had made peace with a Canaanite and was on such hospitable terms with the Canaanites that the commander fled to his tent in a time of battle! How far Israel has strayed from God's command to make no alliance with the people of Canaan! But we will see that if Heber was the leader in this decision, his wife was only following his hospitality superficially, for she was most hospitable to Sisera. She comforted him by telling him not to be afraid (as she wooed him into her own trap). Furthermore, she not only answered his request for water but also went beyond it to give him milk (a nice thing to do until we remember that she is about to crush his skull!).

70

Then she covered him, as if she was assuring his stay. Sisera, in a word to save himself, spoke to the very one from whom his death would come and told her to hide him from any pursuers. But the pursuer was Jael herself, and once Sisera was fast asleep she confidently and boldly drove a tent peg into his temple with a hammer, killing him and making the number of the army that was destroyed complete. Again we see that a woman is doing what the men should have done but failed to do.

Jael went out to meet Barak before he could reach his desired foe and kill him with his own sword. This too betrays Barak's desire to receive the glory for himself. Deborah had already prophesied that he would not receive the glory, but he was running full force after it anyway.[9] Indeed the road that he was going on did not lead to his glory, but to the Lord's, for God sold Sisera into the hand of Jael. While the story line may make us cringe, this is what Israel was supposed to be doing—totally annihilating the Canaanites. Remember what kind of people we are dealing with. One look at 5:30 puts Sisera's execution in context; Sisera's mom was comforting herself concerning her son's delayed arrival with the thought that rape and pillage take time.

Ultimately the prophecy of 4:9 is fulfilled by the Lord's doing. The narrator gives God all the glory for subduing the king of Canaan before Israel and for his destruction at the hand of the Israelites. We too must give him the glory. The note of rest that we expect at this point will have to wait until 5:31, "and the land had rest for forty years."

II. The Lord Raises up a Song of Praise by Deborah (5:1–31)

So often what is difficult to communicate through prose is easily and magnificently communicated through song. Here we have chapter 4 put to a tune in chapter 5, adding new information to the previous narrative and amplifying it with emotion. The only other place in Scripture in which we have two parallel accounts, one in prose and one in poetry, is in Exodus 14–15, which is a celebration of the Lord's deliverance of Israel from Egypt through the Red Sea.[10] The song breaks into three

9. Block, *Judges, Ruth*, 208.
10. Ibid., 176.

major divisions (5:2–11c, 11d–23, 24–30), which each revolve around
a contrast (Israel's silent submission to enemies vs. the Lord's action on
behalf of his people; the faithful tribes vs. the unfaithful tribes; and the
most blessed of women, Jael, vs. the poorest of women, Sisera's mother).[11]

Barak and Deborah bless the Lord for the leadership of Israel taking
the lead and the people offering themselves willingly. They recognized
that this was nothing of their own merit, but that it was all of grace.
Before kings and princes Barak and Deborah sing to the Lord. They
give honor where honor is due, recognizing that the true King is in
heaven. They sing of the past faithfulness of the Lord. It was the Lord
who faithfully brought them through the wilderness, made the covenant with them at Sinai, and brought them to Zion (5:4–5). And it is
the Lord who will march out on their behalf again. We do not serve a
God who is afraid to move on behalf of his people. All through history,
the Lord reveals himself as the active God of the universe, fighting on
behalf of his people.

Another historical note referencing the time of the judges (5:6)
reveals that in the days of Shamgar the highways were not even safe places
to travel. The villagers ceased, but then Deborah arose as a mother in
Israel (5:7). Israel was found without shield or spear. Evidently they had
fallen into silent submission before their enemies (5:8). Again Deborah
blesses the Lord and recognizes that it was by his grace that the com-
manders of Israel offered themselves willingly among the people (5:9).

Deborah calls on all the people, whether wealthy rulers or the
poorer classes who walked by the way. When they rested at the public
watering places (usual places of gossip and celebrations of events[12]), they
were to repeat the righteous triumphs of the Lord, and thus the righteous
triumphs of his people, to the villagers in Israel (5:10–11). Down to the
gates (the fortified cities of Canaan) march the people of the Lord (the
only time this phrase is used in the book and the name which conveys
the ideal covenant relationship established at Sinai).[13] The call to worship

11. Davis, *Judges*, 82.
12. Block, *Judges, Ruth*, 229.
13. Ibid., 230.

closes with a note for Deborah to awake in song and Barak to arise in action to lead away his captives.

The people of the Lord marched from the gates (5:11) into the valley. But only some of the tribes were faithful to march into battle. We clearly see here a picture of a fragmented Israel during the time of the judges. Although they were united by their covenant with the Lord in principle, they were anything but one nation spiritually, politically, and militarily.[14] The tribes of Ephraim, Benjamin, Manasseh (Machir), Zebulun, Issachar, and Naphtali were praised. But the tribes of Reuben, Gad (Gilead), Dan, and Asher were questioned as to their faithfulness. It is clear from the text that they were not oblivious. The text says there were "searchings of heart" (5:15, 16). In other words Reuben thought about it, weighed the options, and decided it would be better for them not to go.

Can we identify with this? Has the Lord called us to do something, and we give it deep consideration, weigh the pros and cons, and decide against it because it would bring us more harm than good, even though in the long run our disobedience to the Lord's call brings us more harm? Or what about Dan? He seemed to stay behind with the ships in order to not miss out on wealth from trade. Have we ever put wealth before the Lord?

The battle is described in 5:19–22. The kings fought at the waters of Megiddo but got no spoils of silver (in other words, they lost). Even the stars of heaven and the waters of the Kishon were on the Lord's side. The Canaanites learned that nature, rather than being ruled by their gods, was underneath the hand of the almighty God of Israel. Such a display of God's power through the flooding waters of the Kishon (recalling the Lord's victory over Egypt at the Red Sea[15]) put the horses in a full-speed gallop. But not only do these verses recall the great historical redemptive event of the Lord's deliverance of his people through the exodus, they also anticipate the second exodus, the deliverance of God's

14. K. Lawson Younger Jr., *Judges/Ruth*, The NIV Application Commentary (Grand Rapids: Zondervan, 2002), 152.
15. Block, *Judges, Ruth*, 237.

people from this world full of pain and suffering into the new heaven and the new earth.

We read of a curse in 5:23 on the inhabitants of Meroz (exact location is unknown[16]) for not coming to the help of the Lord in defending Israel. This city stands as a representative for all those in Israel who have taken their stand against the Lord by not coming to his help and thus deserve his covenant curses.[17] Have we ever sat idly by while others are speaking or acting against our Lord and not come to his defense? The blessing and praise that Deborah gives to Jael will stand in stark contrast to this curse. It is a serious thing to oppose the will of God. His children are to be his helpers. His enemies are to be our enemies. Though our warfare is different on this side of the cross (see Eph. 6:10–20), we are still called to be in the Lord's army and fight with him against the spiritual rulers of this world.

The woman who receives the highest blessing and praise in the song is Jael, the wife of Heber the Kenite, a tent-dwelling woman. Not only did she woo Sisera by her hospitality that went above what he asked for, she boldly killed him with the tent peg, crushing his head and shattering his temple. Then in two climactic verses (5:26–27) we read five different times of the action of Jael in killing Sisera and three times of the result of Sisera's death. In vivid imagery, the song forces us to slow down, first hearing of her hand that went to the tent peg, then her hand that held the mallet, then her striking Sisera, crushing his head and shattering his pierced temple. As for the result, we read once that Sisera sank, two times that he fell, one time that he lay still, and finally that he fell dead.

In 5:28 the third woman in the song is introduced (the first two being Deborah and Jael): Sisera's mother. The song paints the picture of his mother waiting in expectation for his victorious arrival. She wonders at how long he is taking, and her princesses comfort her by speaking of his victory, sure that he will come home with spoil, women to use and abuse, and dyed materials that were embroidered. This is their reason-

16. Ibid., 238.
17. Younger, *Judges/Ruth*, 154.

ing for why he tarries, but ironically he lies dead between the feet of another woman.

Sisera represents all the enemies of Israel, and Deborah cries out that they might all perish like he did. Deborah's song and seeming applause of Jael's murder may come as a surprise to us, but it doesn't receive condemnation by the Lord. He is the Warrior of Holy War. The key is keeping our eyes on the salvation that he has wrought through Jael on behalf of his people. But this is only one key. The greater key is seeing that this overthrow of Sisera and the king of Canaan anticipates the greater overthrow of all God's enemies on the final day of judgment. We join Deborah in her prayer when we pray the Lord's Prayer. For to pray "thy kingdom come" is to pray that the Lord would come in final judgment.

For the Lord's friends, Deborah calls down a blessing that they will be like "the sun as he rises in his might" (5:31). This phrase recalls the ancient Near Eastern belief that the sun was a god and rose in triumph across the sky each day.[18] But for Deborah, it is the Lord who rides forth victoriously on his chariot in the heavens, as the Warrior of all warriors, to win the victory for his people. And as a woman of God, "while she does not displace men in officially established positions of leadership, her gender does not disqualify her from significant service for God."[19] As such, she serves as a wonderful testimony of God's faithfulness to use his daughters in the history of redemption to declare his glory. May we follow in her footsteps and be faithful to do the same!

The Lord's friends are those who love him with all their heart, mind, and soul. This was Israel's greatest responsibility, and it still remains the greatest responsibility for the people of God. Do we love him? Do we really love him with all our heart, soul, and mind? Or are we more taken with the gods of this world than we are with him? If we do not love him, then we side with the enemies and fall under the curse of God's judgment, but if we love him, then we are his friends and in Christ will be hidden from destruction and ushered into eternal salvation.

18. Block, *Judges, Ruth*, 244.
19. Ibid.

Finally we have the note that we anticipated at the end of chapter 4: "And the land had rest for forty years" (5:31). Grace. God's grace. God's amazing grace. He delights in giving his people rest. And of course this note simply anticipates the eternal rest to come in glory that our Lord and Savior Jesus Christ will usher in when he comes again. Come quickly, Lord Jesus. But even now Christ offers us peace and rest in him as we await that final day.

CONCLUSION

The Lord has graciously provided me with Christian brothers in my life who have encouraged me to fulfill the design of helper that the Lord has ordained for me (and all women; see Gen. 2:18) and who have applauded my service in the kingdom of God. I am truly grateful for that, for I know that not all have had that same experience. Let us be encouraged by our heavenly Father today, as he has included one of his daughters, Deborah, in the pages of Scripture to encourage his other daughters to take their stand beside her to sing of the glorious words and works of the Lord. May we be faithful to our God-ordained design, proclaiming his excellencies among the nations and leading others to do the same!

LESSON 6

Judges 6:1–40

PLEASE USE THE QUESTION paradigm from pages 301–2 as you work through the following. See the introductory comments there that explain each part of the process below in more detail.

- **Pray.**
- **Ponder the Passage.** Read Judges 6:1–40 once a day from different translations for the entire week, looking for its:
    - Point
    - Persons
    - Problem
    - Patterns
    - Persons of the Trinity
    - Puzzling Parts
- **Put It in Perspective.**
    - Place in Scripture. Skim Judges 1:1–3:6.
    - Passages from Other Parts of Scripture. See below.

1. Based on your observations of the text, what is the basic content of this passage? Try to summarize it in your own words, using a sentence or two.

2. Compare 6:1–6 with 2:11–15; 6:7–10 with 2:1–5; and 6:14 with 2:16.

3. Who gives the Israelites into the hand of oppressors (6:1)? Who are these oppressors? See Genesis 25:2–4; Exodus 2:15–22; 3:1–4:23; 18:1–27; Numbers 25:6–18. What is Israel's reaction to these oppressors and why (6:2–6)? Who are the Amalekites (6:3)? See Genesis 36:12, 16; Exodus 17:8–16; Numbers 24:20–21.

4. Compare 6:3–6 with Deuteronomy 28:15–63. Why has the Lord brought this oppression on Israel? How long does it last? How is God's grace displayed in this length of time?

5. How does the Lord first respond to the people's cry, with action or with word (6:7–10)? What time in the life of Israel do these verses recall? Where do you find covenantal language in these verses? Why is this significant in the context? What specific command of the Ten Commandments has Israel broken (6:10)?

6. Who is the angel of the Lord in 6:11? Compare this with Exodus 3:2. How does the angel of the Lord address Gideon (6:12), and how does Gideon respond (6:13)? How does this reveal Israel's attitude toward the Lord at this time in history?

7. What is the Lord's second word to Gideon (6:14)? How is this key to the story as a whole? What is Gideon's response (6:15)? Where else in Scripture do we see that (1) someone called by the Lord hesitates to respond to the call because of human inadequacy, and (2) the Lord uses the weak and humble of the world to display his glory (there are several examples of this)?

8. What is the Lord's third word to Gideon (6:16)? How is this language covenantal language? What is Gideon's response (6:17–18a) and the Lord's response to Gideon (6:18b)? How does Gideon, striking the Midianites as one man, foreshadow David striking Goliath and ultimately Christ striking Satan on the cross?

9. Compare the sign in 6:20–21 with Exodus 3. What does Gideon's fear of seeing the Lord face to face allude to in Exodus 10:28?

What is Gideon's response (6:22–24)? Who are the Abiezrites (see Num. 26:30; Josh. 17:1–2)?

10. How does the sign prepare Gideon for the Lord's command in 6:25–26? What is Gideon called to do? How does this reveal the state of Israel during this time and the Lord's covenant stipulations? What is Gideon's response (6:27)?

11. What is the response of the men of the town to Gideon's action (6:28–30)? What is ironic about them searching for Gideon to put him to death? According to the Mosaic law, who should have been put to death (Deut. 17:1–7)?

12. Who comes to Gideon's defense (6:31)? Why is Gideon's new name significant (6:32)? Who is the greater Gideon who breaks down the strongholds of this world and is actually put to death as the innocent man by his own people? How does the name that those crucifying him gave him (Luke 23:38) reveal the truth (even though it was done in mockery)?

13. How is 6:34 key for the Gideon story? Compare this to Zechariah 4:6.

14. How does Gideon betray by his own words, "as you have said," that he is not trusting in the word of the Lord when he asks for another sign after one has already been given (6:36–40)? What does the Mosaic law say about testing the Lord (Deut. 6:16), and what wilderness event does Gideon's testing recall? How does the Lord display his grace to Gideon despite his testing? From your previous answers, how do you know this is not a paradigm for finding God's will for your life? Who and what has he given you to guide you in making decisions?

- **Principles and Points of Application.**
1. In what present circumstances are you wondering if the Lord has forsaken you? How does Judges 6 encourage you? Take your honest emotions before the Lord, crying out to him and placing your trust in his promises that he will never leave you nor forsake you.

2. So often in Scripture the Lord chooses the least likely candidate and humblest of means. How does this encourage you? How can you relate?

3. In what area of your life do you need the Lord to be your peace right now? Pray to him today, recognizing his Spirit is in your heart to bring you peace.

4. Can you relate to Gideon's fear? In what situation are you afraid to speak or act boldly for the Lord? Recognize that the Lord has given you the strength and boldness you need by his Spirit. Then speak boldly and confidently for him today.

5. How do you exercise justice on behalf of those falsely accused? How has the Lord convicted you of being wrong at times and used that conviction to bring you to defense of the weak?

6. Only when we are clothed in God's Spirit can we be effective for God's kingdom. In whose power are you serving and living? Confess this today and ask God to fill you with the Holy Spirit (Eph. 5:18b).

7. As New Testament believers we have the completed revelation of God's Word. We are not to test the Lord with fleeces. What has the Lord asked you to do that you are unsure about? Recognize that he has given us his Word to reveal his will to us. For specific circumstances, such as whether to marry Christian man A or Christian man B, whether or not to pursue a certain career, whether or not to move, etc., godly counsel can be very helpful from the leadership of your local church. But remember that whatever counsel you receive must align with biblical principles.

NOTES FOR JUDGES 6:1–40

Ponder the aim of this lesson concerning our:

Mind: What do we need to know from this passage in Scripture?

The Lord delivers his people from the physical and spiritual oppression of the Midianites through one man, Gideon, anticipating his deliverance of his people from physical and spiritual oppression through the one God-man, Jesus Christ, on the cross.

Heart: How does what we learn from this passage affect our internal relationship with the Lord?

It prepares us to be kingdom disciples who recognize God is with us in Christ and that we are clothed with the power of the Holy Spirit to reject the gods of this world.

Hands: How does what we learn from this passage translate into action for God's kingdom?

It enables us to:

1. Recognize that the Lord will never leave us nor forsake us.
2. Recognize and be encouraged that the Lord so often chooses the least likely and most humble means to accomplish his great purposes.
3. Embrace the Lord's peace in the difficult circumstances of our present life.
4. Recognize that the Holy Spirit helps us in our weakness to speak boldly on behalf of God.
5. Defend our brothers and sisters in Christ who are unjustly accused when proclaiming the Word of God and tearing down the gods of this world.
6. Recognize it is only when we are clothed with God's Spirit that we can be effective for God's service.

INTRODUCTION

As women, we often serve as the gatekeepers of our homes. If we are mothers (and we are all mothers to somebody even if not biologically), we often have the task of keeping those things out of our homes that are ungodly and the task of keeping those things a part of our home that are godly. Most significantly, we have the opportunity to be prayer warriors for our husbands and our children from the "prayer closets" of our homes. We have been sent into our families and the world to proclaim the salvation of the Lord, but we do not go alone nor do we go in our own power. The Covenant Lord has promised to be with us. The Holy Spirit has given us the peace of God. And the Lord has overcome the god of this world on the cross of Calvary.

But the task of tearing down the altars to false gods in our own hearts and homes, as well as in the church, is not easy. We often falter and are overwhelmed with fear and timidity. This is when we must cling to God's promise to be with us in the power of his Spirit. The Lord is looking for women who will pull down the idols of false worship in their hearts and homes and uphold the truth of God's Word. While we may be looking for miracles and quick fixes, the Lord is looking for servants who are sure and steady by being rooted in his Word. It is in his Word that we will find the spiritual weapons to fight against the gods of this world. Judges 6:1–40 has much to say about being kingdom disciples who recognize that God is with us in Christ and that we are clothed with the power of the Holy Spirit to reject the gods of this world.

We can divide the lesson into four sections:

 I. The Lord Gives Israel into the Hand of Midian (6:1–10)
 II. The Lord Calls Gideon to Save Israel from the Hand of Midian (6:11–27)
 III. The Lord Changes Gideon's Name and Clothes Him with the Spirit of the Lord (6:28–35)
 IV. The Lord Graciously Answers Gideon's Lack of Faith in His Request for a Sign (6:36–40)

I. The Lord Gives Israel into the Hand of Midian (6:1–10)

Although the Lord had graciously given the land rest for forty years after delivering the Israelites from the Canaanites, the Israelites did not follow in the Lord's ways, but again did what was evil in the Lord's sight. As a result, the Lord gave them over to the hand of Midian for seven years. The Midianites, descendants of Abraham by his second wife, Keturah (Gen. 25:2–4), had a history of being problematic for Israel. On the one hand, Genesis 37:25–36 tells us that the Midianites were part of Joseph's being sold into slavery in Egypt. On the other hand, the Midianites gave Moses a place to stay when he fled from Pharaoh (Ex. 2:15) and Moses' wife was the daughter of Jethro, a Midianite priest who helped Moses reorganize leadership of the nation (Ex. 2:15–22; 18:1–27). It was also in Midian that Moses received his call from the Lord (Ex. 3:1–4:23). At Mount Sinai the Israelites were brought into covenant relationship with the Lord and received the Mosaic law (Ex. 19–Num. 10:10). However, after the Israelites departed from Sinai, things went downhill. In fact, we learn from Numbers 25:6–18 that because the Midianites actively tried to lead Israel away from the Covenant Lord in the matter of Baal worship at Peor, the Lord called for Israel to harass and strike the Midianites.[1]

The oppression by the Midianites, as well as the Amalekites and the people of the East, was so bad that "Israel made for themselves the dens that are in the mountains and the caves and the strongholds" (6:2) as places of refuge. We have already discussed the Midianites, but who are the Amalekites and the people of the East? The Amalekites were descendants of Esau (Gen. 36:12, 16). In Exodus 17:8–16, Israel defeated Amalek through Moses' upheld hand and Joshua's sword. After their victory, the Lord told Moses to write the victory down as a memorial in a book and recite it in the ears of Joshua, that he would utterly blot out the memory of Amalek from under heaven. Moses built an altar at that place and named it "The LORD Is My Banner" and said, "A hand upon the throne of the LORD! The LORD will have war with Amalek from generation to generation" (Ex. 17:15–16). Balaam curses the Amalekites in Numbers 24:20, and 1 Samuel 15 tells us that Samuel killed their last king. But most recently, we saw in 3:13 that these Amalekites had allied with Eglon of Moab to bring distress on Israel. The "people of the

1. Daniel I. Block, *The New American Commentary*, vol. 6, *Judges, Ruth* (Nashville: Broadman & Holman, 1999), 251–52.

East" were probably another desert tribe that joined with the Midianites and Amalekites to bring disaster on Israel.[2] The Lord judged Israel with famine that he brought on them by the Midianites laying waste to their land. This of course was one of the covenant curses (Deut. 28:15–63). It was during this time that the people again called out for help to the Lord. Again, this should not be taken as repentance, but a desperate plea for help under oppressive circumstances (see 10:14).

When the people cried out to the Lord, in his grace he sent a prophet to the people of Israel (6:7–10). (We have seen this before in the previous story of Deborah and Barak; right after the people cried out in distress, he sent them Deborah the prophetess.[3]) God reminded the people through the prophet of his great act of redemption in bringing them out of Egypt and into a covenant relationship with him. Because they were in covenant with him, they were not to fear the gods of the Amorites in whose land they dwelled. However, Israel had not obeyed the Lord, and so he had given them into the hand of the Midianites. The people should have already known this. The Lord had made the blessings and the curses, as well as the law, clear to his people. But in his grace he told them why they were undergoing oppression. Not only that, the Lord was going to save them from such oppression through Gideon.

Have you ever been in the Israelites' shoes? Have you ever cried out to the Lord in your distress, and instead of answering you with a mighty act of deliverance from your chronic pain, from infertility, from a difficult marriage, from a life-threatening disease, from depression, from the death of a loved one, from caring for an elderly parent, from your adult child who has turned away from the faith, or (you fill in the blank), he has given you his sure and solid Word instead? Has he ever, instead of giving you immediate relief, given you the immeasurable treasure of his Word? There is not a verse in the Bible that says God's purpose is for us to be happy, although in his grace he often gives us happy times, but there are many verses that speak of God's will for us to be holy. If he delivered us from our pain every time we cried out in

2. Ibid., 252.
3. Ibid., 254.

84

distress, we would never learn the way of the cross. And the way of the cross is the way of Jesus, and Jesus is the only way, the only truth, and the only life. Have you come to the living Word today, or are you still waiting for the wonder of deliverance apart from Jesus? The wonder of deliverance will never come apart from Christ.

II. The Lord Calls Gideon to Save Israel from the Hand of Midian (6:11–27)

Note the contrast between the previous verse, "But you have not obeyed my voice" (6:10), and "The angel of the LORD came and sat" (6:11). What a merciful and gracious God we serve! The Covenant Lord condescends to his people. He does not leave us in our disobedience but comes to us in love and grace to save us from our sin. Of course, the ultimate condescension is seen in Jesus Christ, who came into the world as the perfect God-man to save us from our sin by his death on the cross. And each one of the saviors that the Lord raises up in the book of Judges anticipates him, the greatest and final Savior. Here we see that the angel of the Lord sat under the terebinth at Ophrah, while the son of Joash the Abiezrite, Gideon, was beating out wheat in the winepress to hide it from the Midianites. We have already learned that the Midianites were oppressing the Israelites by coming on their land in droves and destroying the crops (6:3–5). However, some of the Israelites had learned how to keep some food for themselves. Gideon was one such man.

When the angel of the Lord appeared to Gideon, he both assured him of the Lord's presence with him and assured him of the might and valor that he had because the Lord was with him. This of course is key to the story of Gideon. It would not be by Gideon's might or power, but by the Lord's, that he would save Israel from the Midianites. But this is also the key to the Christian life. The covenant can be summarized in one phrase, "I . . . will be your God, and you shall be my people" (Lev. 26:12). The great promise of God is that he will be with us. Immanuel means, "God with us." And John 1:14 tells us that it is through Jesus Christ that God dwelt with his people. When Jesus ascended after his resurrection, he promised that he would send

85

another Helper, the Holy Spirit. On the Day of Pentecost the gift of the Holy Spirit was given in a fuller way than he had ever been given before. The church is given marching orders in the Great Commission, but it is also made clear that the Holy Spirit is the one who will open up blind eyes so that they can see. And ultimately it will be God the Father through the Son by the power of the Holy Spirit who ushers in the new heaven and the new earth. Is this promise enough for you? Is God's sure word of promise enough, or are you constantly looking for more confirmation of his love for you? It cannot get any more sure than God the Father sending his only Son into the world to die for you so that you might live with him. He has already given you proof that he will be with you. What have you done with this proof? I hope and pray that you have turned to him and said, "I will be a part of your people; I will serve you all my days, not by might or power, but by your Spirit."

Gideon's response sounds a lot like many of our responses to the Lord today. If the Lord is with us, why have all these bad things happened to us? Why are we living in famine and distress? Where are all the mighty deeds that the previous generations recounted concerning the Lord? The Lord may have delivered us from Egypt, but he's now forsaken us and given us into the hand of the Midianites. Don't we often get it turned around like Gideon? We think that the Lord has forsaken us when it is really that we have forsaken the Lord.

Notice that the Lord does not answer Gideon's questions, but instead tells him to go in his might and save Israel from the hand of Midian. Then the Lord asks him a question, "Do not I send you?" (6:14). The only reason Gideon can go in his might to save Israel is because the Lord's might is behind him. He does not go on his own accord but is sent by the Lord. We need to remember that it is the Lord who sends us into the world to be ambassadors for him and that we do not go in our own might but in his. The Holy Spirit has been given to the church so that we can go and make disciples of all nations. We have been given our marching orders, and the Lord's might is behind us. Are we, as members of the church, taking the call seriously?

Gideon falters in his faith as he answers. He questions how he can save Israel after the Lord has just told him. He tells the Lord what he believes to be true but is not: his clan is the weakest in Manasseh and he is the least in his father's house. If his father is the priest of Baal (6:25) and if Gideon is able to bring ten servants with him to tear down the altar to Baal (6:27), then his clan had considerable standing. But even if he was the weakest, isn't this just the way the Lord likes to work? Think of David, the youngest of Jesse's sons, who had not even been considered as a candidate for kingship. Remember, he had been left to keep the sheep. But he was the one whom the Lord chose (1 Sam. 16:6–13). And King David anticipated the greater and final Davidic king, our Lord and Savior Jesus Christ, who was born to a poor, young virgin in the little town of Bethlehem and had no stately form or appearance. Jesus himself teaches that whoever would be great must be a servant, and whoever would be first must be a slave (Matt. 20:26–27).

This time the Lord answers Gideon's question of how he can save Israel. The Lord will be with him, and he will strike the Midianites as one man. Even here we see that the Lord can save his people by one man, which anticipates his salvation of his people through his one and only Son, Jesus Christ.

Gideon is still weak in his faith, in spite of the fact that the Lord has spoken with him. So he asks for a sign. The Lord, in his grace, agrees and waits for Gideon to retrieve the props for the sign. Gideon returns to the terebinth with a young goat, unleavened cakes, meat, and broth and presents them to the Lord. Notice that it is the angel of God who tells him what to do. He is to put the meat and unleavened cakes on the rock and pour the broth over them. So Gideon obeys. The angel of the Lord touches the tip of his staff to the meat and unleavened cakes, and fire springs up from the rock and consumes them. And the angel of the Lord vanishes. Now fires don't come from rocks. You can't burn a fire on a rock, unless you're the Lord—the same Lord who appeared to Moses in the burning bush without consuming the bush. This fire also served to reveal to Gideon that he had been speaking with the angel of the Lord. Fire so often accompanies the Lord's presence in the Scriptures.

Gideon was afraid because he had seen the Lord face to face, which, if you remember, was something that not even Moses was allowed to do, lest he die (Ex. 33:23). But the Lord graciously blessed him with his peace. And he told him not to fear, because he would not die. What was Gideon's response? He built an altar to the Lord and called it "The LORD Is Peace" (6:24). The author tells us that at the time of his writing it still stood at Ophrah, which belonged to the Abiezrites. The Abiezrites were a clan of Manasseh that had been given land on both sides of the Jordan (Josh. 17:2; 1 Chron. 7:18).[4]

In what area of your life are you full of doubts concerning the Lord's call to you and in desperate need of his peace? Asking for signs is not the answer. Following God's Word is. Though the Bible does not give us the answer to our specific questions, such as whether or not to change jobs, move to a specific location, marry a specific man, use infertility drugs, or (you fill in the blank), the Bible does give us clear principles for us to follow. For example, although the Bible does not tell us exactly whom to marry, the Bible does make it clear that if we marry (and we don't have to marry), we must marry a man and he must be a Christian. The Lord has also given us the Holy Spirit to lead us in our decisions, and he has given us the elders of our church and the body of believers to provide us with wise counsel.

After giving Gideon his peace, the Lord asked him to do something that would interrupt the peace of his family. He asked him to fulfill his name's meaning, "hacker, hewer."[5] He was to hack down the altar of Baal that his father had by using two bulls and cut down the Asherah ("the female counterpart to Baal in the fertility religion"[6]) that was beside it. In its place he was to build an altar to the Lord and offer the second bull as a sacrifice by using the wood from the Asherah pole for the fire. The Lord wanted to show Israel that worship of the true God and worship of idols couldn't coexist. Jesus puts it another way: "No one can serve two masters, for either he will hate the one and love the other, or he

4. Ibid., 258.
5. Ibid., 257.
6. Ibid., 267.

will be devoted to the one and despise the other" (Matt. 6:24). But isn't this what we so often do? Aren't our lives so often a mix of worshiping the gods of beauty, materialism, comfort, security, marriage and family, independence, career, and our own plans? The Lord still calls us to pull down the idols from the pedestals in our hearts and in their place, "by the mercies of God, to present [our] bodies as a living sacrifice, holy and acceptable to God, which is [our] spiritual worship" (Rom. 12:1).

So Gideon took ten of his servants and obeyed, but because he was afraid of his family and the men of the town, he did it at night. Can we really blame him? How many times has the Lord called us to do something that we do, but we do it in fear and in hiding, being anything but bold for him? How often do we hide our testimony from those around us because we are embarrassed and afraid of what they will say? How often are we afraid of what persecution might be involved if we state our faith clearly and boldly to our friends and families? Yet, as we will see, the Lord continues to respond graciously to his weak servants. In spite of the Israelites' seeming desire to destroy themselves, the Lord graciously preserves his people. And the same is true today.

III. The Lord Changes Gideon's Name and Clothes Him with the Spirit of the Lord (6:28–35)

We quickly learn that Gideon had good reason to be afraid. As soon as the next day dawns, the men of the town see what has happened and seek the culprit. Determining it was Gideon, they set out to kill him. Isn't this ironic? According to the Mosaic law in Deuteronomy 17:2–7, it should have been the men of the town who were put to death, but Israel had become so evil that the godly among the nation who were following the Lord were being sought for death. However, Gideon's father Joash (the priest of Baal!) speaks out on his behalf. Ironically, Joash questions whether they should contend for a god (Baal) who could not save himself. If they do, Joash says they will be put to death the next morning. Do we come to the defense of those who are persecuted for their work in the name of the Lord? How do we exercise justice on behalf of those unjustly accused?

Gideon's name was changed to Jerubbaal, "Let Baal contend against him" (6:32), because he broke down Baal's altar. Thus Gideon/Jerubbaal serves to remind the people that the Lord is God, not Baal. This of course was the real problem for the Israelites: not the oppression of the Midianites, but the possession of their gods. They had forsaken their covenant commitment to not have any other gods before the Lord.

The Lord used this event to stir up the Midianites, Amalekites, and the people of the East in battle against the Israelites. But the Lord did not leave his people defenseless. Instead he clothed Gideon with his Spirit. "Not by might, nor by power, but by my Spirit, says the LORD of hosts" (Zech. 4:6). Here we see Gideon call some of the Israelites together (Manasseh, Asher, Zebulun, and Naphtali) to fight against their enemies, and more importantly, the Lord's enemies, which anticipates the final battle at the end of history between the people of God and all God's enemies.

The greater Gideon who pulled down the powers of darkness and principalities of this world on the cross was also sought by the ungodly to be put to death as an innocent man. But his Father did not speak out on his behalf as Joash did. Instead the Father forsook the Son so that all God's children would be saved. The righteous died for the unrighteous. The true Jerubbaal is Jesus Christ; he is the one whom Satan contended with, but Satan lost at the cross. Jesus Christ has broken down the altar and in its place has raised up the altar of the cross, on which he was laid as the perfect and true sacrifice to reconcile God the Father with his children.

IV. The Lord Graciously Answers Gideon's Lack of Faith in His Request for a Sign (6:36–40)

Now Gideon requests another sign from the Lord. However, he clearly acknowledges that the Lord has already told him that he will save Israel by Gideon's hand. Thus this sign exposes Gideon's weakness and doubt in light of the Lord's clear word. Indeed Gideon even says that he is testing the Lord, which Deuteronomy 6:16 clearly states Israel is not to do. Amazingly, the Lord in his grace still answers Gideon's request.

Because Gideon is displaying weakness here, this is not a pattern for us to follow. The word of the Lord should have been enough for Gideon to obey. But instead he asks for more proof before he will follow. God's Word is enough for us to obey as well. The amazing thing is that the Lord, in his grace, so often helps his children who are floundering along the path of obedience with sure signs as well as his sure Word. But these signs are not to be sought; God's Word is enough for those who look to him in faith.

CONCLUSION

In what family has the Lord placed you? What strongholds and altars need to be pulled down? Begin with your own heart first. Remember that the Lord is with you. He has clothed you with the Holy Spirit as a believer in Jesus Christ and has given you everything that you need to live a life of godliness. Jesus Christ has contended for you on the cross. Satan can no longer contend against Jesus Christ, because Christ has secured the victory for us on the cross. There is no other sign that we need. The sign of Jesus Christ crucified is the greatest sign ever given. And the promise, "I will walk among you and will be your God, and you shall be my people" (Lev. 26:12) has been fulfilled in him.

LESSON 7

Judges 7:1–8:32

PLEASE USE THE QUESTION paradigm from pages 301–2 as you work through the following. See the introductory comments there that explain each part of the process below in more detail.

- **Pray.**
- **Ponder the Passage.** Read Judges 7:1–8:32 once a day from different translations for the entire week, looking for its:
  - Point
  - Persons
  - Problem
  - Patterns
  - Persons of the Trinity
  - Puzzling Parts
- **Put It in Perspective.**
  - Place in Scripture. Skim Judges 1–2.
  - Passages from Other Parts of Scripture. Read Exodus 23:20–33; Deuteronomy 9:13–29; 17:14–20; 28:15–63.

1. Based on your observations of the text, what is the basic content of this passage? Try to summarize it in your own words, using a sentence or two.

2. How does 7:1 relate to 6:33–35?

3. How many people are with Gideon at first (7:3)? Why does the Lord send some away? What characterized those who are sent home?

4. How many people are with Gideon the second time? Why does the Lord say that they are still too many (7:2)? What test does the Lord use to send more men away? How many men remained with Gideon? What would the Lord do with these men (7:7)?

5. When does the Lord send Gideon and his men against the Midianites (7:9)? What promise does he give to Gideon (7:9)? What emotion is Gideon feeling (7:10–11)? How does the Lord display his grace to Gideon (7:10–11)? What will be the result (7:11a)?

6. Compare the description of the Midianites, Amalekites, and people of the East (7:12) with the description of the Israelites in God's promise to Abraham (Gen. 22:17).

7. What does the Lord use to encourage Gideon (7:13)? What else does the Lord provide (7:14)? Where else in Scripture has the Lord used the dream of a non-Israelite and its interpretation to encourage his people?

8. What is Gideon's immediate response to the interpretation of the dream (7:15a)? Then what does he do (7:15b–16)? Compare the instructions that Gideon gives to the three hundred men with the instructions that Joshua gave to the Israelites at the battle of Jericho (Josh. 6).

9. When do Gideon and his men attack the Midianite camp (7:19)? What do the men do (7:19–21)? What does the Lord do (7:22)? Which tribes are called out to assist Gideon in the battle (7:23)?

10. Which tribe is called to capture the waters against the Midianites (7:24)? What is their initial response (7:24–25)? What is the result? What do they bring to Gideon (7:25)?

11. What is Ephraim's accusation against Gideon (8:1)? How does Gideon strategically reply to diffuse the animosity (8:2–3)? Does his strategy work (8:3)?

12. During Gideon's pursuit of the two Midianite kings, from which two cities does he ask for assistance (8:5, 8)? How does each respond (8:6, 8)? How does this reflect the lack of unity in Israel at this time? What does Gideon promise to do as a result (8:7, 9)? How does this promise reflect a change in Gideon's attitude from chapter 7 and his reliance on the Lord?

13. How many men are left with the two kings (8:10)? How many are destroyed by the sword (8:10)? By whose sword are they destroyed (7:22)?

14. In contrast to the first attack (7:19), how does Gideon attack the second time (8:11)? What is the result (8:12)? Does Gideon fulfill his promise to Succoth and Penuel (8:13–17)? Whom specifically does he kill from Penuel (8:17)?

15. Why was Gideon pursuing the two Midianite kings so fiercely (8:19)? Whom does Gideon ask to kill them and what is his response (8:20)? Whom do the two kings challenge to kill them and what is the result (8:21)? What does Gideon take from their camels (8:21)?

16. What do the men of Israel request of Gideon (8:22)? Compare their request with the laws concerning Israel's kings in Deuteronomy 17:14–20. What is Gideon's response (8:23)? Does he prove his response with his actions or does he act as king anyway (8:24–32)? In light of Deuteronomy 17:17 and the description of Gideon in 8:24–32, was Gideon a good choice for the men of Israel to make to be their king? Explain why or why not. How does this anticipate the Davidic dynasty?

17. What does Gideon make with the spoil he acquires (8:27)? Where does he put it? Why is this ironic in light of his earlier action at Ophrah in 6:25–27? What is the result of Gideon's action (8:27)? How is Gideon's name of Jerubbal ("Let Baal contend against him") ironic? When they contended, who won?

18. How does the note of rest in 8:28 reflect God's grace in Israel during this time of apostasy? Compare the years of oppression (6:1) with the years of rest (8:28).

19. What character is introduced in 8:31 for the next story (ch. 9)?

20. How does the story of Gideon saving the Israelites from the hand of the Midianites anticipate Christ? What character flaws and failures point to the need for One greater than Gideon?

- **Principles and Points of Application.**

1. In what area of your life are you facing a seemingly impossible situation? How does the fact that the Lord purposely narrowed Gideon's army from thirty-two thousand to ten thousand to three hundred, so that he would receive the glory, encourage you?

2. Think of a recent time when the Lord graciously gave you a word of encouragement through his Word or another person, which gave you the confidence to carry through with what he wanted you to do. Spend time worshiping and thanking him for this today.

3. How did the death of the two kings and their ornaments end up being a snare for Gideon? Was his personal vengeance right? Who is the only one who has the right to vengeance? What situation in your life do you need to leave for the Lord to avenge? How were you deserving of vengeance before being saved? Spend time thanking Jesus Christ today that he has atoned for your sin on the cross.

4. How do you point others to the Lord's rule when they want you to lead them and guide them? Although we have significant responsibilities as mothers and grandmothers (whether physical mothers and grandmothers or spiritual mothers and grandmothers), we must always prioritize pointing the children that the Lord has entrusted to us to him. Spend time in prayer today, asking the Lord to strengthen you as a mother or grandmother and committing the children that he has entrusted to your care to him.

5. How can you relate to the men of Ephraim who exemplified hurt pride or to the men of the cities of Succoth and Penuel who were

more focused on their security than helping their fellow brothers in need? In what area of your life are you displaying hurt pride in a relationship with your husband, your sibling, your parent or in-law, your friend or neighbor, or your brother or sister in Christ? In what area are you more concerned about your own security or comfort than you are about helping someone in need? Confess this to the Lord today, humbling yourself before him and seeking comfort and security from him alone.

6. What in your life right now has become a snare to you? In other words, what is taking your focus off of Christ? Anxiousness, external beauty, career, depression, finances, gossip, health, infertility, loneliness in singleness, a difficult marriage, physical or emotional pain, rebelliousness of a child, a turn of circumstances contrary to what you wanted, a whirlwind schedule, or (you fill in the blank)? Confess any snares to the Lord, recognizing that he has given you everything you need to live a life of godliness though the power of the Holy Spirit.

7. Spend time today remembering how the Lord has displayed his power of deliverance in your life, and commit to displaying loyalty to him by relying on the Holy Spirit.

NOTES FOR JUDGES 7:1-8:32

Ponder the aim of this lesson concerning our:

Mind: What do we need to know from this passage in Scripture?

> The Lord delivers Midian into Gideon's hands by three hundred men in order to display his power and glory.

Heart: How does what we learn from this passage affect our internal relationship with the Lord?

> It prepares us to be kingdom disciples who trust the Lord to deliver us even in the least likely of circumstances for the sake of his name.

Hands: How does what we learn from this passage translate into action for God's kingdom?

It enables us to:

1. Recognize, be encouraged, and rest in the fact that the Lord often uses the humblest of means and circumstances in order to display his glory.
2. Encourage another sister in Christ with the encouragement that we have received from the Lord in a certain circumstance.
3. Repent of any anger toward another person for their wrongdoing or injustice toward us and leave vengeance with the Lord.
4. Point our children and/or grandchildren and those in our circle of influence to the Word of God.
5. Repent of any "snare" in our life, recognizing that the Lord has given us the power of the Spirit to resist it.
6. Remember and give thanks to the Lord this week for his display of power and deliverance in a recent circumstance in our life and to display loyalty to him as we walk by the Spirit.

INTRODUCTION

As I write, our house is on the market. It went on the market on Labor Day weekend, and it is now the beginning of November. We have had one showing in two months. Several people have told me that this is a horrible time to try to sell. Not only is the economy really bad, this time of year doesn't bring much traffic for home sales. But that simply means that those who come to see the home are usually serious buyers. The reason we are moving is because we want to be closer to our church family. We have a contingency contract down on another home that is being built and will be ready by the end of January. We have done all that we can to make our home in good condition. We are in a good location. And we are priced to sell. But we need the Lord to bring the buyer. We are not hoping in the realtor, the condition of our home, its location, or the price's being right; we are hoping in the Lord. And as hard as it is,

I have to submit to his timing and, ultimately, I have to remember that he may not want us to move right now. That is hard, but that is not the point of my telling you this story. The point is that the Lord often uses the least likely of circumstances to display his power and glory. So every time I am told that it is a horrible economy in which to sell a house or it is a bad time of year, I smile and think to myself, "That is just the way the Lord often has it so that he will receive the glory."[1]

Judges 7:1–8:32 has much to say about being kingdom disciples who trust the Lord to deliver us, even in the least likely of circumstances, for the sake of his glorious name.

We can divide the lesson into three sections:

I. The Lord Chooses Three Hundred Men to Defeat Midian (7:1–25)
II. Gideon Captures the Kings of Midian and Teaches the Men of Succoth and Penuel a Lesson (8:1–21)
III. Gideon's Snare and Death (8:22–32)

I. The Lord Chooses Three Hundred Men to Defeat Midian (7:1–25)

The preparations for the battle that began in 6:33–35 resumed; Gideon and all who were with him encamped by the spring of Harod (ironically, "spring of trembling"[2]), south of the Midianite camp. Now, if I had been oppressed by the Midianites for seven years, I would want as many men on my side as possible to defeat the enemy, but this is not the Lord's way. The Lord desires his own glory and knew man's heart would boast in the victory himself if there were enough men to destroy Midian from a human standpoint. So he had Gideon release twenty-two thousand of the men who were fearful and trembling so that they could return home. This left ten thousand men, but that was still too many for the Lord. So the Lord tested them at the water by the way that they

---

1. Eight months and forty-nine showings later the Lord brought a buyer!
2. Daniel I. Block, *The New American Commentary*, vol. 6, *Judges, Ruth* (Nashville: Broadman & Holman, 1999), 275.

drank water. Those who lapped the water, three hundred of the men, were the ones the Lord would use to overcome the Midianites. The text leaves no impression that the lappers were better than the kneelers. In fact, it would seem quite the opposite. But the point of the text is that the Lord is going to magnify his power in the weakness of three hundred men lapping like dogs. And I would think that the posture of three hundred lapping men is exactly where the Lord wanted them: on their knees and faces lapping up water in thirst before the Lord with no strength or power of their own. And as we will later see, these water-lappers will simply become trumpet blowers and torch lighters, for the victory belongs to the Lord.

It is the way of the Lord to make his power perfect in weakness. He displayed this on the cross of Calvary most of all, but he continues to display this in the life of his servants. Paul said that a thorn was given him in the flesh (2 Cor. 12:7–8). We don't know what this thorn was, but we know that it caused Paul great distress, for three times he *pleaded* with the Lord to have it leave him. Have you been there? Have you had the thorn of cancer; chronic pain; death of a loved one; depression; financial insecurity; foreclosure; infertility; insults from family and friends; loneliness in singleness; loneliness in marriage; marriage difficulties; pain of a prodigal son or daughter, sister or brother, mother or father; traumatic circumstances; emotional and spiritual shipwrecks; unwanted events; or (you fill in the blank)? Hear the Lord say to you, as he did to Paul in 2 Corinthians 12:9, "My grace is sufficient for you, for my power is made perfect in weakness." How did Paul respond? "Therefore I will boast all the more gladly of my weaknesses, so that the power of Christ may rest upon me. For the sake of Christ, then, I am content with weaknesses, insults, hardships, persecutions, and calamities. For when I am weak, then I am strong" (2 Cor. 12:9–10).

This is hardly the picture that the world paints of strong women. Usually we are given the superwoman model in which we can have it all and do it all. We can make it as the full-time career woman and the full-time mom at the same time. We can sidestep beauty on the inside as long as we clean ourselves up really well on the outside. We can have financial success, but not without paying the price of long hours, late nights, and mommy guilt. We can keep running our household, cleaning our house, and doing the other chores even when we are exhausted and in a great deal of physical pain. We can keep up with the men while still having the flair of a woman even when something deep down in our hearts cries out that we are different and want to be different.

But the Scriptures give us the true picture of a woman of strength. She is portrayed in the book of Genesis as a helper created in the image of God (Gen. 1:27; 2:18) and as the mother of all living (3:20). In Proverbs 31:10–31 she is described as an excellent wife who is trustworthy, a doer of good, a worker with willing hands, a bringer of food, a provider of food for her family, fruitful with her hands, wise in financial decisions, dressed with strength, gracious to the poor and needy, full of dignity, filled with laughter, wise, kind, engaged in her household's needs, blessed by her children, praised by her husband, and worthy of praise because she fears the Lord. In Titus 2 she is described as the younger woman who loves her husband and children, who is self-controlled, pure, working at home, kind, and submissive to her own husband. She is the older woman who is reverent in behavior, not a slanderer, not given over to addictive behaviors, who teaches what is good and trains the younger women in their God-given design. And in the midst of fulfilling our design that the Lord has given us as women, we will hear him say, "My grace is sufficient for you, for my power is made perfect in weakness" (2 Cor. 12:9).

That night the Lord told Gideon to arise and go down against the camp because he had given it into his hand. But the Lord knew that Gideon would be afraid, and he knew Gideon's track record of wanting the Lord's word plus a sign. The word of the Lord was enough to obey, but the Lord in his graciousness gave Gideon another sign without even a request for one. He told Gideon to go with Purah his servant to the Midianite camp to hear what they would say in order that his hands might be strengthened for battle.

The covenantal language the Lord used with Abraham describing his descendants being as the sand of the seashore (Gen. 22:17) is now used to speak of the innumerable Midianites, Amalekites, and people of the East at the camp (7:12). Remember that the Lord had stripped Gideon's men to only three hundred! The Lord uses a man's dream and the interpretation of it by his comrade to encourage Gideon's heart and strengthen him to go against the Midianites. Even the enemies declared that God had given into Gideon's hand Midian and all the camp. Don't miss the irony here; Gideon refused to believe the direct word of God but readily believed a pagan's ambiguous dream.[3]

Can you relate to Gideon? How often do you doubt or refuse to hear God's Word while running to a friend, counselor, or self-help book for your answers to life's problems? It is God's Word that has the counsel that we need in the muck and the mire, the trials and the temptations, the pain and persecutions of life. Why are we so hesitant to go to the Scriptures and so quick to go to anyone or anywhere else?

Gideon's response was the right response here. He worshiped and obeyed. He returned to the camp to muster the troops, telling them that the Lord had given Midian into their hands. Gideon divided the three hundred men into three camps, putting "weapons" of trumpets and torch-filled jars into their hands. He led the way and told the men to follow. When they got to the camp, he would blow the trumpet, and the others were to blow theirs and shout, "For the LORD and for Gideon" (7:18). The Lord was teaching those who did not know the Lord or the work that he had done for Israel (2:10) the lesson that he taught Joshua's generation at the battle of Jericho (Josh. 6). But there was one problem with the battle cry: "and for Gideon." The Lord alone was to receive the glory for victory.

When Gideon and the three hundred men got to the Midianite camp, they blew the trumpets and broke the jars while crying out, "A sword for the LORD and for Gideon!" (7:20). Ironically there was no sword used, only some trumpets and jars![4] This caused great chaos among the Midianites, and the Lord turned every Midianite man's sword against his comrade and all the army. And Midian fled in a southeastern direction with the men from the tribes of Naphtali, Asher, and Manasseh pursuing them.

3. I am indebted to Dr. Iain Duguid for this thought.
4. Block, *Judges, Ruth*, 282.

Then Gideon sent messengers to call Ephraim to capture the Midianites before they fled through the waters of the Jordan and Beth-barah. And they did. They also captured the two princes of Midian (Oreb and Zeeb), killed them, and brought the heads to Gideon.

II. Gideon Captures the Kings of Midian and Teaches the Men of Succoth and Penuel a Lesson (8:1–21)

Now comes conflict that displays the lack of unity between Israel's tribes during this time. We have seen Gideon battle Baal (ch. 6), we have seen him battle the Midianites (ch. 7), but now we see him face a battle with his own people, Israel (ch. 8).[5] However, with masterful peacemaking skills Gideon heads off the battle with Israel. Ephraim is not happy that they were not called when Gideon went to fight against the Midianites, and they take it personally. "What is this that you [Gideon] have done to us [Ephraimites]?" (8:1).

Remember this hurt pride of the Ephraimites, because we will see it again in 12:1–6.[6] They accused him fiercely, but he put the focus on their victory over the princes of Midian and the fact that the Lord had put them into their hands in comparison with what he had done. By elevating their achievement over his, he pacified their anger and avoided a huge intertribal conflict.

Can we identify with the hurt pride of Ephraim? Have we ever been upset that we have not been asked to join in a ministry opportunity or that someone else stole our thunder when it was really our idea? Or perhaps we have been on Gideon's end and have been falsely and fiercely accused of not including someone in a ministry plan or venture. Life with the people of God sometimes hurts and wounds deeply. Fierce, cutting words have a way of leaving us feeling discouraged and defeated. But Gideon's response is not far off from what the writer of Proverbs tells us in 15:1, "A soft answer turns away wrath." Perhaps today you need the Lord to give you the grace to give a soft answer to fierce words

---

5. Dale Ralph Davis, *Judges: Such a Great Salvation* (Fearn, Great Britain: Christian Focus, 2000), 107.

6. Block, *Judges, Ruth*, 286.

from a spouse, a child, a friend, a neighbor, or a sister in Christ. He has already done so. Recognize his grace and respond in words seasoned with grace today.

Although Gideon continues to pursue the kings of Midian, the story takes a distinctive turn. While the previous account highlights the Lord's work through Gideon, here we see the portrait of a blood-hungry Gideon pursuing his oppressors in a ranting rage. Remember, this is the same Gideon we met in 6:15: "My clan is the weakest in Manasseh, and I am the least in my father's house."[7] He presumes that the Lord will give these kings into his hands (8:7) while he pursues vengeance for himself. It is no mistake that the Lord's name is only mentioned in this chapter's dialogue, whereas he has been an active part of the story line in the previous two chapters.

While he asked the men of both Succoth and Penuel to give his men food, both refused because Gideon did not have the kings of Midian in his hands nor did they seem to think he would, which brought the threat and promise of torture or death by Gideon among these cities after he had killed the kings. Gideon's pride had been hurt, and he was enraged that they would even question his victory over the two kings. The way of torture would be by the flailing of flesh (for Succoth) and the way of death by bringing a tower down on the people (for Penuel). But Succoth and Penuel were also in the wrong to look after number one (themselves) before looking after their fellow Israelites. They were concerned for their safety more than they were concerned for taking care of their own.[8]

We are guilty of this today as well. There are many times when we are concerned more for our own safety or security than we are concerned about taking care of those in our covenant family who are in real need. There are women who are hungry on the streets, there are abortion clinics that need to know that not all women are for the choice of abortion, there are people in other countries suffering from dysentery because of bad water, there are sisters being put in prison in the Middle East because they won't recant their faith, there are families in our churches

7. Ibid., 287.
8. Davis, *Judges*, 108.

that are going through unemployment and need us to give groceries or meals, and there are widows and divorced women who need us to share our time with our husbands so he can mow their yard or fix up their home. Are we willing to be squeezed a little tighter with our time and money? Are we willing to be in an uncomfortable place like the streets of downtown for the sake of our Savior?

Gideon continued his bloodthirsty pursuit and caught up with the Midianites in a time and place in which they were feeling secure, but the two kings of Midian fled. Gideon pursued them and captured them, throwing the Midianite army into a panic.

After returning from battle, Gideon fulfilled his earlier threat to the men of Succoth and Penuel. He brought the two Midianite kings to show them that he had done what they had thought he could not do, their doubt being their reason for not giving his men food. In an act of rage and self-righteous vengeance, Gideon flailed the flesh of the Succoth men and brought the tower down on the men of Penuel. He fulfilled his own self-righteous prophecy.

Then he turned to the kings of Midian and questioned them about the men of Tabor, those who were his brothers, the sons of his mother. Interestingly and significantly it is the Midianite kings who first introduce the term "king" in the book with regard to Gideon's family.[9] Gideon told the kings that if they had not killed his brothers, he would not have killed them, but in an act of vengeance he asked his firstborn son to kill them. Jether his firstborn would not do it, though, because he was still young and full of fear. How we, as readers, side with Jether here instead of the one called by the Lord! And how many "Jethers" there are in this world who need us to side with them and intervene for them! How many parents sacrifice their children in the name of religion, financial gain, emotional instability, and the like; the children of our world are crying out, full of fear. The children involved in sex trafficking; the children involved in sweat shops; the children dying of starvation; the children in our communities who are sexually, physically, and verbally abused. Do we hear their cries? Are we responding?

9. Block, *Judges, Ruth*, 294.

Because Jether refused, the two kings challenged Gideon to do it himself. Gideon gladly accepted the challenge, at last living up to his name, "Hacker," while taking the crescent ornaments that were on their camels' necks. Gideon may have brought the Midianite crisis to a close, but he did so in a way that was less than attractive.[10]

III. Gideon's Snare and Death (8:22–32)

Now the Israelites did not recognize that the Lord had saved them from the Midianites. Instead they gave the glory to Gideon. This is just what the Lord had predicted and why he had pared the army down to three hundred men. But Israel still did not get it! They still did not give glory to the Lord. They wanted Gideon as a king, a desire that was opposed to the requirements that the Lord had given them for a king (Deut. 17:14–20). Although he tells them that neither he nor his son will rule over them but only the Lord, Gideon is not as pious as he sounds here. We will soon see that for all practical purposes Gideon does act as king (and we will learn in chapter 9 that his son does too[11]). And evidently he considers himself their king, as we see when he names his son Abimelech, which means "The king [Gideon] is my father."[12]

First he asked for the Ishmaelites' golden earrings that were in the Israelites' spoil. The Israelites heralded Gideon so much that they willingly complied. The weight of all the gold from the earrings—along with the crescent ornaments, pendants, and purple garments of the Midianite kings and the collars that were around the camels' necks—was enormous (forty-three pounds![13]). So much so that Gideon made an ephod out of the gold and put the golden ephod in his city. The one who had been so graciously clothed by the Spirit of the Lord now clothes his city in syncretism, denying the Lord the glory that he alone deserves. Baal has indeed contended with Jerubbaal ("Let Baal contend against him"), and Baal has seemingly won. Gideon in Ophrah now resurrects the Baal

10. Ibid., 296.
11. K. Lawson Younger Jr., *Judges/Ruth*, The NIV Application Commentary (Grand Rapids: Zondervan, 2002), 210.
12. Block, *Judges, Ruth*, 304.
13. Ibid., 300.

worship that previously characterized Ophrah and that the Lord had used Gideon to destroy.[14]

This is another repeat of the golden calf incident at the bottom of Mount Sinai. The people, not knowing what had become of Moses, asked Aaron to make them gods who would go before them. So Aaron told the men to take off the earrings that were in the ears of their wives, sons, and daughters and bring them to him. The people followed Aaron's instructions, and Aaron made a golden calf out of the gold. The people worshiped the golden calf as the god who had brought them out of Egypt. And when Aaron saw this he built an altar before it (Ex. 32:1–6).

It is not a total disregard of the Lord. It is the "Lord plus" (syncretism). What was the point of this ephod? One commentator argues well that this was most likely a priestly garment made to obtain direction from the Lord, much like the Urim and Thummim were attached to the priest's ephod to give direction from the Lord (1 Sam. 23:9–12; 30:7–8).[15] Gideon had already been visited directly by the Lord earlier; now he could seek the Lord's will like the priests and be another channel of grace for Israel, which the people would love.[16] Not only did it become a snare for the Israelites, but for Gideon and his family as well. They sought more than what the Lord had graciously provided through his means.

Are we any different? How many times I have longed for a postcard in the mail or a bright flashing sign in the sky telling me if this is the seminary I am supposed to go to, if this is the man I am to marry, if this is the ministry opportunity I am to take, if now is the time to try to conceive a baby, if this is the right home to buy, etc., etc., etc.! But the Lord has provided us with his Word, the means of grace (baptism and the Lord's Supper), and godly leaders in our churches to encourage our hearts and lead us in the right way.

Despite Gideon's failures and imperfect record as a judge, the Lord was gracious to use him to defeat the Midianites and give the land rest for forty years during Gideon's days. Significantly, this is the last time we will read this note of rest in the book. Remember that the book of

14. Ibid., 208.
15. Davis, *Judges*, 114.
16. Ibid.

Judges is not just cyclical but is a downward spiral, a progression of deeper and deeper apostasy. And in every story the implied message is the same: "All have sinned and fall short of the glory of God" (Rom. 3:23) and "Salvation belongs to the LORD!" (Jonah 2:9). But the book reminds us that not all will be saved. Only those who come to Jesus Christ in faith and believe in him will be saved from an eternity in hell.

Let us stop for a moment and ponder this. Many, if not all, of us have been disappointed with leadership in the church at one time or another. Perhaps it's been far removed from you, and you have only heard about the youth pastor who molested someone's daughter on the youth trip, or the deacon's wife and the pastor who were caught in adultery, or the church treasurer who stole money from the local congregation. Or perhaps it has hit closer to home. Perhaps the pastor's wife has stung you instead of encouraged you with words, maybe your pastor gave you poor counsel and you've struggled to forgive him, maybe your sister in Christ broke trust in your friendship, or perhaps the women's ministry director hasn't shepherded well. Maybe you're struggling with where the Lord is in the midst of these circumstances. According to Scripture, he is right there in the midst of them using them for your good and his glory (Gen. 50:20; Acts 2:23; Rom. 8:28). And even in the midst of them he has extended his rest and peace to you (Matt. 11:28; John 14:27).

While we would expect the narrative to move on at this point to the next judge, we receive some added information to introduce another story of one of Gideon's descendants, his son Abimelech (ch. 9), which is part of the entire Gideon story (ch. 6–9). Before the note of Gideon's death is sounded, we receive the birth note of one of his seventy sons, Abimelech. The fact that Gideon had seventy sons and many wives, plus a concubine, further confirms what was suspected in the previous verses: Gideon's refusal of kingship was lip service. He indeed lived as a king over the Israelites.[17] But he lived as an imperfect king, pointing to the need for a perfect One to come.

This indeed would happen in time. First the Lord would establish his covenant with King David, but ultimately it is God's own Son, Jesus

17. Block, *Judges, Ruth*, 302–4.

Christ, who is the only one fit for kingship. And King he is. One greater than Gideon is here. His kingdom has already been inaugurated, and one day soon it will be consummated. Are you ready? Have you believed in the Lord Jesus Christ? Are you displaying loyalty to him by the power of the Holy Spirit?

CONCLUSION

Perhaps you too are waiting for a home to sell. Or maybe you are waiting to be delivered from another set of difficult and seemingly impossible circumstances. The story of Gideon reminds us that the Lord often uses the most humble of means to deliver us in order to display his glorious grace and power through our lives. With the deliverance of the Israelites from the Midianites, he took the men from thirty-two thousand down to three hundred. But with the deliverance of his people from the slavery of sin, he took the number down to one man. And it is this one God-man, Jesus Christ, who stretched out his arms for God's people, who beckons you to come and drink from the water of life that delivers you from the snare of the Enemy forever.

Judges 8:33–9:57

PLEASE USE THE QUESTION paradigm from pages 301–2 as you work through the following. See the introductory comments there that explain each part of the process below in more detail.

- **Pray.**
- **Ponder the Passage.** Read Judges 8:33–9:57 once a day from different translations for the entire week, looking for its:
  - Point
  - Persons
  - Problem
  - Patterns
  - Persons of the Trinity
  - Puzzling Parts
- **Put It in Perspective.**
  - Place in Scripture. Read Deuteronomy 17:14–20 and skim Judges 1–2.
  - Passages from Other Parts of Scripture

1. Based on your observations of the text, what is the basic content of this passage? Try to summarize it in your own words, using a sentence or two.

2. What happens after Gideon's death (8:33–35)?

3. What is Abimelech's argument to the people in order to persuade them to make him king (9:1–2)? What is his mother's relatives' response (9:3)? What do they give him and from where (9:4)? What does Abimelech do with this gift (9:5)? Why does Abimelech go to Ophrah (9:5)? What title does this earn him (9:6)?

4. Read Deuteronomy 17:14–20 in light of 9:6. Should Israel have made Abimelech king? Why or why not?

5. How does the youngest of the seventy sons of Jerubbaal escape Abimelech (9:5)? What is his response to Abimelech's vengeful actions (9:7)?

6. Look up Deuteronomy 27:11–14. What is ironic about Jotham standing on Mount Gerizim to tell his fable (9:7)? What four things are sought by the trees in the fable and why (9:8–15)? What are their responses (9:8–15)?

7. What is the point of Jotham's fable (9:16, 19–20)? What is Jotham's indictment against the leaders of Shechem (9:17–18)? What is the blessing that he pronounces and on what condition (9:19)? What is the curse that he pronounces and on what condition (9:20)?

8. How long does Abimelech rule over Israel (9:22)? What does God send at the end of this time (9:23)? Are the actions of the leaders of Shechem right (see Deut. 32:35, 43)? How do you explain this seeming tension (see Gen. 50:20; Acts 2:23)?

9. What new leader comes to Shechem and stirs up the people against Abimelech (9:26)? What is the people's response (9:27)? How does this display the state of apostasy in Israel during the time of the judges? What is Gaal's real motive (9:29)?

10. What is the response of Zebul, the ruler of the city (9:30)? What does he command Abimelech to do (9:31–33)?

11. What is Zebul's strategy to delay Gaal (9:36)? What is Zebul's taunt (9:38)? What does he command Gaal to do (9:38)? What is Gaal's response (9:39)?

12. How does Abimelech capture the city and what does he do to it (9:42–45)? Was the city ever rebuilt (see 1 Kings 12:25)?

13. Compare Abimelech's action against the Tower of Shechem and the people within it, as well as the tower in Thebez and the people in it, with his father's action against the tower of Penuel (8:17).

14. What happens when Abimelech gets to the door of the tower to burn it down (9:53)? Compare this "certain woman" with Jael in 4:17–22. What is Abimelech's dying response to his armor-bearer and what is the result (9:54)?

15. How does 9:56–57 connect with 9:23 and give us the key to the interpretation of the story of Abimelech?

16. How does the story of Abimelech anticipate the vengeance of the Lord on the last day of judgment? How does it point to the need for a godly king? How is this fulfilled in the history of redemption (see 2 Sam. 7; Heb. 2:7)?

- **Principles and Points of Application.**
  1. In what areas of your life right now are you tempted to do things in your own way in order to get what you want when you want it? Spend time repenting of this attitude today and submit your will to the Lord's will and timing for your life.

  2. Jotham tells the Shechemites to listen to him that God may listen to them. Where do we see a similar principle in the New Testament (read 1 Peter 3:7)? What sin in your life is hindering your prayers to God? Spend time in confession and repentance today so that your prayer life might be restored.

  3. In what area(s) of your life are you acting selfishly instead of selflessly? Recognize that the Holy Spirit will help you, and walk in the Spirit today.

  4. Is there a situation in your present life where you are tempted to take vengeance into your own hands? Meditate on Romans 12:19; Hebrews 10:30; Revelation 6:10. Now read Matthew 5:38–48. Forgive those against whom you are holding a grudge today, regardless of whether they have asked for forgiveness.

NOTES FOR JUDGES 8:33–9:57

Ponder the aim of this lesson concerning our:

Mind: What do we need to know from this passage in Scripture?

> The Lord displays his judgment on those who try to take the kingship illicitly.

Heart: How does what we learn from this passage affect our internal relationship with the Lord?

> It prepares us to be kingdom disciples who recognize Jesus Christ is the only One with the right of kingship for the eternal throne.

Hands: How does what we learn from this passage translate into action for God's kingdom?

> It enables us to:

1. Repent of seeking position, power, and prestige in our own ways and to rest in the Lord's position for us, power in us, and his prestige.
2. Listen to and heed God's Word.
3. Act in good faith and integrity in areas where we're tempted to act selfishly.
4. Leave vengeance to the Lord and rest in his justice this week.

INTRODUCTION

I am sure it doesn't come as a surprise to you that leadership in America is in a crisis. Both inside and outside the church, true leaders are hard to find. The focus has too often been on the charisma of the person rather than the character, the makeup rather than the morals, the humor rather than the humility, their power and prestige rather than their prayer lives, their money rather than their motives, their speech rather than their spirituality, and their drive rather than their devotion to the Lord.

J. Oswald Sanders wrote a wonderful book called *Spiritual Leadership*, which made a lasting impression on me as a young high school girl. I learned that there were essential qualities for leadership that included discipline, vision, wisdom, decision, courage, humility, integrity, sincerity, appropriate humor, righteous anger, patience, friendship, the ability to deal with others sensitively and to manage delicate situations well, the power of inspiring others to service and sacrifice, good organizational skills, mastery of the art of listening, and the ability to correspond with others through writing.[1] But Sanders goes on to speak of those qualities that are not just essential but that are indispensable. One is to be Spirit-filled, and the other is to be a person of fervent prayer.[2]

Some of you are seeking leadership positions, some of you have been asked to assume a leadership position, and others are in the position of choosing leaders. Perhaps you feel called to run for a political office, or perhaps the Lord has chosen to make you a mother and you will be leading a child. Maybe you are the candidate for the headmaster of a Christian school or the principal of a public school. Perhaps you are head of the nurses' ward. Maybe you have been asked to be a leader in your corporation, or maybe you have been asked to be a small group leader in your church. Perhaps you are the one who has the responsibility of choosing leaders for the women's ministry at your church, or of voting for those running for public office. Choosing leaders and being leaders is part of life and we must do so wisely, with humility, and with a great deal of prayer.

Judges 8:33–9:57 is a story about leadership. From the time of the fall in the garden of Eden, men and women have failed to be godly leaders. And this theme is woven all throughout the Bible. All have sinned and fallen short of the glory of God (Rom. 3:23). It should come as no surprise to us then that we need a Savior.

We can divide the lesson into five sections:

I. Israel Returns to Idolatry (8:33–35)

✦ II. Abimelech Gains the Kingship in an Evil Way (9:1–6)

---

1. J. Oswald Sanders, *Spiritual Leadership* (Chicago: Moody, 1994), 51–76.
2. Ibid., 79, 85.

III. God Warns the Men of Shechem by Jotham (9:7–21)
IV. Abimelech Gains the City of Shechem in an Evil Way (9:22–49)
V. God Brings Curse of Jotham on Men of Shechem (9:50–57)

I. Israel's Return to Idolatry (8:33–35)

We saw in the previous verses (8:29–32) that, before Gideon's death is mentioned, we receive the birth note of one of his seventy sons, Abimelech ("My father is king"), which further confirmed that Gideon considered himself a king in Israel. Here we see the spiritual death note of the sons of Israel who again whored after the Baals and made Baal-berith ("lord of the covenant"[3]) their god after Gideon died. They did not remember the true Lord of the covenant, the one who had delivered them from their enemies on every side. Sure, they knew the story, they knew the history, but it made no difference in their lives. They were like so many today who have heard Scripture and catechism from an early age but do whatever seems right in their own eyes. The Israelites also did not show steadfast love to Gideon's family for what good he had done to Israel by being the Lord's instrument to deliver them from the oppression of the Midianites. While we are not to idolize our favorite preachers, Bible study leaders, or seminar speakers, we are to honor such servants of the King who pour out their hearts in service to the Lord (1 Thess. 5:12–13). Notice here that when people don't honor the King, neither do they honor the servants of the King.

II. Abimelech Gains the Kingship in an Evil Way (9:1–6)

The story of Abimelech begins and ends on a negative note. Contrary to what we may think given the length of the narrative, Abimelech was not a deliverer that the Lord raised up to save Israel from oppression. Instead Abimelech was the oppressor who rose up from within Israel and took his name "My father is king" as license to become king in Israel.[4]

3. K. Lawson Younger Jr., *Judges/Ruth*, The NIV Application Commentary (Grand Rapids: Zondervan, 2002), 218.
4. Daniel I. Block, *The New American Commentary*, vol. 6, *Judges, Ruth* (Nashville: Broadman & Holman, 1999), 310.

The church is not always oppressed from without; there are times when it is oppressed by leaders within. Abimelech, the son of Jerubbaal by his concubine (8:31), went to Shechem to his mother's relatives and the whole clan of his mother's family to gain the people's favor. His argument was that it would be better for him, as one man and their own flesh and bone, to rule over them than for seventy of the sons of Jerubbaal to rule over them.

His mother's relatives agreed with his argument and spoke favorably of him to the leaders of Shechem. Their hearts found this scenario favorable, for Abimelech was their brother by flesh and bone. So they gave him seventy pieces of silver out of the house of Baal-berith, another indication of the depth of apostasy in Israel at this time. The number of shekels is the same number of the brothers that Abimelech will kill to secure his kingship. Obviously he placed little value on their lives.[5] Furthermore, Abimelech used this silver to hire "worthless and reckless fellows, who followed him" (9:4). To take care of any threat to his devised plan, he went to his father's house at Ophrah and killed sixty-nine of his seventy brothers on one stone. In other words, they were consecutively put on the stone one after another and slaughtered. The youngest brother had hidden himself. While this was an act of sinful personal revenge, the Lord was using it to bring judgment on Gideon's house. It was Gideon who had ruled with a high hand, murdered his own countrymen, and officially sponsored a pagan cult.[6] Interestingly, it was Gideon's firstborn who would not kill the two Midianite kings because of his fear and youth, and now it is the youngest son who hides and will prove to be a voice of indictment against Abimelech's kingship. All the leaders of Shechem and all Beth-millo came together by the oak of the pillar at Shechem and made Abimelech king.

III. God Warns the Men of Shechem by Jotham (9:7–21)

When Jotham, the only son left of Jerubbaal, hears that Abimelech has been anointed king, he goes to stand on Mount Gerizim. It was on this mountain that his tribe had stood with the tribes of Simeon, Levi,

5. Younger, *Judges/Ruth*, 219.
6. Block, *Judges, Ruth*, 312–13.

Judah, Issachar, Ephraim, and Benjamin to bless the Israelites after they had crossed over the Jordan. The other tribes had been commanded by Moses to stand on Mount Ebal to recite the curses (Deut. 27:11–13).

Jotham calls for the leaders of Shechem to listen to him, that God may listen to them (9:7). Then Jotham tells a fable to bring judgment against the Shechemites for anointing such a ruthless ruler over them. God had made the requirements for kingship clear to Israel (Deut. 17:14–20), and Abimelech did not fit the description.

The fable depicts the Shechemites as trees that went out to anoint a king over them. "The first three candidates represent the most prized species of domestic plants in ancient Palestine."[7] The first of the four candidates is described as an olive tree, but he declines because he already has an important job to do. The second candidate is a fig tree, but he too declines because he too is already in a good position. The third candidate is a vine, and he too declines because his job cheers God and men. The fourth and final candidate is a bramble (the plant that had nothing of value[8]), and he agrees as long as they are anointing him in good faith. Otherwise they would be devoured.

What is the point of Jotham's fable? It cannot be that kingship is bad, for the Lord had set forth instructions for choosing kings in Israel (Deut. 17:14–20). No, the point is seen by the almost identical phrases in 9:16 and 19, that voting for one with bad character and poor leadership is a bad move, and yet people do it all the time. I have seen churches do it when they elect the pastor or elders or deacons. But I have also seen women do it when they say yes to a man to be their husband. They make excuses for or overlook his poor leadership and character during the dating period and then show up for counseling after the marriage. We must take great pains to select our leaders. We must spend much time in prayer seeking whom the Lord would have to lead our churches, our children's ministries, our women's ministries, our homes (if we are single and looking toward marriage). How often we look at all the wrong things to select our leaders and forget to look at the heart (1 Sam. 16:7).

7. Ibid., 317.
8. Ibid., 318.

But a more significant point of the fable is the curse. Jotham goes on to reveal his judgment against the Shechemites. He places a blessing on them and on Abimelech if they (1) have acted in good faith and integrity in making Abimelech king and (2) have dealt well with Jerubbaal and his house and have done to him as his deeds deserved (his deeds of delivering them from the oppression of the Midianites), which they have not. And he places a curse on Abimelech if they have not acted in good faith and integrity with Jerubbaal and with his house, which is what they have done. Then Jotham flees because he knows his life is in danger by the hand of Abimelech.

IV. Abimelech Gains the City of Shechem in an Evil Way (9:22–49)

Abimelech ruled over Israel for three years, but the narrator of the book refuses to give him the title of king in the Hebrew. Instead he uses the word for "govern" to describe what Abimelech was doing. Then the text says that God sent an evil spirit between Abimelech and the leaders of Shechem. This translation can be confusing with regard to the Lord's character, so we must understand that the Hebrew word here can have more than one meaning and the one here is not to be interpreted in a moral sense, but in the normal sense of "bad" as opposed to "good." We will see that this spirit produces bad effects or conditions on the intended object. This is no different from the Lord sending other agents of destruction such as fire, the sword, or plagues.[9]

So the leaders of Shechem dealt violently with Abimelech. This evil spirit was sent so that the violence done to the seventy sons of Jerubbaal might come, and their blood be laid, on their murderer, Abimelech, and on the men of Shechem, who had strengthened and supported Abimelech to such an act. The leaders of Shechem put men in ambush against Abimelech, and they robbed all who passed by them on the mountaintops where they were in ambush. We don't know who told Abimelech, but this uprising against him was told to him.

Gaal the son of Ebed and his relatives came to Shechem and stirred up the people against Abimelech. The men of Shechem put their trust

9. Ibid., 323–24.

in Gaal. In celebration of Gaal's arrival, they held a festival and reviled Abimelech in the house of their god. Again, these actions portray how apostate Israel had become during the time of the judges and how much they needed a king after God's own heart. During the festival Gaal discredited Abimelech as their ruler and put doubt in the people's minds concerning him. He also discredited Jerubbaal (the one the Lord had chosen to deliver Israel from the Midianites) and Zebul, Abimelech's officer. Gaal let his own desire for rulership be known and promised that if he were ruler he would remove Abimelech by challenging him to battle.

When Zebul, Abimelech's officer and ruler of the city, heard Gaal's words, he was angry. So he secretly commanded messengers to go to Abimelech and tell him of the riot and instruct him to set an ambush in the field. Then in the morning he was told to rise early and rush on the city. Then he was to do to them what his hand found to do.

Abimelech did as Zebul had commanded and, while Zebul delayed Gaal's reaction by telling him that what he thought were men coming from the mountains were really just shadows, Abimelech made great headway to attack. When Gaal finally realized they really were men, Zebul taunted him for what he had said against Abimelech and urged him to go out and fight. Abimelech chased Gaal, and Gaal fled from before him. Then Zebul finished driving out Gaal and his relatives from Shechem.

But the battle was not over. A second battle was stirring. Those who had once supported Abimelech, those who were of his own flesh and bone, turned against him and went out to battle. But Abimelech rose up against them and killed them. Not only did he kill the people, he also razed the city and sowed it with salt. This may have been an attempt to make sure it would be barren and desolate forever (see also Deut. 29:23).[10] But it may have been a ritual act of invoking a curse on the land that was irreversible.[11] Regardless, the city is rebuilt under the rule of King Jeroboam (1 Kings 12:25).

But some had escaped. All the leaders of the Tower of Shechem entered the stronghold of the house of El-berith (the same as Baal-berith

10. Younger, *Judges/Ruth*, 227.
11. Ibid., 330.

in 9:4 that they had taken silver from to support Abimelech). But when Abimelech found out that they were there, he took his men with him and set the stronghold on fire over them. Like his father Gideon who had broken down the tower of Penuel, killing the men of the city (8:17), so Abimelech burned down the Tower of Shechem, killing about one thousand men and women, fulfilling the curse stated by Jotham in 9:20a.

V. God Brings Curse of Jotham on Men of Shechem (9:50–57)

But Abimelech's bloodthirsty tower days were not over. He went on to capture Thebez, but all the men, women, and leaders of the city took refuge in the roof of the city's tower. Again, Abimelech planned to burn the tower with fire. But just as he drew near to the door to set it on fire, a woman threw an upper millstone on Abimelech's head and crushed his skull, fulfilling the curse stated by Jotham in 9:20b. As he had with Jael (5:24), God had used another woman to kill a bloodthirsty man, but this time the man was an Israelite himself. But in his dying moment, Abimelech's pride was still in place, for he requested his armor-bearer to thrust his sword into him so that it would not be said of him that a woman had killed him. While Abimelech was more than willing to use a woman (his own mother) to gain the kingship (9:1), he was not willing to die by one. So the armor-bearer fulfilled Abimelech's request, and all the men of Israel went home upon seeing Abimelech dead. The Lord had used evil to destroy evil. The evil Abimelech destroyed the men of Shechem, and the evil men of Shechem, along with Thebez, destroyed Abimelech. We will see this again at the end of history when the Antichrist and his followers will hate the very antichrist society they have sown (Rev. 17:16–17).

The narrator concludes on a somber note, but it is the key to the chapter. It was God who returned the evil of Abimelech on his own head, the evil that he had committed against his father by killing his seventy sons. And it was God who also made all the evil of the men of Shechem return on their heads. There is no note of "The LORD raised up 'So-and-So' to deliver Israel from the oppression of Abimelech." No, the Lord himself is the sole Deliverer in this story. What amazing grace!

121

On the Shechemites came the curse of Jotham, the son of Jerubbaal. It is not just an Old Testament principle that the Lord will avenge. The apostle Paul quotes from Deuteronomy 32:35 in Romans 12:19, "Beloved, never avenge yourselves, but leave it to the wrath of God, for it is written, 'Vengeance is mine, I will repay, says the Lord.'" The author of Hebrews quotes the same verse from Deuteronomy in 10:30. And the apostle John, in the book of Revelation, records what he heard from the souls of those who had been slain for the Word of God and for the witness they had borne when the fifth seal was opened: "They cried out with a loud voice, 'O Sovereign Lord, holy and true, how long before you will judge and avenge our blood on those who dwell on the earth?'" (6:10). But the Lord's vengeance is only one side of the story. The other side of the story is the Lord's redemption. Although all deserve his judgment, he has chosen to redeem a people for himself, and he has chosen to do so through his Son, Jesus Christ.

Israel was in need of a better king and a living king. In time the Lord would raise up King David, a man after God's heart, to be king over his people. But Scripture will not hide David's sin from us—his sin of murder and his sin of adultery. Indeed Scripture continuously points out that all have sinned and fallen short of the glory of God (Rom. 3:23) and are in need of a Savior. But God, in the fullness of time, sent his perfect Son, the final and perfect Davidic king, to rule over his people in righteousness and justice, in purity and truth. He is the King who now reigns from the heavenly realms, seated at the right hand of God the Father, Jesus our King and High Priest. Have you considered Jesus, the Apostle and High Priest, who was faithful to the Father who appointed him? He has been counted worthy of the most glory, for he is faithful over God's house as a son. And we are God's house if we hold fast our confidence and boasting in our hope (see Heb. 3:1–6).

CONCLUSION

We need a Savior. We need a leader who will lead us to the throne of grace. We need a leader who will lead us beside paths of righteousness. We need a leader who will grant us wisdom. We need a leader who will give us righteousness. We need a leader who will give us spiritual gifts and spiritual character. The Lord did not find one righteous enough to fulfill his plan except for his own Son, the perfect God-man. Jesus Christ is the only One with the right of kingship for the eternal throne. He is the only Leader worthy of his calling.

But he also makes us worthy of our calling. He clothes us in robes of righteousness. He gives us his Spirit to be our helper. He grants us wisdom through his Word. He teaches us to pray and prays for us. As mothers, as grandmothers, as directors of women's ministry, as women's small group leaders, as women's Bible study teachers, as career women, as women in political office, as women in public service, we acknowledge Jesus Christ as our Leader and we follow in his royal train, leading others to a life of service and sacrifice for him, giving him all glory, honor, and praise and delighting ourselves in him.

Judges 10:1–12:15

PLEASE USE THE QUESTION paradigm from pages 301–2 as you work through the following. See the introductory comments there that explain each part of the process below in more detail.

- **Pray.**
- **Ponder the Passage.** Read Judges 10:1–12:15 once a day from different translations for the entire week, looking for its:
  - Point
  - Persons
  - Problem
  - Patterns
  - Persons of the Trinity
  - Puzzling Parts
- **Put It in Perspective.**
  - Place in Scripture. Skim Judges 1:1–3:6.
  - Passages from Other Parts of Scripture

1. Based on your observations of the text, what is the basic content of this passage? Try to summarize it in your own words, using a sentence or two.

2. In light of Abimelech's leadership, how is the Lord's grace toward Israel displayed in 10:1?

3. List everything the text tells us about Tola (10:1–2). What do you learn?

4. What does the text tell us about Jair (10:3–5)? In light of Deuteronomy 17:14–20, is Jair successful in the Lord's eyes or in man's? Why or why not?

5. How many years of rest from oppressors do Tola and Jair give Israel? How does this display God's grace?

6. How many gods are listed in 10:6? Compare this with Deuteronomy 7:1. What do you learn? Finish reading Deuteronomy 7. Does this explain the Lord's anger in 10:7? How?

7. Into whose hand does the Lord sell his people (10:7)? How long are the Israelites oppressed (10:8)?

8. What is the people's response to this oppression (10:10)? Is this sincere repentance (see the Lord's response in 10:14)?

9. How many nations does the Lord list from which he has saved Israel (10:11)? Compare this with 10:6. Look up Exodus 14:30; Numbers 21:21–35; Judges 3:13–30; 4. What do you learn?

10. What is the Lord's response to the people (10:16)? Is it because of their repentance or because he is impatient over their misery? How does this display God's grace? How is this the key to the theme of the story of Jephthah?

11. How do the Gileadites choose their leader (10:17–18)? Contrast this with 1:1.

12. Describe Jephthah's background (11:1–3). How does this further show the apostasy in Israel during the time of the judges?

13. How does Jephthah respond to the Gileadites' request of him to be leader over them (11:7)? How is the choice of Jephthah to be deliverer different from earlier accounts in the book in which the Lord himself raised up or called the deliverer?

14. What are the words that Jephthah sends to the king of the Ammonites (11:12–27)? Try and make a brief list of the points of

the argument. What is the bottom line of the argument (11:27)? Does the king of the Ammonites listen (11:28)?

15. How does Jephthah deliver Israel from the Ammonites (11:29)? Compare this with Zechariah 4:6.

16. What is the motivation behind Jephthah's vow (11:30)? Who gives the Ammonites into Jephthah's hand (11:32)? What is the result of Jephthah's vow (11:39)? In light of this vow, read Leviticus 27:1–8; Deuteronomy 12:31. What do you learn? What custom in Israel was a result of the fulfillment of Jephthah's vow (11:40)? How did this serve as an annual reminder of a sinful and tragic event?

17. Compare Ephraim's response to Gideon in 8:1 with their response to Jephthah in 12:1. What common sin do you see? How does the Lord judge Ephraim's sin (12:6)? How does this intertribal war display the disunity of Israel during this period of redemptive history?

18. How does the Lord's judgment of Ephraim's pride with death anticipate the judgment by eternal death of all those who die apart from Christ?

19. How do Jephthah's faults and failure as a leader point toward the need of the Davidic dynasty, which culminates in Jesus Christ?

20. What do you learn about Ibzan (12:8–10), Elon (12:11), and Abdon (12:13–15)?

- **Principles and Points of Application.**
1. Spend time today giving thanks to the Lord that, despite our sin, he is committed to his plan of redemption.
2. How does it encourage you that the Lord records his people's names and knows the places where they live?
3. How do you need to embrace your role as helper, mother, teacher, and trainer of other women today while glorifying God and enjoying him?
4. What sin in your life do you need to repent of today that is hindering your relationship with the Lord? Spend time meditating on 1 John 1:9.

5. Spend time today evaluating any wrong thinking you have with regard to the Lord's forgiveness being conditional, recognizing that his deliverance is not conditioned on our obedience, but on that of his Son, Jesus Christ. Then spend time in thanksgiving for this wonderful truth.

6. In what areas of your life are you responsible to choose leaders? How do you go about doing so? If you are responsible to choose leaders in one of your church's ministries, spend time today identifying and implementing biblical ways of choosing leaders based on God's Word.

7. How do you choose your friends? Spend time evaluating your friendships and praying that the Lord will give you wisdom from his Word in choosing friends.

8. Sing, speak, or write a song of praise today for the deliverance from sin and death that is yours through Jesus Christ if you have placed your trust in him.

9. Whom in your life do you need to point away from flawed and failure-filled leaders to the perfect Savior and Leader, Jesus Christ? Ask the Lord to open a door of opportunity for you to do that this week.

10. In what ways are you pursuing power, possessions, or prestige, instead of pursuing the work God has for you?

NOTES FOR JUDGES 10:1–12:15

Ponder the aim of this lesson concerning our:

Mind: What do we need to know from this passage in Scripture?

> In spite of Israel's apostasy, the Lord was impatient over the misery of Israel and delivered them from the Ammonites through Jephthah.

Heart: How does what we learn from this passage affect our internal relationship with the Lord?

It prepares us to be kingdom disciples who recognize that the Lord is moved to compassion before we clean ourselves up, because he sees us robed in the righteousness of Christ.

Hands: How does what we learn from this passage translate into action for God's kingdom?

It enables us to:

1. Give thanks to the Lord that, despite our sin, he is committed to his plan of redemption.
2. Recognize that we serve a personal God who knows us by name and knows our location.
3. Embrace our role as helpers, mothers, teachers and trainers of other women while glorifying God and enjoying him.
4. Confess and repent of any sin that is hindering our relationship with the Lord.
5. Evaluate any wrong thinking with regard to the Lord's forgiveness being conditional, recognizing that his deliverance is not conditioned on our obedience, but on that of his Son, Jesus Christ.
6. Identify and implement biblical ways of choosing leaders for the women's ministries in our local church.
7. Evaluate our friendships and pray that the Lord will give us wisdom in choosing friends.
8. Sing a song of praise for the deliverance from sin and death that is ours through Jesus Christ.
9. Point others away from flawed and failure-filled leaders to the perfect Savior, Jesus Christ.

INTRODUCTION

Carrie sat in her car looking at the women walking into the church for Thursday morning Bible study.[1] The Bible study leader had invited

---

1. Carrie represents many different women whom I have counseled over the years.

her several weeks ago, but this was the first morning she had gotten up the courage to come to the church. She was used to going to Sunday morning services, but the church was so large that she felt she could at least hide then. Now she felt so vulnerable. The Bible study only had about thirty women, and they broke down into small groups. What if someone found out about the past couple years of her life? Surely they would disapprove of her.

Carrie's first marriage had been disastrous. She knew she shouldn't have married whom and when she did, but she had, and it had been a painful experience. However, there had been no biblical ground for divorce, so she had stuck it out as long as she had thought she could. But one day she had had it, so she had made biblical grounds for divorce by having an affair. Knowing that she had made the wrong decision, she had ended the affair, but it had been too late. The marriage was in shreds, divorce papers were signed, and Carrie was free again. But it wasn't the freedom that she had expected. She felt enslaved to her past and lived under guilt and condemnation every day of her life. She knew she had failed her parents' expectations, her church's expectations, and her own expectations. She had felt unworthy to set foot in the church for a long time. But finally she had begun coming on Sundays.

To try to make herself feel more acceptable, Carrie had consistently spent time reading the Bible each night, had gotten involved in feeding the homeless with a local church on Friday nights, had volunteered for every advertised need at the church, and was trying to be perfect during the days. But she still couldn't shake her feeling of unworthiness about herself. She knew that she was the Lord's. She loved him, and she had always believed that he loved her. But now she doubted that his love extended to her now that she had lived in the way she had. Carrie believed that the Lord's love was conditional. She believed that if she was good, then he would love and accept her, but if she was bad, then he was disappointed and might reject her.

Carrie is like so many women in the church today who have blown it in the past and think they must clean themselves up before God accepts them again. But there is a problem with that thinking. We cannot clean ourselves up. That is why God the Father sent his Son, Jesus Christ, into the world—to save us from our sin. If we are in Christ, we wear his robes of righteousness. "If we confess our sins, he is faithful and just to forgive us our sins and to cleanse us from all unrighteousness" (1 John 1:9). Judges 10:1–12:15 has much to say about being kingdom disciples who recognize that the Lord is moved to compassion before we clean ourselves up, because he sees us robed in the righteousness of Christ.

We can divide the lesson into six sections:

    I. The Lord Raises Up Tola and Jair to Deliver Israel (10:1–5)
   II. The Lord Raises Up Jephthah to Deliver Israel (10:6–11:28)
  III. The Lord Gives the Ammonites into Jephthah's Hand (11:29–33)
  IV. The Tragic Result of Jephthah's Vow (11:34–40)
   V. Jephthah and the Men of Gilead Defeat the Ephraimites (12:1–7)
  VI. Ibzan, Elon, and Abdon Judge Israel (12:8–15)

I. The Lord Raises Up Tola and Jair to Deliver Israel (10:1–5)

It would not be surprising to read, "After Abimelech there arose to destroy Israel . . ." But instead the amazing grace of God abounds. After the story of Abimelech, it is only a gracious God who would save Israel again. They continue into a downward spiral into apostasy, and yet the Lord will not let them go. He is committed to his plan of redemption; the promised Messiah will come through his chosen people, Israel. Thus he preserves them through the darkness of apostasy until the time is ripe to introduce the Davidic dynasty onto the scene, which will ultimately lead to the perfect, final, and eternal King, Jesus Christ.

Although we don't know much about Tola, we know that he was the son of Puah, son of Dodo, a man of Issachar. Family names and lines are important in Scripture and are a wonderful reminder to us that we serve a personal God who knows us by name and records us by name. Tola lived at Shamir in the hill country of Ephraim. We not only serve a God who knows who we are, but also where we are. Tola judged Israel for twenty-three years. This is amazing grace. The Lord had only allowed Abimelech, a horrible and destructive leader, to rule for three years. The

131

length of time in the book of Judges of the oppressors is always shorter than the time of rest that the Lord graciously grants his people. Here we see that he gave the land rest for twenty-three years. But there's more.

Not only did the Lord give Israel rest for twenty-three years, there seems to be no oppression (at least that is recorded) between the time of Tola and Jair. Jair ruled Israel for twenty-two years, making a total of forty-five years of rest for Israel. Jair was a Gileadite, which is important to note because he is meant to stand in contrast with the next Gileadite introduced in the book—Jephthah. Jair had thirty sons, who will stand in contrast to Jephthah, who had no sons and only one daughter; Jair's sons rode on thirty donkeys, and they had thirty cities in the land of Gilead. While this all sounds very positive and successful, it should wave a red flag to us since we have studied Deuteronomy 17:14–20 in past lessons and learned the laws that the Lord gave concerning Israel's kings. While Jair was not a king in the technical sense of the word, he was still a ruler, and many of the same principles apply. For example, if Jair had thirty sons, he most likely had several wives, which Deuteronomy 17:17 warns against lest they turn his heart away from the Lord. While it was not Jair, but his sons, who had thirty donkeys, we are reminded of Deuteronomy 17:16, which warns against acquiring many horses. And, when we read of the cities they have, we are reminded of Deuteronomy 17:17, which warns against acquiring excessive wealth.

Our hearts may resonate with someone like Jair. His biography sounds much more glamorous than that of Tola before him. Don't many women want to have a large family? Don't we as mothers and grandmothers want to say that our children or grandchildren are successful? Don't we want to secure our future financially? This is the world's way, but it is not the covenant way. The covenant way is one of absolute trust and reliance on the Lord. While we rejoice in the family that the Lord chooses to give us, we don't become embittered if he chooses not to give us children or as many children as we wanted. While we praise our children for their success, we make sure to point them to the one who gave them the ability to succeed. While we are wise with our finances and planning for our future, we are not bound by our finances and plans in such a way that we forego the opportunity to graciously give to others in need or follow God's call to foreign missions. We must be women with a mission, but our mission must be to glorify God with our lives, delight in him, and fulfill our design as helpers (Gen. 2:20), as mothers (Gen. 3:20), as teachers and trainers of other women (Titus 2), and as proclaimers of the gospel to the nations (Matt. 28:19–20).

II. The Lord Raises Up Jephthah to Deliver Israel (10:6–11:28)

The Israelites again did evil in the sight of the Lord, and they served other gods. This is by far the book of Judges' most extensive list of the gods that they served. Not only does the author tell us that they served the Baals and Ashtaroth, but also the gods of Syria, the gods of Sidon, the gods of Moab, the gods of the Ammonites, and the gods of the Philistines. These seven foreign gods correspond to the list of the seven Canaanite nations listed in Deuteronomy 7:1, emphasizing the total apostasy of Israel.[2] What was the result? They forsook the Lord and did not serve him. Jesus later says in the gospel of Matthew, "No one can serve two masters, for either he will hate the one and love the other, or he will be devoted to the one and despise the other" (6:24). So we again see that the anger of the Lord is kindled against the Israelites, and he sells them into the oppressive hand of the Philistines in the west (see the Samson narrative in chs. 13–16) and the Ammonites in the east for eighteen years. The narrator specifically names the oppressed as the Israelites in the land of the Amorites, which was in Gilead, as well as the tribes of Judah, Benjamin, and Ephraim that were across the Jordan.

As we have read so many times before, the people of Israel cried out to the Lord. This time, though, there seems to be recognition of their sin. They admit to sinning against the Lord by forsaking him and serving the Baals. Was this true repentance? We will have to keep reading.

The Lord reminds them of his past deliverance that they had forgotten by a list of seven enemies (10:11–12). He had saved them from the hand of the Egyptians when he parted the waters of the Red Sea,

---

2. Daniel I. Block, *The New American Commentary*, vol. 6, *Judges, Ruth* (Nashville: Broadman & Holman, 1999), 344.

allowing Israel to cross on dry land, but immediately afterward made the waters cover the Egyptians' chariots and the horsemen in the Red Sea so that none survived (Ex. 14:30). The Lord had delivered them from the Amorites when Sihon and Og were defeated during the time of Moses (Num. 21:21–35).[3] The Lord had delivered them from the Ammonites and Amalekites by the hand of Ehud (3:13–30). He delivered them from the hand of the Philistines by way of Shamgar (3:31). He delivered them from the Sidonians (the Canaanites) by Barak (ch. 4). He delivered them from the Maonites, most likely associates of the Meunites in the region of the Midianites.[4] Yet they continued to forsake him and serve other gods, so he says that he will save them no more (10:13). Then we have the key verse that illuminates our understanding of their previous cries to the Lord. They were not cries of repentance but simply cries of distress, because the Lord tells them to cry out to the gods whom they have chosen in order to let them save Israel in their time of distress (10:14).

Perhaps you can relate to Israel. Maybe there have been many times when you have cried out to the Lord in distress, but you were not repentant. You wanted relief, but you didn't want the relationship with him that true repentance entails. This is how many interact with the Lord in our society today. They think that they need to have knowledge of him or have a home church just in case they go through a crisis and need him. But if they are doing just fine on their own, they leave the Lord behind. As we will see, this is not the way of the Lord, and this is not the covenant way of dealing with him. When we are in covenant with the Lord, we are in relationship with him through his Son, Jesus Christ. And what Christ has made possible (our reconciliation with the Father) is not to be shirked but embraced.

Again the people acknowledge that they have sinned and tell the Lord to do whatever seems good to him, but they ask that he please deliver them that day. This time there seems to be a sign of repentance, because the narrator tells us that they put away the foreign gods from

3. Ibid., 346.
4. Ibid., 347.

among them and served the Lord. But was there, or was this, the same old superficial cry as before? What was the result? The Lord became impatient over the misery of Israel, which seems to signify that the people may have really repented this time. But did they? The text doesn't say that the Lord became impatient over Israel's oppression because of their repentance. It says that he became impatient over their misery.

Now step back for a minute. We are in the book of Judges. This book of the Bible paints a picture of the sheer apostasy of Israel. And many have wrongly understood that it paints only an Old Testament God of judgment. But here we see God's grace again in the middle of the book in which Israel is at one of its most apostate points. God becomes impatient with their misery. Reflect on that for a moment. If you are one who has always thought that God wants you to be miserable because that is what your sin deserves, think again. Look at his Word. Over and over again the Covenant God intervenes on behalf of his covenant people in order to bring them out of their misery of slavery in sin and into relationship with him. And the climax of it all is when he sends his only Son, Jesus Christ, into the world to save his children from their misery in slavery to sin. Jesus Christ is the Savior of all saviors, and the book of Judges serves to point us evermore toward him.

The next verse takes us by surprise (10:17). Who called the Ammonites to arms? If it was the Lord, how is this the answer to the people's request and his impatience over the misery of Israel? We shall soon see. The Ammonites encamp in Gilead, while the Israelites come together (don't miss the fact that they actually come together!) and encamp at Mizpah in Gilead. And then the discussion of leadership begins. Who will be head over all the inhabitants of Gilead? Unlike 1:1, in which they inquired of the Lord, here they seem to make a random decision. The one who begins to fight against the Ammonites will lead.

This is never a good way to choose leaders! Making random choices will always lead to disastrous results. Our choice of leaders must be purposeful and based on God's Word. As one who has been involved in women's ministry for many years, I have had the privilege of choosing leaders several times. And I always start with the Word of God. What qualities and characteristics does the Lord desire for his people to have? Does the woman love the Lord and his church? Does she embrace her design as helper in her marriage and in her church? Does she have a submissive spirit to those whom the Lord has placed in authority over her? Does she exhibit the fruit of the Spirit? Does she serve the church with her gifts? Does she embrace her calling to teach and train younger women? Does she have a teachable and trainable spirit? Does she embrace and teach sound doctrine? These are just a few questions, but they are most important. The choice of leaders is of utmost importance, for they are shaping the women in our churches, who are shaping the next generation of believers, who will shape the following generation, and on and on it goes.

At this point we may well expect to read 11:29 as the next verse, "Then the Spirit of the LORD was upon Jephthah, and he passed through Gilead and Manasseh and passed on to Mizpah of Gilead, and from Mizpah of Gilead he passed on to the Ammonites." But instead we have a brief account of Jephthah's background, the people's choosing him as leader, and Jephthah's questioning of the king of the Ammonites (11:1–28).

Jephthah was a mighty warrior, but he was the son of a prostitute. Gilead, his father, also had a wife who had borne him sons, and when they grew up they drove Jephthah out of their house, declaring that he had no share of the inheritance since he was an illegitimate child. Both the fact that his father visited prostitutes and the fact that his brothers treated him as they did leaves no doubt of the apostasy in Israel at the time. Nothing good came of Jephthah either, for he fled to the land of Tob, where "worthless fellows" collected around him and "went out with him" (11:3).

Choosing friends is important. Those whom we surround ourselves with will have the greatest impact and influence on our lives. Women are relational beings, and our friendships with other women are imperative. But they must be friendships of grace. Our closest friends should be our sisters in Christ. And they should be sisters who are willing to sharpen us with the Word of God. That doesn't mean that everyone we are friends with will be a believer. But it does mean that those in our closest circle of influence, those whom we bear our deepest desires and secrets to, and those from whom we seek counsel should be.

Interestingly, when the Ammonites made war against Israel, it was Jephthah whom the elders of Gilead sought to be leader over them. Jephthah asks the question that we wonder when we read, "Why would they choose Jephthah, the one they kicked out of their house and treated as worthless?" Evidently the fact that he was "a mighty warrior" (11:1) was reason enough. Jephthah agrees to be their head if they bring him home to fight against the Ammonites, and the Lord gives them over to him. There is no piety in this statement though. Like Abimelech, Jephthah is driven by his own selfish motives.[5] So the elders agree and take him home, where he is made leader over them.

"And Jephthah spoke all his words before the LORD at Mizpah" (11:11). What does this mean? This seems to be another attempt to manipulate the circumstances and appear pious while the heart remains proud and self-centered.

This is not just a story about the Gileadites and Jephthah. This is a story about Israel and the Lord. Israel was treating the Lord just as the Gileadites were treating Jephthah. They wanted nothing to do with him until they needed a mighty warrior, and then suddenly Jephthah wasn't looking so bad after all. The Jews wanted nothing to do with Jesus either when he came to save Israel. They cast him out, which was good news for the Gentiles. But the Jews will one day understand that the only one who can save them is the one whom they once rejected (Matt. 23:39; Rom. 9–11).[6]

Instead of going straight to battle, Jephthah sends messengers to the king of the Ammonites to ask why he has come to fight against his land, Gilead. And the king answers that it was because Israel, on coming out of Egypt, took away his land from him, from the Arnon to the Jabbok and to the Jordan. The king wants it restored peaceably. But Jephthah knows Israel's history and declares that Israel had not taken the land of

5. Ibid., 355.
6. Dale Ralph Davis, *Judges: Such a Great Salvation* (Fearn, Great Britain: Christian Focus, 2000), 139.

Moab or the Ammonites, but instead had gone through the wilderness to the Red Sea and into Kadesh. At that point they requested to pass through Edom, but the king of Edom refused. So they asked the king of Moab, but he also refused. So Israel remained at Kadesh. Then they went through the wilderness, around Edom and Moab, and arrived on the east side of Moab, camping on the other side of the Arnon (the boundary of Moab). But they never entered Moab. Then they requested that Sihon king of the Amorites let them pass through his land, but Sihon didn't trust them and actually fought against them. However, the Lord was with his people, and he gave the Amorites into Israel's hand, so Israel gained possession of the land of the Amorites.

All through Scripture we read of the Lord delivering his people out of others' hands or delivering other people into his people's hands. Though the exodus through the Red Sea is better known than the Lord's delivering the Amorites into Israel's hands, this is occasion for us to pause and sing a song of praise to our Redeemer for what he has done in Israel's past that anticipated our deliverance on the cross from the power of sin and death and to sing a song of praise for our deliverance today.

At this point Jephthah challenges the king of the Ammonites. If the Lord dispossessed the Amorites from Israel, who does the king of the Ammonites think he is to take possession of them? Then he taunts him a little by saying that he is to take what his god, Chemosh, had given him and leave Israel what the true God had given them. Now the god of Chemosh is the god of Moab, not Ammon. But it is very possible that the influence of Chemosh spread far beyond Moab's borders and even that Ammon's god, Milcom/Molech, may have been a local manifestation (along with Chemosh) of the same god.[7]

Jephthah goes on to challenge the king by questioning whether he is better than Balak king of Moab who fought against Israel (Josh. 24:9–10). Indeed the Lord delivered them out of the hand of Moab. Furthermore, if the king really has a right to claim the land, why has he waited so long to claim it (11:26)? Jephthah finishes by declaring his innocence and accusing the king of the Ammonites of doing wrong against him.

7. Ibid., 142.

Then he says, "The LORD, the Judge, decide this day between the people of Israel and the people of Ammon" (11:27). But the king of the Ammonites does not listen.

We may be thinking at this point that finally Israel has a good, strong, solid, and godly leader whom the Lord is going to use to turn Israel around. But as we read on, we are going to be sorely disappointed.

III. The Lord Gives the Ammonites into Jephthah's Hand (11:29–33)

Then the Spirit of the Lord was on Jephthah. We have come to learn in our study of Judges that this is the key to all Israel's deliverances. It is "not by might, nor by power, but by my Spirit, says the LORD of hosts" (Zech. 4:6). The Lord chooses the "least" of humankind and the "foolish" in order to glorify and exalt his name. He did it by using Jephthah, he will do it again in his choice of David, and ultimately he will bring his own Son into the world through a poor virgin in an obscure place and have him die the most shameful death on a cross.

Jephthah passes through Gilead to the Ammonites. On his way he makes a vow to the Lord, promising to give whatever/whoever comes out from the doors of his house as a burnt offering when he returns from the Ammonites if the Lord will give them into his hand (11:30–31). Again he is manipulating. What or whom did he have in mind? Because the masculine gender is used in the Hebrew for "whatever/whoever," some commentators believe that Jephthah thought sheep or cattle would be the first out of his house, which was typical since one of the four rooms of a typical home then would have housed animals.[8] However, other commentators believe that Jephthah was so determined to gain victory over the Ammonites that he was willing to sacrifice his own child to guarantee success. The phrase "whatever [or whoever] comes out from the doors of my house to meet me" envisions the joyful greeting by children of a father who has been away for military reasons.[9] If Jephthah simply

8. K. Lawson Younger Jr., *Judges/Ruth*, The NIV Application Commentary (Grand Rapids: Zondervan, 2002), 263.
9. Block, *Judges, Ruth*, 368.

had promised an offering, it still would have shown his manipulative motives, but he wouldn't have been nearly so rash. But to put on such a qualifier as this displayed not only his manipulation but also his rashness.

Perhaps you, like me, can relate to Jephthah as you look back over your lifetime. Have there been times when you have used your words rashly to manipulate either the Lord or others, and it led to disaster? Do we try to control the Lord by our prayers and our service, trying to get him to do what we want if we pray the right words or serve him in the "right ways"? The Lord cannot be manipulated. He sees through our motives and calls us into account. We are as foolish as Jephthah if we think we can get him to change his ways by making deals. And if he ever does deliver what we ask when we have done so, it is an expression of his marvelous grace, not an indication that we have gone about the matter in the right way.

So Jephthah crossed over into the land of Ammon, and the Lord gave the Ammonites into his hand. He struck twenty cities with a great blow, and the Ammonites were subdued before Israel. Though the Gileadites chose Jephthah as their leader without inquiring of the Lord, the Lord graciously used him to deliver his people.

IV. The Tragic Result of Jephthah's Vow (11:34–40)

The narrator records that Jephthah came home to Mizpah after defeating the Ammonites, and with an emphatic "behold" tells us that Jephthah's daughter came out to meet him with tambourines and dances of victory, celebrating her father's subduing of the Ammonites. In contrast to Jair and Gideon, who had numerous children, Jephthah only had one child, a daughter, as the narrator is careful to record. As soon as he saw her, he was overwhelmed with grief, for he had not forgotten the vow that he had made to the Lord. But he had forgotten that the Lord had made provision for vows that were made without fully reflecting on their ramifications (Lev. 27:1–8).[10]

When Jephthah told his daughter that he had made a vow to the Lord, she was quick to tell him to fulfill it, now that the Lord had avenged

10. Ibid., 265.

his enemies. She only asked for two months to go and mourn her virginity with her companions in the mountains. So Jephthah granted her request and on her return fulfilled the vow that he had made, sacrificing his daughter on the altar.[11]

Though the Israelites had been saved from the Ammonites, Jephthah's daughter was not saved from her father's foolish vow. So Jephthah's daughter died without knowing a man, but the memory of her lived on in the thoughts and actions of the daughters of Israel, for they went every year to lament the daughter of Jephthah for four days in the mountains. This custom would have served as an annual reminder of a tragic and sinful event. With Jephthah's daughter went Jephthah's future line, for there was no other child to carry on the family name. While he tried to secure his present with his words, he ultimately lost his future.

What a stark contrast to the story we read in chapter 1 of Caleb's vow concerning his daughter. Caleb vowed to give his daughter in marriage to the man who captured Kiriath-sepher, which ended up being Othniel. Instead of having to ask for two months to mourn her virginity, Achsah asked for a blessing—springs of water in the Negeb—to perpetuate life for her family. One woman died; the other woman lived. One father spoke a foolish and rash vow; the other spoke a responsible one. One deliverer actually delivered; the other one delivered only to turn around and became the oppressor of his own daughter. The question of justice cries out from this story. Who will deliver us from the injustice of this world? Only the one in whom "steadfast love and faithfulness meet; righteousness and peace kiss each other" (Ps. 85:10). But all of us who are in Christ are called to cry out because of the injustice in this world. Are we crying out on behalf of the unborn, the orphan, the widow, and the poor? Are we serving Jesus by serving them?

11. Not all commentators agree that Jephthah sacrificed his daughter on the altar. Some (S. G. De Graaf, *Promise and Deliverance*, vol. 2, *The Failure of Israel's Theocracy* [St. Catharines, Canada: Paideia, 1978], 32) believe that she was relegated to a life of singleness and loneliness. But others (Davis, 145; Block, 372–74; Younger, 262–63; Matthew Henry, *Commentary on the Whole Bible: Complete and Unabridged in One Volume* [Peabody, MA: Hendrickson Publishers, 1991], 354) believe that she was offered as a human sacrifice on an altar.

V. Jephthah and the Men of Gilead Defeat the Ephraimites (12:1–7)

Just as the Ephraimites in their hurt pride questioned Gideon in 8:1 for not calling them when he went to fight against Midian, here we see them question Jephthah for not calling them to go with him to fight the Ammonites. Their supreme arrogance led to supreme anger, and they threatened to burn his house over him with fire. Jephthah responded by saying that he had called them when his life was in danger by the Ammonites, but since they had not responded, he had taken his life into his own hands and crossed over for battle. He then attributed the victory to the Lord and questioned why they had come up to fight him when they had not responded to his request for help. So Jephthah gathered all the men of Gilead and fought against the Ephraimites. The Gileadites struck the Ephraimites because they called them fugitives of Ephraim. Remember that the Ephraimites are not their enemies, but their own tribal brothers. Just as Jephthah struck his own daughter in death, now he leads in the striking of his brothers. How far Israel has fallen!

So the Gileadites captured the fords of the Jordan and strategically used phonetics to destroy them; forty-two thousand of the Ephraimites died because their accent gave them away to the Gileadites. The Lord had judged the pride of the Ephraimites through death. Ultimately, all those who remain in their own pride apart from a relationship with Jesus Christ will be judged by eternal death. Only those whose lives are hidden with Christ will be saved.

The story of Jephthah closes with the duration of his reign, which was a mere six years. Then he died and was buried in Gilead. The account of Jephthah again leaves us hopeless. While Jephthah saved Israel from the Ammonites for a time, he was from an illegitimate ancestry, he was appointed as judge by the elders of Gilead, he was surrounded by worthless fellows, and he was the author of a foolish vow that resulted in his only child's death. He again points us to a need for a Savior in Israel. He points us forward to the need for a true Savior and King, which anticipates the coming line of David that will culminate in our Lord and Savior Jesus Christ.

Jesus Christ was from the legitimate ancestry of the tribe of Judah. There are no flaws or failures in him; he is the perfect God-man. The triune God appointed him as the Savior of the world before the creation of the world. He was surrounded by disciples when he walked this earth and is surrounded by God the Father, the Holy Spirit, and the myriads of angels in the heavenly realm at his present seat in heaven. He made no foolish vow but fulfilled the covenant vow that he had made as God's Son to be sent into the world to reconcile God the Father with his children. And his rule on the Davidic throne lasts for all eternity.

VI. Ibzan, Elon, and Abdon Judge Israel (12:8–15)

As with Shamgar (3:31), Tola (10:1–2), and Jair (10:3–5), we don't receive extensive information about Ibzan, Elon, or Abdon. Yet we know that they are significant because they are recorded in Scripture for us. What is the purpose of listing these three judges here? From the little information we have, it seems these judges are dominated by power, possessions, and prestige. They do not seem at all interested in saving Israel but rather in making a name for themselves. In the end though, they die, taking nothing with them from this world and saving no one, not even themselves. It's another reminder of the decline of Israel and the desperate need for a true deliverer.

Ibzan had his sons marry women from other places and sent his daughters to marry men outside his clan for political reasons. He was securing a kingdom for himself. But his kingdom did not last; he died.

We don't learn much about Elon, except that his rule lasted for ten years, but Abdon's family and extended family was clearly wealthy enough to ride on donkeys, which means he secured wealth for himself and for his family. The Lord had commanded rulers not to acquire many horses for themselves (Deut. 17:16); he knew that possessions would become their master rather than him. Like Ibzan, Abdon couldn't take his wealth with him. He died too and wasn't even buried in Israel's land, an indication that Israel had failed to possess it as they had been commanded.[12]

In what ways are you pursuing power, possessions, or a prestigious position instead of pursuing the work God has for you?

12. Younger, *Judges/Ruth*, 279.

CONCLUSION

Carrie is still active and involved with feeding the homeless and serving at her church, but no longer does she serve out of guilt and with the motive of trying to earn a righteous standing before the Lord. Now she serves out of thanksgiving and joy because of what Jesus Christ has done for his people, including her, on the cross. Now she knows that the Lord doesn't look on her and see a sinner but looks on her and sees a saint, because she is clothed in the righteousness of Christ.

Perhaps you can relate to Carrie. Perhaps you have blown it and you are trying to clean yourself up before coming back to the Father. I pray that you will meditate on the story of Israel and Jephthah this week and be encouraged that the Lord was impatient over the misery of Israel and delivered them from the hand of the Ammonites before they cleaned themselves up and got right with him. In God's grace he extends his arms out to those of us who are prone to wander and calls us to come home again. Out of the gutter and into his grace, out of our rags and into his robes, out of our famine and into his feast. Sister, come home.

LESSON 10

Judges 13–14

PLEASE USE THE QUESTION paradigm from pages 301–2 as you work through the following. See the introductory comments there that explain each part of the process below in more detail.

- **Pray.**
- **Ponder the Passage.** Read Judges 13–14 once a day from different translations for the entire week, looking for its:
  - Point
  - Persons
  - Problem
  - Patterns
  - Persons of the Trinity
  - Puzzling Parts
- **Put It in Perspective.**
  - Place in Scripture. Read Judges 1–2; Numbers 6:1–21.
  - Passages from Other Parts of Scripture

1. Based on your observations of the text, what is the basic content of this passage? Try to summarize it in your own words, using a sentence or two.
2. Compare 13:1 with 3:9, 15; 4:3; 6:6; 10:10. What is missing?

3. Compare the angel of the Lord's appearance to Manoah's wife with the Lord's appearance to Abraham (with Sarah overhearing) in Genesis 18:1–15, with the angel of the Lord's appearance to Zechariah in Luke 1:8–25, and with the angel Gabriel's appearance to Mary in Luke 1:26–38.

4. What does the angel of the Lord promise Manoah's wife? What conditions are set forth? Why? What do you learn from Numbers 6:1–21 about Nazirites? Are all the conditions set forth in Numbers 6:1–21 mentioned in Judges 13:4–5, 14? If not, which ones are missing?

5. What is the first thing Manoah's wife does after the angel of the Lord appears to her (13:6–7)? Who does she think the angel of the Lord is? Does she repeat his words correctly?

6. What is Manoah's response and why (13:8)? What is God's response to Manoah (13:9a)? How does God answer Manoah's request (13:9b)? Does this surprise/encourage you? What does Manoah's wife do when the angel of the Lord appears to her the second time (13:10)? What is Manoah's response (13:11a)?

7. What questions does Manoah ask the angel of the Lord (13:11b–12)? What does the phrase, "Now when your words come true," in the middle of his questioning reveal about Manoah during this encounter (13:12a)? What is the angel of the Lord's response? Compare this with 13:3–5?

8. How does the angel of the Lord reveal his true identity to Manoah and his wife (13:15–21)? Compare 13:18 with Isaiah 9:6. Who is the angel of the Lord?

9. What is Manoah's fear after seeing God (13:22)? Compare this with Genesis 32:30; Exodus 33:20; Judges 6:22–24. How does Manoah's wife respond to him (13:23)? What does this reveal about her character and how she fulfills her helper design as a wife?

10. How is 13:25 key to the entire Samson story? Who is behind all of it and guiding the events?

11. Who does Samson see and desire from Timnah (14:1–2)? What is the response of his parents (14:3)? Why might this be (see Deut. 7:3–4)? How does Samson respond to his father (14:3)? Compare this with Exodus 20:12; Judges 21:25.

12. How is 14:4 the key verse not only to 14:1–3 but also to the entire chapter? Compare this verse with Genesis 50:20; Acts 2:23.

13. Describe the events in 14:5–7 and 14:8–9. Compare this with Numbers 6:1–21. What do you learn about Samson?

14. How does Samson's riddle that he poses to the thirty Philistines display a weakness in his faith and character?

15. How do the Philistines use Samson's wife to learn the riddle's answer? Contrast Samson's wife with Manoah's wife (Samson's mother)? How does Samson's wife fail to fulfill her God-given design as helper?

16. What does Samson learn (the hard way) about the Philistines from this incident? What is his response in words (14:18b) and in action (14:19)? Who is behind these actions (14:19)? Compare this with 14:4. How is it a fulfillment of 14:4?

17. What happens to Samson's wife while he is at Ashkelon and then at his father's house (14:20)?

18. How does the birth narrative of Samson (the Lord raising up a deliverer from one not yet born), and Samson's defeat of the thirty Philistines by himself, anticipate our Lord and Savior Jesus Christ? How do Samson's weaknesses point to the need for One greater than Samson?

• **Principles and Points of Application.**

1. How are you going forth and making disciples of people from every tribe, tongue, and nation? If you're not, pray and ask God to show you specific ways that you can be involved with discipleship through your church. If you are, spend time in prayer for new opportunities and for those whom you are discipling.

2. Spend time in thanksgiving and prayer as you meditate on Romans 8:28, committing the outcome of any present difficulty to the Lord and embracing the suffering as from his hand.

3. How poor, hopeless, and lost we would be if the Lord waited for us to cry out to him before he reached out and helped us! Write a poem, a letter, or a hymn to God the Father today, thanking him for sending his Son, Jesus Christ, into this world to reconcile us to him through the cross.

4. Spend time in prayer for those you know struggling with infertility today, asking the Lord to open up their womb, if he is willing, and praying for his grace to overwhelm their hearts and minds as they struggle through this season. Consider sending a note or making a phone call or visit to those you are praying for to let them know that you are praying and to encourage them during this difficult season.

5. Are you prepared to fully support your son or daughter or grandchild if they feel called to missions, to politics, to a career that you would not choose but that God has chosen for them? Are you willing to sacrifice time and resources in your personal life for the betterment of your children and grandchildren? If you are a mother or grandmother, spend time committing your children or grandchildren to the Lord today, asking him to prepare your heart for his calling for their lives.

6. In what present decision are you struggling to know God's will that you would like a postcard or blinking light in the sky telling you what to do? The Lord does not give us postcards from heaven or write answers in the sky, but he has given us his Word. Spend time in prayer today and in his Word, committing your decision to him and trusting him to lead you and guide you.

7. If you are married, how does Manoah's wife encourage you and challenge you to be a wife who fulfills your God-given design as helper, who fears the Lord, and who helps point your husband to the Lord? In what specific circumstance do you need to be your husband's helper and encourager this week?

8. Have you blown it? Has one of your children blown it? Has your spouse blown it? All is not lost. The Lord works through mysterious ways, even sinful ways, to accomplish his plans and purposes. That

does not excuse or encourage sin, but it reminds us that we serve a gracious and forgiving God who can accomplish his plan even when we blow it. Spend time in confession and repentance today, asking the Lord to redeem a sinful situation for his glory and your good.

NOTES FOR JUDGES 13-14

Ponder the aim of this lesson concerning our:

Mind: What do we need to know from this passage in Scripture?

The Spirit of the Lord shows Samson is a savior for Israel, which anticipates Israel's greatest and final Savior, Jesus Christ.

Heart: How does what we learn from this passage affect our internal relationship with the Lord?

It prepares us to be kingdom disciples who recognize, by the power of the Holy Spirit, that Jesus Christ is the Savior for God's people.

Hands: How does what we learn from this passage translate into action for God's kingdom?

It enables us to:

1. Go forth and make disciples from every tribe, tongue and nation by seeking opportunities this week through the ministries of our local church.
2. Trust the Lord with specific oppression in our life this week, meditating on Romans 8:28 and thanking him for his grace in the midst of it.
3. Write a poem, letter, or hymn of praise for God's condescension to us in Christ Jesus and share it with others.
4. Pray for and encourage those women in our lives whom we know are struggling with infertility.

5. If we are mothers, commit our children and/or grandchildren to the Lord, relinquishing our desires for them so that we can support them in the Lord's calling for them.
6. Trust the Lord to reveal his will regarding present decisions through his Spirit and his Word as we walk by faith.
7. Be wives who are "helpers" and point our husbands to the Word of God.
8. Repent of any present sin in our lives, asking the Lord to redeem the situation for his glory and our good.

INTRODUCTION

Amber was devastated.[1] She had just gotten off the phone with her twenty-five-year-old son. She didn't know what had happened between his high school years and his twenty-fifth year, but the influence of college and career had changed her little boy. She well remembered praying for him long before he was even conceived. She had prayed through Scripture, asking the Lord to save him and give him character that displayed the fruit of the Spirit. She had sung songs filled with Scripture and the old hymns to him when he was a baby and toddler. She had read him Bible stories during the day. She and her husband had taken him to church every Sunday and had lived out a faithful marriage before him. But it all seemed to make no difference now. He was lost in his own rebellion with no glimmer of hope for turning around. Amber continued to pray, but after so many years with no change, she was growing hopeless and discouraged. Did the Lord hear her? Did he care about her son? What was he doing in the midst of all this?

Perhaps you can relate to Amber. Perhaps you have or know of someone who has, or is trying to guard against having, a prodigal. Perhaps you have known the sweetness of the early childhood years when you heard your child sing the great truths of the faith, but now you fight the bitterness of the years when those tunes not only go unsung, but also are flung far away from their hearts. The story of Samson will encourage

1. Name has been changed and some details generalized to represent several women I have counseled and/or prayed for this year with prodigal sons and/or daughters.

your heart, because it will remind you that it is not really a story about Samson, but a story about the Lord and what he is doing in Samson's life.

Samson too had a mother who surely taught him the great truths of the faith. She was a God-fearing woman, and she and her husband were a couple of prayer and faith. Indeed Samson was set apart from before birth to begin saving Israel, and his mother knew it. But God's Word and Samson's life did not line up when he got to his grown years. Samson seemed to be a wayward child who had a hot temper and a love for unbelieving women.

But if we keep our eyes on Samson, we'll miss the point of the story. Just as, if we keep our eyes on our children, we will miss the point of what God is doing in their lives. The Lord loves our children more than we do and is more than worthy of our trust that he will fulfill his plan for their lives. We may have to hold fast to his promises through some very deep waters, but hold on we must. For the Lord is not through with his children yet.

Judges 13–14 has much to say about being kingdom disciples who recognize, by the power of the Holy Spirit, that Jesus Christ is the Savior for God's people. And he alone can save and use our prodigal sons and daughters.

We can divide the lesson into two sections:

I. The Lord Promises a Son Who Will Save Israel to Manoah and His Wife (13)
II. The Spirit of the Lord Shows Samson Is a Savior for Israel (14)

I. The Lord Promises a Son Who Will Save Israel to Manoah and His Wife (13)

The story of Samson should be viewed (with regard to time) as parallel to the story of Jephthah. While the Ammonites were oppressing the Israelites in the east, the Philistines were oppressing the Israelites in the west. This oppression by the Philistines lasted for forty years, until the time of Samuel, who finished the deliverance that Samson began. Samson's deliverance may have begun at the time that the ark was carried away and Eli suddenly died (1 Sam. 4).[2] If so, the beautiful story of Hannah takes place during this time in Israel's history and serves, along with the story of Ruth and the story of Samson's parents, as a beautiful reminder that not all of Israel had turned their backs on the Lord during the time of the judges.

All through the history of redemption, the Lord has always preserved a remnant for himself to glorify him and delight in him, to serve him and worship him. Even today when so many are hardened to the gospel message, the Holy Spirit continues his work of opening hearts to the Savior, continuing to build the church of Christ. And we are to be his witnesses, workers, and worshipers dependent on the Holy Spirit, as we go forth and make disciples of people from every tribe, tongue, and nation.

Why did the Philistines oppress the Israelites for forty years? Because the Israelites had done evil in the sight of the Lord, and the Lord gave them over to the Philistines. It should encourage us that the Lord controls the time of oppression. We are not at the mercy of our enemies, but at the mercy of our Lord.

Perhaps you are facing an overwhelming "giant" in your life right now and need to be reminded of this truth. Times of oppression are in the Lord's hand and are always used for his glorification and your good. In the midst of a difficult marriage, infertility, raising young children, dealing with a prodigal, the grief of losing a loved one, the news of cancer, chronic pain, persecution in the workplace, or (you fill in the blank), we can rest in the promises of God's Word, that "for those who love God all things work together for good" (Rom. 8:28).

After we learn that the Lord gave the Israelites into the hand of the Philistines for forty years, we expect to read of their cry of distress. This is the twelfth judge listed in the book of Judges, and all the other stories that are developed speak of Israel's cry of distress, but not this one. Evidently Israel's apostasy had grown so bad that they didn't even seek to be delivered from their enemies anymore. Slavery to foreign peoples was not only tolerated, it seems to have been welcomed. Yet God in his

2. S. G. De Graaf, *Promise and Deliverance*, vol. 2, *The Failure of Israel's Theocracy* (St. Catharines, Canada: Paideia, 1978), 38.

grace does not wait for his people's cry; he reaches out in grace anyway and raises up a savior for Israel.

How poor and hopeless and lost we would be if the Lord waited for us to cry out to him before he reached out and helped us! His Son never would have come! But from all eternity, the Lord has loved his people and condescends to us. Of course, the climax of this is in the incarnation, which had its climax in the death, resurrection, and ascension of Jesus Christ. But all through the Old Testament we see glimpses of his condescension that anticipates the Savior of the world coming.

In this chapter it is as if a curtain is drawn back and we are invited to peer into one small family's life. I say "small" because Manoah, a man of Zorah, of the tribe of the Danites, was living with his wife, but she was barren and they had no children. This undoubtedly would have been very painful for Manoah and his wife, just as it was for Rachel and Leah when they faced barrenness, for Ruth when she had no children at the time of her first husband's death, for Hannah when she was praying in the temple for a child because of her barrenness, and for Elizabeth when she was barren before finally in her old age God gave her a son—John the Baptist. But the Lord, in his grace and mercy, and also in his providence, had great plans for these barren women. What they considered to be loss, he considered great gain. For each one of these women was chosen to bear a special son who would play a significant role in the history of redemption.

Some of you know the pain of barrenness. Some of you know what it is like to long day after day for a child, and month after month conception does not come. Some of you know the difficulty of laying your desire for a family at the feet of Jesus and trusting him with your most precious desire. And some of you know what it means to consider great losses as great gains because of your love and submission to Christ. But some of you also know the glory of receiving a child after a long time of waiting, sometimes through conception, sometimes through adoption. And you revel in the graciousness of your Father who has given you a good gift in his perfect timing. But you recognize at the same time that it was also his gift to deny your desire for a time, for you learned in the trial to be content in him alone. And many of you who are still in the trial today are already learning or have learned the same.

The angel of the Lord, a preincarnate appearance of Jesus Christ, appeared to Manoah's wife and told her at first what she already knew, "You are barren and have not borne children," but then gave her a glorious promise, "But you shall conceive and bear a son" (13:3). Again, perhaps some of us can understand the depth of emotion Manoah's wife must have felt at that moment. Perhaps you too have waited long years to conceive and then did, or perhaps your wait ended in a wonderful adoption of a child from another family. Maybe you are still waiting, trusting in the Lord's sovereign plan for your life. For Manoah's wife, this must have come as quite a surprise and a delightful one at that! Not only was she promised a child, she was promised a son, and not only a son, but a special son. Her son was to be a Nazirite (see Num. 6:1–21) from before he was even born, for he would begin to save Israel from the Philistines. He would begin because David would finish (see 2 Sam. 5:17–25).[3] No razor was to come on her son's head either.

What did this mean for Manoah's wife? It meant that she could not drink any wine or strong drink or eat anything unclean. Even before her son was born, Manoah's wife was learning what it meant to sacrifice for her son on behalf of his calling from the Lord.

This can sometimes be a hard lesson for mothers to learn. Sometimes we have our own plans for our children and are not as supportive as we should be when they come to us and tell us what they believe is the Lord's leading for their lives. Sometimes we push against that and try to discourage them from fulfilling his call because his call means sacrifice for us. And we don't always like to sacrifice. But our children are the Lord's, and we must be ready to sacrifice our own desires for them and for the sake of the Lord.

Manoah's wife, after being visited by the Lord, did what we would expect a wife to do with such significant news. She went and told her husband. We learn from her words that she believed the man to be

---

3. Daniel I. Block, *The New American Commentary*, vol. 6, *Judges, Ruth* (Nashville: Broadman & Holman, 1999), 404.

a prophet ("a man of God"), but that she recognized his appearance to be like that of the angel of God, very awesome. We learn that she did not ask where he was from and he did not reveal his name, but only that he promised her a Nazirite son who would be a Nazirite for his entire life.

Oftentimes the Lord does not give us all the information that we might like to have when he calls us to a position. We are given one instruction book and that is the Word of God, but too often we are discontent because it is not specific enough to answer our specific questions concerning God's will for our lives. But he has given us enough, and it is wrong for us to seek postcards in the mail from heaven or handwriting in the sky. The Lord wants us to grow up into maturity in him, making decisions based on his sure Word, led by his Holy Spirit, and guided by faith in him. This does not mean that we cannot seek the counsel of others. The Lord has given us pastors, elders, deacons, and godly laypeople in our churches who can oftentimes be of great benefit in making tough decisions. But we should always remember that God's Word trumps all man's opinions, and when we do receive counsel, it must align with his Word.

The first thing Manoah did was pray to the Lord. He asked for the Lord to send the man of God again to teach them what they were to do with the child once he was born. This is an important prayer, and one that should be heeded by parents today. Do we ask the Lord to teach us what we are to do with our children once they are born? As mothers, we can sometimes fall into the trap of believing that they are ours and that we get to raise them the way we want to raise them. But we must always remember that our children are the Lord's, and we must raise them according to his Word, not ours.

The Lord listened to Manoah's voice, despite the fact that Manoah proves to be less than a spiritually mature man of God. The fact that God listened to Manoah's prayer displays God's patience with us. We serve not only a loving God, but also a listening God. I can think of nothing more important for your life and your ministry than to be a woman of prayer. Our effectiveness should be judged more by the knobs on our knees than the accolades on our walls or the perfection of our homes. If we have a listening God, let us be faithful to give him something to listen to from the lips of his daughters. Let us cry out in praise and petition for our families, our churches, our neighbors, our city, our country, and our world.

"And the angel of God came again to the woman as she sat in the field" (13:9). Interestingly, Manoah was not with her again. This should encourage us that the Lord is pleased to reveal himself to women as well as to men. It is also an encouragement to women whose husbands may not be acting as spiritual leaders in the home. Manoah's wife is the one who shines as the spiritually mature one in these verses, and God honors her. However, Manoah's wife, gracious, submissive, and the helper of her husband that she was, ran quickly and told her husband so that he would not miss the man again.

It is difficult to live with husbands who are not fulfilling their calling as spiritual leader in the home. But we should take encouragement from the many women in the books of Judges and Ruth, that God honors God-fearing women and uses them in the lives of the men around us. We need to pray for our husbands to be the men that God wants them to be and live with them in a humble and gracious manner. We should continue to grow in the grace and knowledge of Jesus Christ, setting an example as ones who love the Lord and seek his will for our lives. And we should remember that God uses us in the lives of our husbands to encourage and strengthen their faith.

Manoah, believing his wife's word, arose and went after her and came to the man. It is important to notice that Manoah does not question the word that has already been given to his wife, for he says, "Now when your words come true" (13:12). Instead he asks what is to be the child's manner of life and mission. But the answer to this question was already in the word that the angel had spoken to Manoah's wife. So the Lord repeats that Manoah's wife may not drink any strong drink or eat any unclean thing and adds that she is not to eat anything that comes from the vine. Why? The child's life was to be strengthened by the Lord alone. It was the Spirit of the Lord who would strengthen this child, not anything else. Not even his hair should be cut, as a sign that his consecration to the Lord had not been broken.[4]

This word was important for Manoah to hear, for he would need to support his wife in this calling. She was called to bear a savior of Israel, and this was a great calling indeed. The Lord did not use a man who was already living in Israel to deliver them from the Philistines. He implanted one in a womb. Before Samson was on anyone's radar, he was on the Lord's. God's plan is from eternity. He does not have plan B's. Indeed this would not be the last woman who would be called to bear a savior of Israel. There would be another, and her name would be Mary. It was Mary who was chosen to be the bearer of the final and perfect Savior, Jesus Christ. And Jesus Christ would be the true finisher of what Samson, Samuel, and David had begun. He would deliver his people from the Enemy for all eternity. And that was God's plan from the beginning.

Since Manoah believed that he was speaking with a prophet rather than the person of the Lord, he asked to detain him and prepare a young goat for him. But no one can detain the Lord. He has work to do that we do not know and is detained by no one. He did suggest that Manoah prepare a burnt offering to the Lord though. When Manoah asked for his name so that they could honor him when his words came true, the Lord responded by questioning why Manoah should ask his name when he should have seen that it is wonderful. The prophet Isaiah, many years later, would prophesy of Christ, saying, "And his name shall be called Wonderful Counselor" (Isa. 9:6). So often our eyes are blinded to the wonderful words and works of the Lord. We seek someone or something to attribute them to, while all the time we should be glorifying the Lord for the wonderful things that he has done and the wonderful person that he is.

Manoah took the sacrifice and offered it on the rock to the Lord, to the one who works wonders, and the Lord worked a wonder for Manoah and his wife. When the flame of the sacrifice went up toward heaven from the altar, the angel of the Lord went up in the same flame.

4. De Graaf, *Promise and Deliverance*, 39.

It was at that moment that Manoah and his wife realized that they had met with the Lord himself, and they fell on their faces to the ground.

Perhaps you know the posture of being facedown on the ground before the Lord. If you don't, you should. It is not only an appropriate place to be, but also it is a glorious place to be. As the author of Hebrews says, "Therefore let us be grateful for receiving a kingdom that cannot be shaken, and thus let us offer to God acceptable worship, with reverence and awe, for our God is a consuming fire" (Heb. 12:28–29).

That was the last that Manoah and his wife saw of the angel of the Lord, but it was enough for them to know that it had been God whom they had seen. Yet this instilled great fear into Manoah. Perhaps this is understandable since the Lord had told Moses that no one could see his face and live (Ex. 33:20). Or perhaps this was grounded in unfounded fear in the midst of a culture that had strayed far from the Lord and forgotten that the Lord was a Covenant Lord; he had willingly bound himself to his people in a personal way. Regardless, Manoah's wife comes alongside Manoah as his helper and one who points her husband to the truth and sharpens him like iron, who tells him that if the Lord had meant to kill them, he would not have shown them all that he had, or announced what he had, or accepted their offering as he had done. Here is a beautiful picture of a godly wife who knows and believes the word of the Lord and submissively, lovingly, and respectfully encourages her husband to do so also.

There are times in our marriages when we need to do the same. There are times when our husbands will doubt the sure word of the Lord and we need to be there as their helpers, submissively, lovingly, and respectfully pointing them toward the truth of God's Word. It has often been said by godly men that godly men have godlier women standing behind them. We have the opportunity in our marriages to help our husbands be godly men as we stand behind them as godly women.

I had the opportunity in my own marriage to do this recently. My husband was in the depths of great grief, and he asked me to hold him and comfort him. I had nothing left to say after days of already doing so, but I knew that the Lord still had much to say. So I took my Bible upstairs to the bedroom and held him as he wept and I read the Psalms over him. When he couldn't feel Jesus' loving arms, he could feel mine. And the Lord used that time to strengthen him and encourage him. Don't ever be afraid to be God's spokesperson to your husband. There are times when our husbands, leaders that they are, need our help to fix their eyes on Christ.

In the closing verses of this chapter we have part of the promise fulfilled. Manoah's wife bore a son, and they called him Samson, which means "Little sun" or "Sunny boy"! Though it may be tempting to interpret it positively, pointing to Samson's birth as a ray of light in the dark time of the judges, it is probably better to see it as a reference to the sun god, Shemesh.[5] Of course this is shocking in light of the truth that this child was promised by Yahweh and is named after a pagan god.[6]

Samson "grew, and the Lord blessed him," and "the Spirit of the Lord began to stir him" (13:24, 25). These are key phrases that we must not forget as we read and teach the story of Samson. We never want our study to be moralistic. The theme of this story is not, "Be a Samson." Samson did nothing in his own strength. The Lord blessed him and the Spirit of the Lord accomplished great things through him. This is the story of how the Lord began to save Israel from the Philistines through one mighty man, anticipating his saving his people from the Enemy through one greater mighty man, our Lord and Savior Jesus Christ through the cross of Calvary.

II. The Spirit of the Lord Shows Samson Is a Savior for Israel (14)

In 13:25 we learned that the Spirit of the Lord began to stir Samson in Mahaneh-dan, between Zorah and Eshtaol. This is different from the Mahaneh-dan mentioned in 18:12, which was west of Kiriath-jearim in Judah, but the exact meaning is unclear. Is it another Mahaneh-dan, or is it simply a way of referring to a Danite camp? According to

5. Block, *Judges, Ruth*, 417.
6. I am indebted to Dr. Iain Duguid for this thought.

commentators, the latter is more likely.[7] Regardless, it was within the part of the Danite tribe that lived near the border of the Philistines.[8] When Samson was at the age to desire a wife, he went down[9] to Timnah, located in the border region between Israel and Philistia, and evidently still controlled by Philistia, although it had been allotted to Dan (Josh. 19:43).[10] It was there at Timnah that Samson saw one of the daughters of the Philistines and desired her for a wife. As we will soon learn, Samson's eyes are one of his biggest problems; his eyes will continue to be hungry for women whom he is not supposed to have. To marry a Philistine was sin for an Israelite, for the Lord had made it clear that they were not to intermarry with the Canaanites because Canaanites would turn them away from following the Lord to serve other gods (Deut. 7:3–4). But Samson did not regard the Word of the Lord. Instead he did what was right in his own eyes, just as all of Israel did what was right in their own eyes during the time of the judges. The story of Samson is a microcosm of what was true of Israel as a whole (see 21:25).

Samson went up to the camp of Dan where his parents lived and told them[11] that he had seen one of the daughters of the Philistines at Timnah and requested that they get her for him as a wife. Now we know from chapter 13 that Manoah and his wife were God-fearing people and took the Lord's Word seriously and recognized the Lord. So it is not surprising that they urged Samson to take a wife from among the Israelites. Surely they knew Deuteronomy 7:3. But Samson did not honor his father and mother. Instead he demanded what was right in his own eyes.

Manoah and his wife could not have known that the Lord would use the sin of Samson to show that he was savior of Israel in the midst

7. Block, *Judges, Ruth*, 423; and Younger, *Judges/Ruth*, 292.

8. De Graaf, *Promise and Deliverance*, 42.

9. The verb "to go down" is used five times in this chapter and divides it structurally. See Dale Ralph Davis, *Judges: Such a Great Salvation* (Fearn, Great Britain: Christian Focus, 2000), 167.

10. Block, *Judges, Ruth*, 424.

11. The verb "to tell" occurs fourteen times in the Hebrew Bible in this chapter, which is the main theme of the chapter. As Davis says, "The whole chapter then is about telling, or, should I say, not telling. It's all about what people don't know"; *Judges*, 167.

of Philistine oppression. This does not excuse Samson's sin. But in the Lord's sovereign and providential plan that is exactly what happens.

This should encourage us. Some of us struggle with sin in our past and believe that our indulgence messed up God's plan for our lives. But the Lord is more than able to, and often does, use sin to accomplish his providential will. Have you blown it? Has one of your children blown it? Has your spouse blown it? All is not lost. The Lord works through mysterious ways, even sinful ways, to accomplish his plans and purposes. That does not excuse or encourage sin, but it reminds us that we serve a gracious and forgiving God who can accomplish his plan even when we blow it.

Because the Lord had set apart Samson as savior within Israel from the Philistines, he graciously revealed to him the strength that he had been given by the Lord for such a calling. The Lord did this first by way of a young lion that came roaring toward Samson. The Spirit of the Lord came on Samson and enabled him to kill the lion with his bare hands, as if he were merely tearing a young goat. Evidently Samson had veered from the path that his parents were on and was alone in the vineyards when this occurred. What was he doing in the vineyards as a Nazarite? Part of the Nazarite vow was that he separate himself from wine and strong drink and any juice of grapes produced by the grapevine (Num. 6:1–4). Yet Samson was not all alone, for the Spirit of the Lord appeared and even was on him. This too was a precursor of what was to come when he killed the thirty Philistines (14:19).

Samson did not tell his father or mother what he had done. As a Nazarite, if someone or something died in his presence, he was to go to the tabernacle for an eight-day ritual that included shaving his head, offering a sin and burnt offering, rededicating himself to the Nazarite vow, and offering a year-old male lamb as a guilt offering (Num. 6:9–12). But Samson didn't want to do any of this, so he kept the matter to himself in order to move on to getting the Philistine woman he wanted.[12] So he went down and talked with the Philistine woman who was right in

---

12. K. Lawson Younger Jr., *Judges/Ruth*, The NIV Application Commentary (Grand Rapids: Zondervan, 2002), 302.

his eyes. Again we are reminded of the refrain that will close the book, "Everyone did what was right in his own eyes" (21:25).

After some days Samson returned to Timnah to take the Philistine woman as his wife. On the way he turned to see the carcass of the lion, and there was a swarm of bees and honey inside. He scraped it into his hands, eating as he went. That he did not regard the bees as a problem is not surprising, since he had single-handedly killed the lion. What harm could bees do when a lion could not do any harm? Plenty, since this was a violation of his Nazirite vow, for this was a carcass and he was a Nazirite (see Num. 6:1–21).

Samson's father went down to the Philistine woman, and Samson, according to the Philistines' custom (which he should not have been following!), prepared a feast. When the people saw him preparing the feast, they brought thirty Philistine companions to be with him. And Samson put a riddle to them. But this was foolish. He had no business preparing a feast or speaking a riddle; Samson should have been running in the opposite direction of the Philistines or else killing them!

Thirty linen garments and thirty changes of clothes were the reward for the winner, and the riddle had to be answered within the seven-day feast. The first three days went by and still no answer was put forth. On the fourth day the Philistines began to question Samson's wife. They threatened to burn her and her father's house with fire. They used guilt tactics saying, "Have you invited us here [to your wedding feast] to impoverish us?" (14:15). Samson's new wife turned up the emotion and tried to make him feel guilty for not loving her by telling her the riddle. On the seventh day of the feast, after listening to his wife pressing him hard for several days, Samson finally told her, and she immediately told her people. She was more loyal to her own people than she was to her husband. And Samson was more loyal to his Philistine wife than he was to the Lord. In this way he was an example of the nation of Israel that had been more loyal to the pagan gods than to the Covenant Lord.

What a contrast between the unnamed wife of Manoah in chapter 13 and the unnamed wife of Samson in chapter 14. Manoah's wife is a woman who fears the Lord and is a true helper of her husband. Samson's wife does not know the Lord and is a manipulative wife who does not prove to be a helper to her husband at all. If we are married, let us ask what kind of wife we are. Do we seek to control and pressure our husbands to get what we want, or are we truly women who fear the Lord, submit to our husbands, and are their helpers? Manoah's wife's life, though not without difficulty and pain, was blessed. Samson's wife's life, as we will see, will be with difficulty and pain and is not blessed.

The Philistines tell Samson the riddle. But Samson calls them on their deceitful way of learning it. Thus he sees that they are a deceitful lot and are truly his enemies, not his companions. Through this incident, the Lord uses Samson's anger against the Philistines to defeat them. The Spirit of the Lord rushed on Samson, and Samson went down to Ashkelon and struck thirty men of the town (since thirty men had deceived him at the wedding feast), took their spoil, and gave their garments to the companions who had won the contest of the riddle. In his hot anger he went back to his father's house without his wife. So she was given to Samson's best man. Evidently it was assumed that Samson would never return for her.

What do we do with the last incident recorded in this chapter of Scripture? We must see it as the fulfillment of 14:4, "for [the LORD] was seeking an opportunity against the Philistines."[13] We may not like Samson's temper, we may not like his choice of a pagan wife, we may not be impressed that he only killed thirty Philistines, but in the end we must recognize and grapple with the fact that this was the Lord's doing. There will often be times when we do not understand the Lord's ways. Who would have thought that the King of Kings would come as a baby to the poor of this world? Who would have planned to have him nailed to a cross to die a shameful death in place of his people? What kind of plan is that? It is God's plan, and it is good, and we must join Paul in saying,

> Oh, the depth of the riches and wisdom and knowledge of God! How unsearchable are his judgments and how inscrutable his ways!

> "For who has known the mind of the Lord,
>   or who has been his counselor?"

13. Davis, *Judges*, 173.

> "Or who has given a gift to him
>> that he might be repaid?"

For from him and through him and to him are all things. To him be the glory forever. Amen. (Rom. 11:33–36)

CONCLUSION

Perhaps you are praying for a prodigal whose life seems just as dark and hopeless as Samson's. Perhaps you are devastated at the life that seems wasted. But remember that the Lord saves, and is able to save our sons and daughters, even on their deathbeds. Samson's parents must have spent many dark nights in prayer. Yet the Lord used Samson to begin to save Israel from the Philistines, which is a testimony of his grace. What began as God's plan was not thwarted by way of Samson's sin. He who begins a good work in his children will bring it to completion at the day of Jesus Christ (Phil. 1:6).

LESSON 11

Judges 15–16

PLEASE USE THE QUESTION paradigm from pages 301–2 as you work through the following. See the introductory comments there that explain each part of the process below in more detail.

- **Pray.**
- **Ponder the Passage.** Read Judges 15–16 once a day from different translations for the entire week, looking for its:
  - Point
  - Persons
  - Problem
  - Patterns
  - Persons of the Trinity
  - Puzzling Parts
- **Put It in Perspective.**
  - Place in Scripture. Skim Judges 1–2.
  - Passages from Other Parts of Scripture

1. Based on your observations of the text, what is the basic content of this passage? Try to summarize it in your own words, using a sentence or two.

2. What is Samson's "innocent" plan of harm against the Philistines (15:3–5)? How do they respond (15:6)? How does Samson react (15:8)?

3. How do the Philistines respond to Samson striking them (15:9)? How do the men of Judah respond (15:10a)? What does this say about their lack of recognition that the Lord had raised up a deliverer in their midst? Where else in Scripture do we see a Savior whom the Lord has raised up, but bound and given over to the enemy by his own people?

4. Who breaks the ropes and melts the bonds off of Samson (15:14)? Whose power is behind Samson's striking one thousand Philistines? To whom does Samson give the credit (15:16)? What does he name the place (15:17)? Does this name reflect anything about the Lord?

5. How does the Lord humble Samson (15:18)? To whom does Samson give credit in his prayer for striking the one thousand Philistines? How does the Lord display his grace to Samson in his answer (15:19)? Compare this with Exodus 17:1–7. To whom does the rock that provides water in both incidents ultimately point? What name is given to this place? Contrast this with the name given in 15:17. How does this reflect Samson's recognition of the Lord?

6. Compare 15:20 and 16:31 with 3:11, 30; 5:31c; 8:28. What note is missing from 15:20 and 16:31? Why is this significant in the broader context of a downward spiral of apostasy in the book?

7. What weakness of Samson's occurs again in 16:1, 4 (see also 14:1–2)? How does the Lord display his grace in the midst of Samson's sinful ways (16:3)? How should this have been a sign to Israel that their enemies could not withstand God's chosen deliverer? How does this ultimately point to Christ?

8. Contrast Delilah with Samson's mother. How does Samson's mother fulfill her design as helper (see Gen. 2:18), while Delilah plays the role of deceiver?

9. Describe the four attempts of Delilah to seduce Samson in order to see where his great strength lay. How is the fourth one differ-

ent from the others? How is Samson's weakness displayed? What is the Lord's response (16:20)? How does this situation appear hopeless (the savior of Israel is in the hand of the enemy)?

10. For whose sake would Samson be raised to deliver Israel again? Think about God's greater plan of redemption.

11. How does the Lord use the time that Samson is grinding at the mill in the prison to humble him and remind him of his calling? What is the result (16:28–30)? How does Samson's deliverance, not only during his life but even more so in his death, anticipate Christ's deliverance of his people on the cross?

12. Where is Samson buried? In light of his life of sin and disobedience, how does this display God's grace? Read Hebrews 11:32–34. For what is Samson remembered? How does this further display God's grace in light of all the weaknesses we have seen of Samson in chapters 14–16?

- **Principles and Points of Application.**
1. Do you recognize the Savior in the midst of your daily life? How? Do you recognize that the Lord has already delivered you from the Enemy through the cross of Calvary? How? Spend time in prayer and thanksgiving today, thanking the Lord for his deliverance and acknowledging him in the midst of your everyday life.

2. What have you done with Jesus? Have you relegated him to your bookshelves as a historical figure who was a good man and a moral teacher, or have you embraced him as the living God, the Savior of the world?

3. How often are we like the men of Judah? How often do we help the Enemy rather than stand strong as a soldier in the Lord's army?

4. How have you been on "jawbone hill" recently? You know, the place where you boasted in your own strength and your own accomplishments, the place where you thought that you could make it on your own, the place where you gave yourself the

credit. Go to the Lord in prayer today, acknowledging that you have nothing to boast in except for Jesus Christ.

5. Come to the "spring of him who called" today and call on the Lord for his strength and his power for your difficult marriage, for your rebellious child, for your physical illness, for your infertility, for your unbelieving parent, or (you fill in the blank). Lay down your own means and rest in the Lord today.

6. Is there some sin in your past or present that you feel has disqualified you for the Lord's service? Come to the Lord today in confession and repentance. Then quit thinking that is who you are. You are not that; you are a child of God (meditate on 1 Cor. 6:9–11). And the God of the covenant redeems us from the slavery of sin into service for his kingdom.

7. Delilah reminds us that as women we have the potential to greatly influence our husbands for good or for bad. Read Genesis 2:18. Does "helper" describe you as a wife? Or can you relate more to Delilah? Are you manipulative and deceitful in order to get what you want when you want it? Spend time in prayer for your marriage today (or, if you are single, for the marriage of a friend), asking the Lord to give you (or her) wisdom in how to best help your (or her) husband.

NOTES FOR JUDGES 15–16

Ponder the aim of this lesson concerning our:

Mind: What do we need to know from this passage in Scripture?

The Spirit of the Lord shows Samson is a savior for Israel, which anticipates Israel's greatest and final Savior, Jesus Christ.

Heart: How does what we learn from this passage affect our internal relationship with the Lord?

It prepares us to be kingdom disciples who recognize, by the power of the Holy Spirit, that Jesus Christ is the Savior for God's people.

Hands: How does what we learn from this passage translate into action for God's kingdom?

It enables us to:

1. Recognize the Lord as our Savior in the midst of our everyday life and to spend time in prayer and thanksgiving for his accomplishment on the cross.
2. Embrace Jesus Christ as the living God, the Savior of the world.
3. Resist the enemy and stand strong as a soldier of Jesus Christ.
4. Repent from boasting in ourselves and to boast in the Lord Jesus Christ.
5. Drink from "the spring of him who called" in the middle of difficult circumstances this week.
6. Confess any sin in our lives that we feel has disqualified us from the Lord's service, and then to rest in his grace while we begin serving him again.
7. Pray for wisdom of how to fulfill our God-given design as helper to our husband in our marriage (if we are married) or to intercede for another's marriage (if we are single).

INTRODUCTION

I am sure that you have learned the truth that God's children are messy people. But I hope that you have also learned that, by God's grace, our heavenly Father does not see us that way. Instead he sees us robed in the righteousness of Christ. But you and I well know that until glory we will still struggle with the sin nature inside us, be tempted by the world and often indulge in it, and be tempted by Satan and oftentimes be ensnared.

Maybe you, like me, have struggled with an addiction (mine was anorexia) in the past. Possibly you, like me, have been inconsistent in your love for the Lord and your love for others. Perhaps you, like me, well know that if people could observe your life all the time, they would not compliment you like they do. Maybe you, like me, wander into sin every day and often are comfortable there for a while until the Lord graciously reveals to you that you have camped out in the wrong place. Possibly you, like me, have raised your voice at your husband and your children and made life miserable for them on certain days. Perhaps you, like me, have raked yourself over the coals before a ministry engagement, because you knew that your life hasn't proved worthy for you to stand in front of a group of women or children and lead them through the Word. We are messy people, but I hope that you, like me, have realized that we serve a marvelous Savior who doesn't just clean us up, but also makes us new and redeems us from our sinful ways.

The mirror that is held in front of our hearts, if we are in Christ, does not reflect us, but the perfect Lamb of God who has taken away our sin. The Lord does not see us as we see ourselves. He sees us as a spotless and pure bride, covered in the righteousness of our Savior.

Judges 15–16 has much to say about being kingdom disciples who recognize, by the power of the Holy Spirit, that Jesus Christ is the Savior for God's people. The story of Samson was a reminder to Israel, and is a reminder to us today, that there is still time to repent and to return to the Lord our God. We don't have to remain in our sin. We can come home, and we can come before we clean ourselves up or pull ourselves up by our own hopeless ways. The Father's arms are open wide. Jesus has paid the price in full. There is still time for you to turn from your wandering ways and come home.

We can divide the lesson into three sections:

I. The Spirit of the Lord Defeats the Philistines through Samson (15)
II. The Spirit of the Lord Delivers Samson from the Gazites (16:1–3)
III. The Spirit of the Lord Avenges Samson before the Lords of the Philistines (16:4–31)

I. The Spirit of the Lord Defeats the Philistines through Samson (15)

We learned in 14:19–20 that Samson had gone back to his father's house in hot rage after he had killed thirty Philistines and given their garments to the thirty Philistines who had solved the riddle. We also learned that while he was gone his father-in-law gave Samson's new Philistine wife to his best man. Now we learn that Samson wants his wife back. His draw to the Philistine woman will once more lead to trouble, but again 14:4—"it was from the LORD, for he was seeking an opportunity against the Philistines"—must be seen as the key for the interpretation of the Samson story.

When Samson goes to his wife's home, he takes a young goat as a gift of reconciliation and tells her father-in-law that he will go in to his wife in the chamber. But this cannot be, for his father-in-law, thinking Samson hated her, has given her to his best man. He quickly offers his younger daughter instead, whom he claims to be even more beautiful than the older daughter.

Once again the story moves from the individual to the collective. Samson's rage is not just against his wife and father-in-law, but also against the Philistines. However, in his rage, he desires to be innocent when he does them harm (unlike in the last incident). So instead of killing them with his own hand, he destroys their stacked and standing grain and olive orchards by tying together three hundred foxes' tails and putting lit torches between them so that when they run through the grain and orchards they are destroyed. Again we see another sign of Samson's God-given strength, just as in the lion incident. Here he captures three hundred foxes!

When the Philistines saw the destruction, they sought to know who was the culprit behind it. The answer by the Philistines was that it was Samson, but they also stated why. It was because his father-in-law had taken his wife and given her to the best man. So the Philistines actually are the ones who burn Samson's wife and father-in-law with fire. This fulfills the threat that they had made to Samson's wife in 14:15: "Entice your husband to tell us what the riddle is, lest we burn you and your father's house with fire."[1] But this enraged Samson because, despite the wrong, they were his new family, so he swore that he would

---

1. Dale Ralph Davis, *Judges: Such a Great Salvation* (Fearn, Great Britain: Christian Focus, 2000), 179.

be avenged on them. He struck the Philistines with a great blow, and then went down to stay in the cleft of the rock of Etam.[2] Again we see that the Lord has fulfilled another opportunity of vengeance against the Philistines through Samson. The Lord had indeed raised up a savior in Israel, but did Israel see this and believe? The answer is found in asking another question. The Lord himself was the Savior of Israel, living in their midst and delivering them from their enemies, but did Israel see this and believe? Do we? Do we recognize the Savior in the midst of our daily lives? Do we recognize that the Lord has already delivered us from the Enemy through the cross of Calvary?

Samson's act of vengeance provoked the Philistines to make a raid on Lehi. This prompted the men of Judah to ask them why they had come up against them. Their response revealed what the men of Judah did not know. Samson had made a raid on the Philistines. So three thousand men of Judah went down to the cleft of the rock of Etam. Ironically, the very place to which Samson fled for refuge from his Philistine enemies became the place where his own people betrayed him and gave him into enemy hands. What Israel did not realize is that they were binding their own savior whom the Lord had raised up in their midst and throwing him, their hope of deliverance, to their enemy. This would not be the last time in Israel's history that they would not recognize a Savior sent from God to deliver them and would throw their hope and Deliverer into the hands of the enemy (Acts 2:22–23).

What have you done with Jesus? Have you relegated him to your bookshelves as a historical figure who was a good man and a moral teacher, or have you embraced him as the living God, the Savior of the world?

The men of Judah question Samson's actions, for they would never have touched the Philistines. They stood in fear of these rulers over them. And the Lord well knew that they would not touch these rulers. That is why he had raised up Samson. But they were blinded to that. Indeed,

2. The location is uncertain, and the point may be more symbolic than geographical, for Samson sought refuge from the Philistines just as an animal would seek refuge from its predator. Daniel I. Block, *The New American Commentary*, vol. 6, *Judges, Ruth* (Nashville: Broadman & Holman, 1999), 442.

they tell Samson that they have come down to bind him and hand him over to the Philistines. Samson makes them swear that they will not attack him themselves, which they agree they have no intention of doing. They bind him with two *new* ropes and bring him up from the rock.

God's people are not supposed to help the enemy. Genesis 3:15 tells us that the Lord put enmity between the godly line and the ungodly line. From the beginning of God's Word, holy war is declared, and we can trace the war all the way through Scripture to the final book of Revelation. How often are we like the men of Judah, though? How often do we help the enemy rather than stand strong as soldiers in the Lord's army?

The Philistines welcomed Samson at Lehi, in order to kill him, but the Spirit of the Lord rushed on Samson to save the savior of Israel. The *new* ropes that were on his arms were not a deterrent for the Lord; the ropes and bonds easily came off his arms. Samson found a fresh jawbone of a donkey and with it struck down one thousand Philistines. But Samson was not just a man of strength, as we have seen, he was also a man of weakness. And here we see his weakness again, as we did when he gave a riddle to the Philistines at his wedding. Instead of giving glory to the Lord, he boasts in his own strength and gives himself the credit for striking down one thousand Philistines (15:16). A good translation of the Hebrew is "With the jawbone of an ass, I have piled them in a mass!"[3] As soon as he'd finished boasting, he threw the jawbone down and named the place Ramath-lehi ("jawbone hill"[4]).

Maybe you have been on "jawbone hill" recently. You know, the place where you boasted in your own strength and your own accomplishments, the place where you thought that you could make it on your own, the place where you gave yourself the credit. Perhaps you have forgotten that you have nothing to boast in except for Jesus Christ.

Because of his boasting, the Lord taught Samson the lesson of dependence through his thirst. This is the first time that we see Samson

3. Davis, *Judges*, 181.
4. S. G. De Graaf, *Promise and Deliverance*, vol. 2, *The Failure of Israel's Theocracy* (St. Catharines, Canada: Paideia, 1978), 45.

seeking the Lord.[5] Though he could slay one thousand Philistine men, he could not save himself from his deep thirst. The Lord used this incident to bring Samson back to the place of dependence on the Lord. Instead of boasting in his own strength, this time he cried out to the Lord and gave him the glory for granting the great salvation by the hand of his servant. It was then that God split open the hollow place that is at Lehi and water came out of it, and when Samson drank of this water, his spirit returned and he revived. Just as he named the place where he had boasted in himself, so he names the place where he boasted in the Lord, En-hakkore ("the spring of him who called").

Chapter 15 ends with the note, "And [Samson] judged Israel in the days of the Philistines twenty years." Significantly, there is no mention of rest for the land, as there was in 3:11, 30; 5:31. Instead, "in the days of the Philistines," draws attention to the fact that the Philistines rather than the Israelites dominate this period. We are left pondering how such a prideful and self-centered man as Samson could have judged Israel for so long. We must turn back to 14:4 to see that this is a fulfillment of the words, "It was from the LORD, for he was seeking an opportunity against the Philistines. At that time the Philistines ruled over Israel." So Samson was the Lord's vessel who began the work of delivering Israel from the oppressive Philistines (remember David finished this work; 2 Sam. 5:17–25).[6]

The "spring of him who called" is a much better place to be than "jawbone hill." Maybe you need to come to the spring today and call on the Lord to save you from yourself. Maybe you have been living life in your own strength or handling a particular situation in your own strength and you need to come to the "spring of her who called." Call on the Lord today for his strength and his power for your difficult marriage, rebellious child, physical illness, infertility, unbelieving parent, or (you fill in the blank). Lay down your own means and rest in the Lord today.

The Lord had already had an incident at a rock with the Israelites, and again it was a time for the Lord to humble his people and bring

5. Davis, *Judges*, 182.
6. Block, *Judges, Ruth*, 448.

them back into dependence on him (Ex. 17:1–7). Both incidents at the rock pointed to the true Rock, Jesus Christ, the only Savior who provides life-giving water for his people. Apart from our Lord and Savior Jesus Christ, we would die in our thirst and fall with all God's enemies into everlasting punishment in hell. But glory be to the Father and to the Son and to the Holy Spirit, the triune God who has poured out his grace and mercy on his people in Christ Jesus and opened our blind eyes so that we may see our Savior and allow him to rule our hearts and our lives.

The book of Hebrews reminds us that Samson conquered the Philistines through faith and was made strong out of weakness (11:33–34). So we see again that we can never teach women or our children or spiritual children or grandchildren to just "be like Samson." We must always point them to the one in whom they must place their faith, the Lord and Savior Jesus Christ. And this One still speaks through his Word: "My grace is sufficient for you, for my power is made perfect in weakness." Let us therefore "boast all the more gladly of [our] weaknesses, so that the power of Christ may rest upon [us]. For the sake of Christ, then, [let us be] content with weaknesses, insults, hardships, persecutions, and calamities. For when [we are] weak, then [we are] strong" (2 Cor. 12:9–10).

II. The Spirit of the Lord Delivers Samson from the Gazites (16:1–3)

With the note in 15:20, "and he judged Israel in the days of the Philistines twenty years," we expect the Samson narrative to be over, but the author of Judges includes more. As we have seen, one of Samson's weaknesses was also the weakness of Israel as a whole. He intermingled with the Canaanites; more specifically, he intermarried and/or intermingled with Philistine women. We have already seen from Deuteronomy 7 that this was disobedience to the Lord. Yet, in God's grace, the Lord continued to use Samson to deliver Israel from the Philistines despite his sin.

Samson's first Philistine wife had died at the hand of the Philistines (15:6); and Samson went down to Gaza, saw a prostitute, and apparently "she was right in Samson's eyes" (14:7) because "he went in to her" (16:1).

While he was sinfully indulging in the prostitute, the Gazites learned that Samson had come to Gaza. They presumed, correctly, that he would try to leave during the night, so they set an ambush for him all night at the gate of the city in order to kill him. But the Lord was not through with Samson yet. Samson was still the deliverer of Israel whom the Lord had appointed for this time. And so at midnight he arose, took hold of the doors of the gate of the city and posts, pulled them up, put them on his shoulders, and carried them to the top of the hill that is in front of Hebron, a journey of considerable distance since the distance from Gaza to Hebron was forty miles.[7]

From this episode we learn that the Lord's deliverer removed the enemies' gate and laid the city open and bare. Not even the gates of the enemy city were too hard for Israel's deliverer to remove.[8] In this way the story of Samson points to our greater Deliverer, Jesus Christ, the one who told Peter, "I will build my church, and the gates of hell shall not prevail against it" (Matt. 16:18).

Is there some sin in your past or present that you feel has disqualified you for the Lord's service? The Lord is not through with you yet. We serve a gracious and loving God. When we come to him in repentance, he is gracious to forgive us of our sins. And he redeems our past by making us effective servants for him in the present. Whatever your past or present sin, come to the Lord today in confession and repentance. Then quit thinking that is who you are. You are not that; you are a child of God (see 1 Cor. 6:9–11). And the God of the covenant redeems us from the slavery of sin into service for his kingdom.

III. The Spirit of the Lord Avenges Samson before the Lords of the Philistines (16:4–31)

Samson continued to give in to his sin of involving himself with Philistine women. Here is the third Philistine woman with whom we learn Samson has been involved. But this time the woman is named.

7. K. Lawson Younger Jr., *Judges/Ruth*, The NIV Application Commentary (Grand Rapids: Zondervan, 2002), 315.
8. De Graaf, *Promise and Deliverance*, 46.

Delilah was from the Valley of Sorek, and she did not love Samson or the Lord, for she tempted Samson to deny his calling as deliverer of Israel. Her loyalties were with her people, and so when she was asked by the lords of the Philistines to seduce him so that they could trap him, and they held out a reward to her of eleven hundred pieces of silver, Delilah was happy to oblige.

At first Delilah simply asked Samson where his great strength lay, and how he might be bound so that one could subdue him. Samson must have recognized the trap, because he did not answer truthfully, so that when the Philistines carried out the plan, the secret of his strength was not known.

Again, for a second time, Delilah asked for the secret of his strength. But this time she told him that he had mocked her and told her lies. Again Samson recognized the trap and spoke deceitfully so that the secret of his strength would not be known.

For a third time, Delilah asked for the secret of his strength. And again she told him that he had mocked her and told her lies. Again Samson spoke deceitfully. However, he had weakened, because he came close to telling her the secret of his strength, for the Nazirite vow had to do with his hair. But weaving his hair was not the same as shaving his hair, so Samson escaped the trap again.

However, the fourth time that Delilah asked for the secret of his strength, she turned up the emotion and pressed him so hard day after day that the text says, "His soul was vexed to death." "And he told her all his heart," revealing that he had been a Nazirite to God from his mother's womb and that the secret of his strength lay in his unshaved hair (16:16–17). He had divulged his precious calling to the enemy, and the enemy will deceive. Delilah knew nothing of love. She did not produce what she demanded. She deceived Samson and called the lords of the Philistines to come. During Samson's sleep, Delilah had a man shave his head, and she tormented him.

Delilah reminds us that as women we have the potential to greatly influence our husbands for good or for bad. When the Lord gave Eve to Adam, he gave Adam a helper. But Eve did not end up helping Adam.

Instead she gave him the forbidden fruit (Gen. 3:6). But in Christ we are able to fulfill our God-given design as helpers again. And that is what we are to be for our husbands. We are to help them in the ways of the Lord. Does that describe you as a wife? Or can you relate more to Delilah? Are you manipulative and deceitful in order to get what you want when you want it? Or are you respectful and loving, submitting to your husband out of reverence for Christ?

During his sleep and unknown haircut, the strength left Samson, but he did not know it. So when Delilah awoke him and told him that the Philistines were on him, he went out as if nothing had changed. But everything had changed. The Lord had left him. And the Philistines gouged out his eyes. Ironically, this is exactly what Samson should have done much earlier. It was his eyes that had gotten him in so much trouble with the women. Jesus' words in his Sermon on the Mount, speaking of lust, are appropriate to remember here: "If your right eye causes you to sin, tear it out and throw it away. For it is better that you lose one of your members than that your whole body be thrown into hell" (Matt. 5:29).

Samson had no strength apart from the Lord. This is why we can never say, "Be a Samson." Samson was nobody apart from the Lord. His strength was not his own but the Lord's strength. However, the Lord never leaves his people for good. So in the midst of humbling agony, in blindness and the labor of grinding at the mill in the prison, the Lord began to restore Samson's strength by growing his hair again.

Before we move on, let us pause and consider the seriousness of the situation. Israel's deliverer, the one who had been raised up by God from before birth, was in the hand of his enemies. If Israel's God-given deliverer could not save Israel, who could? The situation looked hopeless, but the Lord works in mysterious and glorious ways. This would not be the last time in history that Israel's Deliverer would be in the hand of his enemies. Jesus Christ, the Savior of God's people, was delivered up according to the definite plan and foreknowledge of God, and was crucified and killed by the hands of lawless men at the command of the Jews (Acts 2:23). The situation looked hopeless then too. The Savior of the world was in the hand of his enemies, hanging on a cross. Not only this, he died. But by the power of God he rose again. And because of this, all those who are in Christ Jesus have been raised to new life also. Our debt has been paid, and we have received our inheritance in Christ and are seated with him in the heavenly places already, though this will not be fully realized until glory.

The lords of the Philistines believed that they had cause to rejoice. They believed that their god had given Samson into their hand. But the Philistines did not know that the Lord, the true God, would have the last word. There would be no cause for rejoicing in the end. The only ones who can truly rejoice are those who are hidden in Christ Jesus.

The people, after much drinking, called for Samson to entertain them at the great celebration. They brought blind Samson out of prison and had him stand between the pillars. Now blind Samson asked the young man who led him to let him feel the pillars on which the house was resting. During his stay in prison he must have had much time to reflect on his life and his calling. Evidently he embraced his calling again, for he called to the Lord and asked him to remember him only that one time so that he, the deliverer of Israel, might be avenged on the Philistines for his two eyes. Although the text says that he bowed with all his strength, we know from whom he got his strength. It was the Lord who displayed his grace to Israel and his power over the Philistines that day. The number of Philistines whom Samson killed at his death was greater than the number he had killed during his lifetime.

In time, the Lord used a greater Deliverer to give his life in death so that others might be delivered. The Lord Jesus Christ, the perfect God-man, the only begotten Son of God, was sent to deliver God's people from the enemy of death, but unlike Samson and Israel, who were unfaithful in their callings, he was faithful to his calling. He not only defeated God's enemies by his death and resurrection, but also he enabled God's children to have true rest.

The final note of the Samson stories speaks of his burial and judge-ship. The one who had been set apart from before his birth to begin to save Israel from the hand of the Philistines was not forgotten by his people. Yes, he had sinned. Yes, he had been disobedient. Yes, he had made many mistakes. But he was still an Israelite, and he was still one called by God to be a savior in Israel for twenty years. And so he was laid in the tomb of Manoah his father. Samson took his place among his own people. This should have encouraged Israel, for they too had played the harlot like Samson, but the Lord was calling to them to repent and return to him. He was showing them through Samson that they could still take their place among the people of God.

We too have made many mistakes, are still those who sin, are still those who are disobedient, yet we are part of the covenant community, and because we are covered in the righteousness of Jesus Christ, on our death we too will take our place among our covenant family in the presence of the Lord to the glory of God the Father.

CONCLUSION

Whose camp are you in today? Have you grown comfortable in your sin? Have you blurred the enemy lines? The Lord has put enmity between the godly and the ungodly. We are not to be friends with the enemy. But we also can't be friends with the Lord's army unless the Spirit of the Lord indwells our hearts and minds. But as believers he does. And because of the Holy Spirit, we can put on the full armor of God and stand firm in the midst of a hostile world. And when we do, we will find that we will never die of thirst or fall into the hand of the Enemy, for Jesus says, "Whoever drinks of the water that I will give him will never be thirsty again. The water that I will give him will become in him a spring of water welling up to eternal life" (John 4:14).

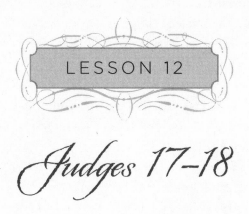

LESSON 12

Judges 17–18

PLEASE USE THE QUESTION paradigm from pages 301–2 as you work through the following. See the introductory comments there that explain each part of the process below in more detail.

- **Pray.**
- **Ponder the Passage.** Read Judges 17–18 once a day from different translations for the entire week, looking for its:
  - Point
  - Persons
  - Problem
  - Patterns
  - Persons of the Trinity
  - Puzzling Parts
- **Put It in Perspective.**
  - Place in Scripture. Skim Judges 1:1–3:6.
  - Passages from Other Parts of Scripture

1. Based on your observations of the text, what is the basic content of this passage? Try to summarize it in your own words, using a sentence or two.

2. Using a concordance, how has the narrator portrayed "Ephraim" throughout the book of Judges?

3. How does Micah's mother respond when she discovers that her money has been taken (17:2)?

4. What is her response to Micah's confession (17:2)? Is this right? How does it display that she is more concerned about money than about keeping the law of the covenant (especially the eighth commandment)?

5. What does Micah's mother dedicate to Micah (17:3)? What does she do with the restored money (17:4)? How does this influence Micah (17:4b)? What does he turn around and do with it (17:5)? Which of the Ten Commandments does this break (see Ex. 20)?

6. How does the narrator of Judges comment on this story (17:6)? Compare this with 18:1; 19:1; 21:25.

7. Read Joshua 21. Why do the Levites not have their own tribal territory (Josh. 13:14)? From Joshua 21 and using a concordance, is Bethlehem one of the forty-eight cities given to the Levites? Why then is this Levite looking for another place to sojourn (17:8)? Skim Leviticus 8–10. In light of these chapters, should the Levite have agreed to stay with Micah?

8. How does Micah reveal his false theology in 17:13? How does this further contribute to the picture of Israelite worship/beliefs during the period of the judges?

9. How do the statements in 17:6; 18:1; 19:1; 21:25 point to the need for the Davidic dynasty that the Lord will raise up after the time of the judges and, ultimately, how do they point to the need of the perfect Davidic king, Jesus Christ?

10. Read Joshua 19:47–48; Judges 1:34. Why is Dan still in need of land? What plan do they make (18:2)? Compare this with Joshua 2:1.

11. How are the Danites deceived by the worship center at Micah's home and the Levitical priest? What are they seeking, and how are they going about it in the wrong way (18:5)? How is the Levite deceived in his own role as priest (18:6)?

12. Describe the land and people of Laish (18:7–10). How do the spies relay the priest's message (18:6, 10)? Were the people commanded by the Lord to take Laish, or was this wrong?

13. How do the six hundred armed Danites assist the five spies in taking the carved image, ephod, gods, and metal image from Micah's house (18:16–18)? How do they respond to the Levite's questioning with their own question? What does the Levite do (18:20)? How does this reveal the apostasy during this time in the period of the judges?

14. Why would the Danites put the little ones, livestock, and goods in front (18:21)? How does Micah respond to finding that his carved image, ephod, gods, and metal image have been taken? How do the Danites bully him? What is his response to this? How does Micah's response (18:24) reveal the emptiness of idolatry (look up "idols" in a concordance to help you answer this)?

15. Which of the Ten Commandments (Ex. 20) do the Danites break by their actions recorded in 18:27? What do the Danites do with Micah's idols (18:30a)?

16. Whom does the narrator finally reveal the Levite to be (18:30)? How does this confirm what we learned in 2:6–10?

17. To what time period might "until the day of the captivity of the land" most likely refer (18:30)? See 2 Kings 15:29.

18. When is the Tent of Meeting put at Shiloh (Josh. 18:1)? What significant event has occurred there (Josh. 22:12)? Look up "Shiloh" in a concordance. What further information do you learn?

19. How do the specific sins we have read about in Judges 17–18 point to the need for a sinless Savior? When in the history of redemption would he come?

• **Principles and Points of Application.**

1. We have the opportunity to bless our children (or spiritual children) when they confess their wrongdoing to us by pointing them to worship Christ for his love, forgiveness, and grace.

How have you taken this opportunity this week? Meditate on 2 Timothy 1:5 today. Pray that you will pass the faith onto the next generation (see also Deut. 4:9–10; 6:7, 20–21; Psalm 48:13–14; 71:18; 78:4, 6; 79:13; 102:18; 145:4). Then make a purposeful plan to do so through your words and actions each day this week.

2. What are the ramifications of doing what is right in our own eyes rather than doing what is right in the Lord's eyes? What situation are you facing right now in which you are tempted to do what you want to do instead of what the Lord wants? Spend time confessing this to the Lord today and relinquishing it to him and his will.

3. For what reasons do you think the Lord will bless you—if you have a quiet time each day, serve his kingdom well, marry a pastor, go into full-time ministry, join a church, or (you fill in the blank)? Recognize today that the Lord does not bless you for any of those reasons, but only because you are in Christ.

4. Whom or what are you tempted to seek to find out if the Lord will bless you or not—counselors, pastors, horoscopes, talk shows, friends, or family? How does this reveal fear and lack of faith and trust in the Lord on your part? What situation are you presently facing in which you are tempted to do this? Confess this today and spend time seeking the Lord in prayer and in his Word this week.

5. In what ways have you set up your own idols in the land that the Lord has graciously provided for you? Remember that an idol is often a good thing that we have made the most important thing. Recognize these idols today, confess them, and walk in the Spirit's delivering power.

NOTES FOR JUDGES 17–18

Ponder the aim of this lesson concerning our:

Mind: What do we need to know from this passage in Scripture?

The judgment on Micah and the Danites (1) anticipates the final judgment of all those who worship false gods and (2) points to the need for a king in Israel, who will come through the Davidic line and culminate in Jesus Christ.

Heart: How does what we learn from this passage affect our internal relationship with the Lord?

It prepares us to be kingdom disciples who repent of the idolatry in our lives and embrace Jesus Christ as the King on the throne of our hearts.

Hands: How does what we learn from this passage translate into action for God's kingdom?

It enables us to:

1. Bless our children, grandchildren, or spiritual children this week when they confess their wrongdoing by pointing them to worship Christ for his love, forgiveness, and grace.
2. Repent of doing what is right in our own eyes rather than what is right in the Lord's eyes, and to relinquish our will to his in our present situations.
3. Recognize today that the Lord does not bless us for any other reason except that we are in Christ Jesus.
4. Confess the temptation to seek the will of God in unworthy means, and to spend time seeking the Lord's will through his Word and prayer.
5. Recognize the idols that we have set up in the life and land that the Lord has graciously provided for us, to confess them, and to walk in the Spirit's delivering power (Gal. 5:16–25).

INTRODUCTION

When we think of idolatry, we usually think of bad things. But all too often our idols are good things that have become bad things because we have made them mandatory to function. Think about your own life. I know that I can look back on mine and see lots of good things that became bad things because I made them gods. I made them gods by placing them on the throne of my heart and bowing down to them. I have bowed down to beauty, so much so that I was enslaved to anorexia. I have bowed down to power and control, so much so that I have tried to usurp the authority of my husband. I have bowed down to family, so much so that sometimes having peace and order in my home has been more important than seeing what God has been doing through seeming chaos. I have bowed down to expectations, so much so that when they have gone unmet, I have slumped into despair. John Calvin was right; our heart is an idol factory.[1] Judges 17–18 has much to say about being kingdom disciples who repent of the idolatry in our lives and embrace Jesus Christ as the King on the throne of our hearts.

We can divide the lesson into three sections:

I. Micah's Confession and His Mother's Unholy Blessing (17:1–6)
II. Micah Wrongly Seeks the Lord's Blessing through the Levitical Priest (17:7–13)
III. The Danites Wrongly Seek Blessing through the Levitical Priest and Micah's Image (18:1–31)

Before we begin, it will be helpful to step back and look at the broader context of this passage and how it relates to the book of Judges and to the entire Bible overall. These final five chapters (17–21) begin the third and final division in the book of Judges. Some commentators have called it a double conclusion, which parallels the double introduction (1:1–2:5 and 2:6–3:6), to the main section of Judges, 3:7–16:31. While the main section of Judges dealt with threats to the nation from non-Israelites, these concluding chapters deal with threats to the nation from their own people. Both stories display the depth of Israel's apostasy. When compared against the

1. John Calvin, *Institutes of the Christian Religion*, vol. 1, ed. John T. McNeill, trans. Ford Lewis Battles (Louisville: Westminster John Knox, 2006), 108.

Ten Commandments, about the only one not mentioned as violated is the Sabbath, and with the others broken, we can safely assume that the Sabbath was broken as well.

We must remember that the Lord had given Israel laws concerning their interaction with Canaanites and concerning kings in Israel. If Israel had paid any attention to the Lord's laws, they would not have fallen into such great apostasy so soon after the great conquests of the land under the godly leader Joshua. But they had not paid attention, and we learn from these last two stories (Micah and the Danites misusing the priesthood and the Levite allowing this misuse in chapters 17–18, and a Levite abusing his concubine in chapter 19) that in the early part of the period of the judges, Israel has fallen into grave sin. They not only need a savior, they need a king. And in the unfolding of the history of redemption the monarchy would come. But even the monarchy would not be enough. Israel would lose the land and go into exile in spite of the monarchy. What Israel needed was a perfect King. And he has come! Jesus Christ, our Lord and Savior, and our Prophet, Priest, and King, has come.

But when he came, Simeon told Mary, his mother, "Behold, this child is appointed for the fall and rising of many in Israel, and for a sign that is opposed (and a sword will pierce through your own soul also), so that thoughts from many hearts may be revealed" (Luke 2:34–35). Indeed this was happening even in the time of the judges; many were falling in Israel, some were rising, but the thoughts from all hearts were being revealed. The Israelites were either found as covenant breakers or covenant keepers. Unfortunately, in these final chapters of Judges, we read of covenant breakers.

All of us have been covenant breakers and still would be, except for the grace of our Lord and Savior Jesus Christ. Let us never forget as we read these chapters that our hearts would be prone to wander to the depths of depravity of which we will read, except for the grace of Christ that has been poured out on our lives. And in light of this, let us cry out in thanksgiving and praise to the one who has saved us as our Prophet, Priest, and King.

I. Micah's Confession and His Mother's Unholy Blessing (17:1–6)

The narrative begins by telling us that "there was a man of the hill country of Ephraim, whose name was Micah" (17:1). The name Micah means "Who is like Yahweh?" anticipating the answer, "No one!"[2] We will soon learn from Micah's life that his name does not reflect his character or beliefs. We have already encountered the Ephraimites before in the book, and each time they have been painted in a negative light. Unfortunately, we will learn that the negative portrayal stays consistent in this story as well.

Ephraim's mother had a large amount of money (eleven hundred pieces of silver). This was the same amount that each of the lords of the Philistines had offered to Delilah if she would seduce her husband (16:5). It was a great deal of money, as we see from Micah's mother's reaction when she discovered that it had been stolen. She uttered a curse, and also spoke it in her son's ears. Surprisingly there is a positive element in the story. Micah actually told his mother that he had stolen the silver and restored it to his mother.

But his mother did no good thing with it. In contrast to her initial curse, she offered a blessing on her son who had returned her money. Evidently she cared more about her money than the fact that her own son had stolen it from her, for there is no word of discipline. She was just thankful to have her riches back. Not only did Micah's mother bless him in the name of the Lord (an unholy blessing), she also dedicated the silver to the Lord from her hand for her son to make a carved image and a metal image. So what Micah had stolen from her, she returned to him so that he could set up this image in his house.

Micah's mother took two hundred (not the eleven hundred that she had promised!) pieces of silver to the silversmith herself and had him make it into a carved and metal image for Micah's house (her breach of promise made the image smaller than it otherwise would have been). But in Micah's house it became a stumbling block, for Micah had a shrine,

2. Daniel I. Block, *The New American Commentary*, vol. 6, *Judges, Ruth* (Nashville: Broadman & Holman, 1999), 478.

and he made an ephod and household gods and ordained one of his sons as his priest. We should not be surprised that Micah was passing unholy and unrighteous living on to his son. He had first learned it from his mother. Micah and his mother should have served the Lord by giving the money to the sanctuary in Shiloh, but instead they wanted to serve the Lord in the way that they thought best in their own eyes. Indeed this is the interpretation we receive from the narrator of the book. He lets us know what he thinks of this first segment of the Micah story: "In those days there was no king in Israel. Everyone did what was right in his own eyes" (17:6). There was a King, but nobody was paying any attention to him. And they weren't paying attention to his requirements for a human king either (Deut. 17:14–20). But in time, as the history of redemption unfolds, the Lord will have mercy on his people and will raise up the Davidic dynasty, which will culminate in his own Son, Jesus Christ, the perfect and final Davidic king.

Nothing much has changed today. We still want to serve the Lord in the ways that we think are best, and on the time schedule that we prefer, and by giving the resources that we deem appropriate. But this is not the covenant way. The covenant way is to honor the Lord with our resources in the ways that he has deemed necessary and appropriate. His Word stands in authority over our reasoning. We must subject ourselves to him and love him with all our heart, mind, soul, and strength. But how do we do this if we are sinners who are totally depraved, dead in our trespasses and sins? It is only in Christ that we can love the Lord as he commands.

Let us pause and ponder the influence that Micah's mother had on Micah. Many of us are mothers or grandmothers (all of us are spiritual mothers as we teach the next generation the covenant way of life) and have the tremendous opportunity to impact our children for Christ and his kingdom. The question is, do we? Are we training and teaching the next generation to fear the Lord (see Deut. 4:9–10; 6:7, 20–21; Ps. 48:13–14; 71:18; 78:4, 6; 79:13; 102:18; 145:4)? Micah's mother led her son in paths of wickedness rather than in paths of righteousness. She led him toward the worship of materialism rather than the worship of the one true God. She taught him that it was okay to worship the Lord however he saw fit, instead of in the way that the Lord had commanded. Let us learn a valuable lesson here. Let us turn to the New Testament and see two other women, Lois and Eunice, Timothy's grandmother and mother, in whom sincere faith dwelt and was passed to the next generation. Lois passed it to Eunice and Eunice passed it to Timothy (2 Tim. 1:5). May we be grandmothers and mothers who do the same for the sake of our Lord and Savior Jesus Christ.

II. Micah Wrongly Seeks the Lord's Blessing through the Levitical Priest (17:7–13)

Micah's shrine wasn't quite complete. Even though he had ordained one of his sons, who had become his priest, Micah thought it would be more pleasing to the Lord if he had a priest from the priestly line that the Lord had ordained, the Levites (Deut. 10:8). At that time a young Judahite from Bethlehem, who was a Levite, left Bethlehem to find a place to live and came to the house of Micah. Micah inquired of his purpose of travel and, on learning that he was looking for a place to live, seized the opportunity to complete his shrine by having a Levite serve as priest. Not only this, Micah asked this "young man" to be his father (here used as a title of respect for his role as priest, one who had spiritual authority and care[3]), another indication that things were not spiritually healthy in Israel during the time of the judges. Micah offers the young man ten pieces of silver a year, a suit of clothes, and his living.

"And the Levite went in" (17:10). Just like that. There was no thinking about it or wrestling with it. He had so lost any sense of being called by God as a Levite to serve the Lord that he immediately went in to serve as a priest in a pagan place. Furthermore, he was content and became like one of Micah's sons. Indeed he evidently replaced Micah's other son whom Micah had ordained as priest earlier, because Micah ordained the Levite to serve as a priest in his house.

The revealing verse as to how Micah viewed the Lord is at the end of the chapter. "Now I know that the LORD will prosper me, because I

3. Ibid., 488.

have a Levite as a priest" (17:13). This phrase has a familiar ring to it in our culture today. Now I know that the Lord will prosper me, because I have had my quiet time this morning. Now I know that the Lord will prosper me, because I have joined a church. Now I know that the Lord will prosper me, because I have a Christian as a spouse, a child, an in-law, or a friend, and he or she is praying for me. Now I know that the Lord will prosper me, because I served him in a specific ministry this week. Now I know that the Lord will prosper me, because I have been a good wife and mom this year. Now I know that the Lord will prosper me, because I have given money to charities recently. And on and on the list grows. We think that we can buy favor with the Lord. But there is only one who could buy favor for us, and he has done that. He is our Lord and Savior Jesus Christ. He is the only way that God will prosper us. The only thing that we can say and the only thing we need to say is, "Now I know that God the Father will prosper me spiritually, because I have Jesus Christ as my High Priest."

III. The Danites Wrongly Seek Blessing through the Levitical Priest and Micah's Image (18:1–31)

Although it is shortened, we have the same refrain from 17:6 in 18:1, "In those days there was no king in Israel." Yet we have seen throughout the book that in his grace and mercy, although the people had rejected the Lord as their King, he was still on the sovereign throne, bringing his purpose in redemptive history to pass. He would preserve his people in spite of themselves until he raised up the Davidic kingship, which would culminate in the coming of the King of Kings, Jesus Christ.

The tribe of Dan had been given territory of its inheritance (Josh. 19:40–48), but we learned in 1:34 that "the Amorites pressed the people of Dan back into the hill country, for they did not allow them to come down to the plain." So here in chapter 18 we see them seeking land for themselves. Just as Joshua had sent two men as spies to view the land of Canaan before they conquered the land (Josh. 2:1), so the people of Dan sent five spies to view the land before they conquered any. However, while the story in Joshua has the Lord's hand of blessing on it because it was done for his name's sake, the story here has the Lord's hand of judgment on it. It would be better to compare it then to the account in Numbers 13:1–24 in which the Lord told Moses to spend spies to spy out the land of Canaan, which he was giving to the people of Israel. The spies, after forty days of spying out the land, brought back a good report about the land and its fruit, but all (except Caleb and Joshua; Num. 13:30; 14:6–9) told the people, out of fear and disobedience to the Lord, that they were not able to go against the stronger people who lived there and overcome them (Num. 13:25–29).

On the way to spy out the land, the spies came to Micah's house and recognized the voice of the Levite as one from their own land. So they inquired of why he was there. When they learned that he was the priest of Micah's shrine, they sought spiritual answers from him. They wanted to know whether or not their journey would be a success. And the Levite assured them that it would be successful, for it was under the eye of the Lord. But both the spies and the Levite were deceived. The men were deceived because they thought they could seek and gain spiritual answers from a pagan priest serving in a sinful shrine; the Levite was deceived because he thought that the Lord would grant him spiritual authority when he had clearly spurned the spiritual authority of the Lord by serving in a man-made shrine. This was man-made religion (idolatry) at its best.

But can we not relate to both the Levite and the spies? How often do we spurn the means of grace through which the Lord communicates his Word to us and seek other sources to discern what the will of the Lord is? How often do we set up our own self-made shrine and worship the Lord as we think convenient and best? All the time! I know women who profess to be Christians who have considered consulting a palm reader to know their future, or who read their horoscopes regularly, or who watch television talk shows as if they are a means of finding truth, or who listen to their best friends as if they have all the answers. We are guilty of wanting what we want when we want it, and there are times when we are willing to consult all kinds of people or things in order to get the answers. We are also people who love our independence, and if the Lord's ways of worship seem too confining for us, we will erect a shrine of our own and worship him the way that we please.

But we must not do this. There is one way to worship, and that is through our Lord and Savior Jesus Christ. The author of Hebrews so eloquently reminds us that we may boldly approach the throne of grace in confidence because we have Jesus as our great High Priest. He is not the Levite who serves God as he pleases; he is the High Priest in the order of Melchizedek who accomplished God's will on the cross and is now seated at the right hand of God the Father as our Prophet, Priest, and King (Heb. 4:14–16). He will never fail us or forsake us or lead us astray. He is faithful to serve as the perfect Priest, in order to lead us in the ways of the Word and true worship at all times.

The spies left the Levite and came to Laish. In Laish they saw what was right in their own eyes. It seemed perfect! The people of Laish were people living in security, quiet and unsuspecting. They lived on fertile ground and possessed great wealth. They had no dealings with anyone, so they would be easy to attack. The five Danite spies took this good news back to the Danite tribe and reported that they had seen the land for their tribe and it was very good land; they even believed that "God [had] given it into [their] hands" (18:10). Remember that they had also been deceived by the self-made shrine of Micah and by the Levite serving in it.

So six hundred men of the tribe of Dan set out from Zorah and Eshtaol (west of Jerusalem) and went north toward Ephraim and came to the house of Micah in the hill country of Ephraim. On their way to rob the people of Laish of their land, they robbed Micah of his loot in his man-made shrine and told the Levite to come with them, reasoning with him that it was better for him to be a priest to a whole tribe than to just one man's family. We would have hoped that the Levite would have had a problem with both, since neither place would bring glory and honor to the Lord, but instead we read, "The priest's heart was glad" (18:20). So he robbed Micah of his things and went along with the Danite people.

Knowing that Micah might come after them, the Danites put the goods along with the little ones and livestock in front of them with the warriors behind to provide protection against the attack. Sure enough, Micah came after the Danites and his priest. Sadly, this was all that Micah believed he had. Everything was the matter with him because he had placed his hope in false religion. He had worshiped and served other gods. He had had chosen a priest according to his own requirements, not God's. And when his self-made religion crumbled, he was devastated. He believed that there was nothing left.

But he found no sympathy from the Danites. Instead they bullied him, and in fear and hopelessness Micah turned and went back to his home. This is the last we see of Micah in the book. And what a depressing picture it is! You can almost see him slump off the pages of Scripture into a meaningless existence. He believed that all was lost. His gods and priest were gone. What he thought gave him purpose and meaning had been stolen right out from under him, and he was facing loss, hopelessness, and fear. If only he had turned to the Covenant God! There was one in his midst who could save him, but Micah was deceived and, as far as we know, remained forever in the trap of man-made religion that always disappoints and never saves.

Perhaps some of us today are where Micah was. Maybe all your self-made religion and worship has crumbled about you and you are left feeling fearful and devastated. Maybe your husband has lost his job and you have realized that financial security was one of your gods. Perhaps you have been diagnosed with cancer and you realize that being healthy and living a long life was most important to you. Maybe you have never married and are not happy about it and have realized that marriage was one of your gods. Perhaps infertility and miscarriage has been your constant companion and you have realized that you thought children would make your family complete. None of these desires in and of themselves are wrong, but we so often lift them to the next level and they become idols that we worship in our lives. But we don't have to turn back in fear and shame and depression like Micah. You can turn today to the Covenant God, and you will find him there. He has always been, is, and will ever be the God who is there.[4] And you can turn today

---

4. I am indebted to Francis Schaeffer for this phrase, which is also the name of one of his many books, *The God Who Is There*.

to Jesus and find that he is the perfect High Priest who is seated at the right hand of God the Father, praying for you.

We should not be surprised that these bullies, the Danites, who had no sympathy for Micah, had no sympathy for the quiet and unsuspecting people of Laish either. We must remember that this was not holy war. The Lord had given them no command to conquer these people. They had not involved the God of the covenant in their decision at all. This was man operating on his own in order to attain his own selfish desires. So they sinfully struck the people of Laish with the sword and burned their city. And they rebuilt the city and lived in it and named it Dan. Here is a microcosm of what happened at the Tower of Babel (Gen. 11:1–9): humans operating independently from God to make names for themselves. Not surprisingly, they set up their own self-made shrine as well. Rather than worshiping according to the way of the covenant, they worshiped according to the way of man. They set up carved images for themselves. And here's the real shocker, the fact that the narrator has kept to himself until now: the Levite had a name. And his name was in the line of Moses. He was Moses' grandson! How far had the Israelites fallen in such a short time! We learned in 2:6–10 that the Israelites forgot the Lord after the generation who saw the exodus and the conquest of the land under Joshua's leadership had died. Here we see evidence of this.

The sons of Jonathan (the Levite) were priests to the tribe of the Danites until the day of the captivity of the land. To what time does this refer? Most likely the time refers to the deportation of Dan by Tiglath-pileser III to Assyria in 734 B.C. (2 Kings 15:29).[5] Judges 18:31 tells us that Micah's carved image remained "as long as the house of God was at Shiloh." This is significant because Shiloh was the place in the middle of the land where the ark was placed before the temple had been built, and which offered the people a central place of worship. But as we have seen, the covenant people did not follow the covenant way of worship. They did what was right in their own eyes because they did not recognize God as their King. They set up their own image in their own convenient place.

5. Block, *Judges, Ruth*, 513.

Although we see in the Scriptures that God destroyed the man-made worship centers of his people all through the history of redemption, we see that by his grace he never destroyed his people. This is because he was raising up the true Temple, the perfect Priest, in his Son, Jesus Christ, one much greater than Moses and Aaron, in order to save his people from their sins. And he has come. This true Temple and perfect Priest came to earth in order to live a life of obedience on our behalf and pay for our sins on the cross to satisfy the justice of God on our behalf, and he is now seated at God's right hand to intercede for us. Glory be to the Father and to the Son and to the Holy Spirit! There is a Redeemer! And he is much greater than the gods and priests we have ever attempted to place on the pedestals in our hearts. He is the God who is there. He is the Savior who has come. And he is the King who is coming again.

CONCLUSION

There is only room for One on the throne of our hearts, and he is our Lord and Savior Jesus Christ, "the radiance of the glory of God and the exact imprint of his nature" (Heb. 1:3). He alone can save us from the "perpetual factory of idols"[6] that our hearts make. And he does. When we are left, like Micah, hopeless and afraid, because everything that we once clung to for protection, position, power, and purpose is gone, God is there. And his Son, Jesus Christ, the true Priest and Temple is there. The way is open for true worship in the midst of the exposure of false worship.

> Now the point in what we are saying is this: we have such a high priest, one who is seated at the right hand of the throne of the Majesty in heaven, a minister in the holy places, in the true tent that the Lord set up, not man. (Heb. 8:1–2)

And "he has appeared once for all . . . to put away sin by the sacrifice of himself . . . so Christ, having been offered once to bear the sins of

6. Calvin, *Institutes*, 108.

many, will appear a second time, not to deal with sin but to save those who are eagerly waiting for him" (Heb. 9:26–28).

> Therefore, [sisters], since we have confidence to enter the holy places by the blood of Jesus . . . since we have a great priest over the house of God, let us draw near with a true heart in full assurance of faith. . . . Let us hold fast the confession of our hope without wavering. . . . And let us consider how to stir up one another to love and good works. (Heb. 10:19–24)

For we serve a gracious and faithful High Priest who alone is worthy of our worship.

LESSON 13

Judges 19–21

PLEASE USE THE QUESTION paradigm from pages 301–2 as you work through the following. See the introductory comments there that explain each part of the process below in more detail.

- **Pray.**
- **Ponder the Passage.** Read Judges 19–21 once a day from different translations for the entire week, looking for its:
  - Point
  - Persons
  - Problem
  - Patterns
  - Persons of the Trinity
  - Puzzling Parts
- **Put It in Perspective.**
  - Place in Scripture. Skim Judges 1:1–3:6.
  - Passages from Other Parts of Scripture

1. Based on your observations of the text, what is the basic content of this passage? Try to summarize it in your own words, using a sentence or two.

2. Skim Numbers 25:1–18; 31:6; Joshua 22:10–34 and compare with Judges 20:27–28. What does this tell us about the chronological time of this last story in the book of Judges? Did it occur early or late in the judges' period?

3. Compare 19:1 with 17:6; 18:1; 21:25. What is one of the main purposes of the book?

4. How long do the concubine and the Levite stay estranged? Who initiates reconciliation and how? What is the father-in-law's response? How does the father-in-law's hospitality contrast/compare with (1) the men of Gibeah (19:15), and (2) the old man from the hill country of Ephraim sojourning in Gibeah (19:16–21)?

5. Ironically, the Levite would not turn aside from Jerusalem because it was a city of foreigners and he wanted to press on to Gibeah, which belonged to the Israelites. But how is he treated at Gibeah (19:15)?

6. Compare 19:22–26 with Genesis 19:1–14. What similarities do you see? What differences?

7. What is the purpose of the Levite's cutting up his concubine and sending her to all the tribes of Israel (19:27–30; 20:6)? What is Israel's reaction (19:30–20:11)?

8. The author stresses the unity of the tribes three times in 20:1, 8, 11. Why is this ironic in light of the rest of the book? Why is this sad in light of the fact that they are united against Benjamites?

9. Is the motivation of Israel godly (20:9–10), or are they taking vengeance instead of leaving it to the Lord?

10. In what way do the Israelites give the larger tribe of Benjamin a way out of battle (20:12–13a)? What is the tribe of Benjamin's response (20:13b)? How many men come out to battle from Benjamite cities (20:15a)? How many from Gibeah specifically (20:15b)? How many from Israel (20:17)?

11. Compare 20:18 with 1:1. What are the similarities? What is the main difference?

12. How does the Lord judge Israel's sinful attitude and motives against the Benjamites (20:9–10) by the first two defeats (20:21, 24–25)?

13. Does the Lord's judgment bring them to repentance (20:26–28)? Do they inquire of the right person (Phinehas the high priest) as to the Lord's will (20:27–28)? How do we know that the people have truly repented (20:28)?

14. Does the Lord fulfill his promise (20:35)? How do the men of Israel turn again to their own ways during the battle and take vengeance into their own hands (20:48)?

15. What had the Israelites sworn at Mizpah (20:1; 21:1)? Are the Israelites' actions at Bethel just sorrow or true repentance (21:3–4)? Do they inquire of the Lord or do they come up with a self-made plan (21:5)? While the Israelites' compassion toward Benjamin seems commendable, the way that they go about it raises suspicion. Why? Again, whom did they treat with violence, the Canaanites or their own people (21:10–11)? Is this holy war or haughty war?

16. To whom does the author attribute the breach in Israel (21:15)? What is the Israelites' plan to restore this breach (21:16–24)? What is God's ultimate plan to restore the breach (Acts 2:22–36)?

17. For whom does 21:25 prepare us (1 Sam. 16:11–13; 2 Sam. 7; Isa. 16:5; Jer. 23:5; Ezek. 34:23–24; 37:24–25; Matt. 1:1; Rev. 5:5; 22:16)?

18. How does the sin of Gibeah and the division among the Israelites point to the need for a different kind of savior from the ones we have seen in the book of Judges? How does God display his grace to the Israelites by preserving the Benjamites, and how does this preservation relate to his greater plan of redemption? Why is the preservation of God's people important?

- **Principles and Points of Application.**
  1. Meditate today on Psalm 133:1; John 17:23; Romans 15:5–6; Colossians 3:12–17. With whom in your life do you need to seek

reconciliation—a spouse, child, sibling, neighbor, friend, or a sister in Christ? Pray and ask the Lord to forgive any wrong that you are responsible for in the relationship, and then seek reconciliation this week through a phone call, a letter, a meeting, etc.

2. How does the culture around us reflect the statement, "There was no king . . . Everyone did what was right in his own eyes" (21:25)? How are you taking the good news to those around you that there is a King and he saves us in order for us to do what is right in God's eyes by his Spirit?

3. In what situation in your life are you aware of injustice? Are you considering it, taking counsel from other godly people about it, and speaking out on behalf of it? How?

4. In what ways are sin and tragedies opportunities to come together as a family (either an individual family or the church family)? What opportunities for this are in your life circumstances right now? How will you take this opportunity and use it to glorify God?

5. Do you inquire of the Lord before making decisions or fighting life's battles? In what area do you need to do that today? Do you worship and give thanks during such times or are you just concerned about petitioning the Lord for what you want when you want it? Spend time in prayer today concerning a present decision you are facing or a present battle you are fighting.

6. How has Christ shown compassion for all God's children who are cut off from him? How has the Lord Jesus stood in the breach and reconciled us to the Father? Read Romans 5:6–11. In what ways are you sharing the message of reconciliation with others (see 2 Cor. 5:17–21)? Ask the Lord to help you see the opportunities around you to share this message this week.

NOTES FOR JUDGES 19–21

Ponder the aim of this lesson concerning our:

Mind: What do we need to know from this passage in Scripture?

The utter depravity of man, as seen in Gibeah, the tribe of Benjamin, and the Israelites' response, requires salvation from the Lord, the final and perfect Davidic king.

Heart: How does what we learn from this passage affect our internal relationship with the Lord?

It prepares us to be kingdom disciples who recognize salvation is from the Lord, and to give thanks for the Spirit's regenerating work in our lives and the righteousness of Jesus Christ that has been applied to our sinful souls.

Hands: How does what we learn from this passage translate into action for God's kingdom?

It enables us to:

1. Confess areas of our life and our church's life where we observe little restraint of sin, to recognize Jesus is our King, and to walk in his ways by the power of the Spirit.
2. Respond to injustice by considering it, taking counsel with the godly about it, and defending those who are victims of injustice.
3. Meet together with those in our family or church and pray for specific sins or struggles presently occurring.
4. Inquire of the Lord first during life's battles and decisions, and to give thanks and worship him while going through such times.
5. Spend time in thanksgiving today that God the Father has shown compassion for those who are cut off from him through the sacrifice of his Son, Jesus Christ, and to give thanks to Christ for standing in the breach and reconciling us to the Father.

INTRODUCTION

Several years ago scrapbooking hit a boom. Churches in the city where I lived had scrapbooking clubs and meetings weekly or monthly, it was talked about a great deal, stores promoted scrapbooking products regularly, and you almost felt bad if you didn't scrapbook. Now it seems that Facebook and blogs have largely replaced traditional scrapbooks. But the idea remains the same. People scrapbook and blog in order to share their memories with others and keep others informed of important events in their lives.

Friends gave me scrapbooking materials as baby gifts, but I have to be honest with you, I rarely used them. I love to journal instead. From the time I was in elementary school, I have kept journals. Journals can capture what pictures can't. Nobody takes pictures of the dark places in life. Have you noticed that? Nobody wants to have photos of his or her deepest valleys. When you open up a scrapbook, you sense that something is missing. The life of the person has been only good. Everything is happy. Vacations and parties abound. But the hard times are not represented. I think this is a shame.

The darkest times of our lives are when God's grace shines the brightest. And when you go back and look, as hard as it is to remember, you are reminded that the Lord graciously pulled you through that addiction, that sin, that foreclosure, that time of unemployment, that sickness, that depression, that rebellious child, that marital difficulty, that struggle with infertility, or (you fill in the blank).

In this lesson we are going to be looking at a story that would have never made it into a scrapbook. In a way, we could say that about the entire book of Judges. But this story is especially gruesome. It is one of those stories that is very difficult to read. You would rather leave it out of the family memories. But it is there, and it is God who has placed it there. Why? Why does he want this story in his scrapbook? He wants it in his scrapbook because his scrapbook is all about his Son. And this story not only shows us the need for our King, but it also shows us the grace of our King, and the priesthood of our King, as he is presently interceding for us in heaven. The book of Judges, especially these final chapters, showcases our Savior. Remember that the next time you scrapbook. Remember to showcase your Savior. There may be a few dark pages, but remember that his grace shines the brightest on those.

These final chapters have much to say about being kingdom disciples who recognize salvation is from the Lord and give thanks for the Spirit's regenerating work in our lives and the righteousness of Jesus Christ that has been applied to our sinful souls. How do you take a picture of that? The picture is Christ on the cross. Make sure you overlay each of your dark pictures with his dark one. For his darkest night turns our darkness to brightness and whiteness. The blood of our King washes our sins away.

We can divide the lesson into three sections:

   I. The People of Gibeah Despise the Holiness of the Lord (19)
  II. The Lord Judges Israel and the Benjamites (20)
 III. The Lord Graciously Spares the Tribe of Benjamin in Spite of Israel's Sin (21)

I. The People of Gibeah Despise the Holiness of the Lord (19)

The events of these last five chapters (17–21) most likely occurred at the beginning of the time of the judges. In the case of this story, the fact that Phinehas the son of Eleazar, son of Aaron, is named as high priest (20:28) leads to this conclusion.[1] So, in the beginning of the period of the judges, when there was no king in Israel, a Levite was sojourning in the remote parts of the hill country of Ephraim and took to himself a concubine from Bethlehem in Judah (despite similarities between the situations, this Levite was not the same one who became Micah's priest in the last story). The fact that he took a concubine does not bring back good memories for the reader. The last time a concubine was mentioned in the book was in the Gideon story (8:31), and she bore him Abimelech, a son who brought great trouble to Israel. We already expect there to be trouble here as well. While the ESV says she "was unfaithful to him" (19:2), a better translation is probably that of the Septuagint: "she became angry with him." She left and went back to her father's house at Bethlehem.

---

1. S. G. De Graaf, *Promise and Deliverance*, vol. 2, *The Failure of Israel's Theocracy* (St. Catharines, Canada: Paideia, 1978), 49.

After four long months, the Levite finally arose and went after her, taking his servant and a couple of donkeys with him. He spoke kindly to her and won favor in her eyes and in his father-in-law's eyes. Interestingly, despite the way the Levite has treated his father-in-law's daughter (his concubine), the father-in-law's hospitality is overly emphasized in the story. But we will see that this serves as a stark contrast to the lack of hospitality the Levite will receive in Gibeah. Although the Levite intended to stay only three days, he ended up staying five. The father-in-law asked him to stay until the sixth day since it was evening at the time of departure, but the Levite refused and went on his way, taking his concubine, young man, and donkeys with him.

When they came to Jerusalem, the servant suggested they lodge there for the night, but the Levite refused because he did not think it wise to stay among foreigners. Does this statement hit you as odd? Why would Jerusalem be a place of foreigners? Wasn't Jerusalem supposed to be Israelite land? Yes, it was. Remember 1:21, though, where we read, "But the people of Benjamin did not drive out the Jebusites who lived in Jerusalem, so the Jebusites have lived with the people of Benjamin in Jerusalem to this day." As we will see, their failure to conquer Jerusalem led to serious consequences.

So the Levite continued onto Gibeah, which belonged to the tribe of Benjamin, and sought lodging there. But the group could not find anyone among their own people to give them lodging for the night. So they sat down in the open square of the city. Finally an old man passed by on his way home from work. He was just a sojourner in Gibeah; he too was from the hill country of Ephraim, as the Levite was. After inquiring of his situation and realizing that they simply needed a place to stay, the old man offered them lodging at his home. At first he seems very hospitable. He gave the donkeys feed, even though the Levite had told him that they had already had that. And he gave them food and drink, even though they had those supplies as well. But such great hospitality would not last, at least not for the concubine.

While the Levite, his concubine, and his servant were enjoying the old man's hospitality, wicked men of the city surrounded his house and beat on the door. Evidently they had observed the Levite go into the home, and they had wickedly desired to have him in order to have sex with him. Though the old man showed some kind of conscience by begging them not to act so wickedly, he still did a disgraceful thing by offering the man's concubine and his own virgin daughter to the wicked men. The old man even gave them permission to violate them and do what seemed good in their eyes, as long as they left the Levite alone. The Levite stood for God's holiness. The Levite was the one who had been set apart by God for priestly duties. But the men of Gibeah wanted nothing to do with the Lord's holiness. They were sinful men, seeking another opportunity for sin. That is why they would not listen to the old man.

While we would expect the old man to be the one to push the concubine and virgin daughter among the men, it was the Levite who seized his concubine (you know, the one he had gone to retrieve in kindness from his father-in-law) and made her go out to them. And the wicked men raped her and abused her all night. In fact, by the end of it all, after they let her go, it was all she could do to stumble to the home where she should have had protection, but had not received it. One wonders why she went back there, but evidently it was her only hope.

Her hope was short-lived, for her life was almost over. When her master opened the door to be on his way, she was lying at the door with her hands on the threshold and was unresponsive to his less-than-sensitive command, "Get up, let us be going" (19:28). The Levite saw her as an object, rather than his wife to be loved. He carried her home on his donkey and cut her into twelve pieces, sending one piece to each tribe of Israel. What was the purpose of this? The purpose was to bring war against Gibeah from the rest of Israel. How did the people respond? They were shocked. Nothing like this had happened since they had come out of Egypt. And they were not going to dismiss it.

How Israel has fallen! We are reminded of Sodom in Genesis 19, but now it is happening in Benjamite land, except no angels came to rescue from evil or urge the people to flee. It is as if the Lord has withheld help for the moment in order to display his judgment and reveal man's

207

desperate need of repentance. The ways of Canaan had won among this tribe of Israel. In Genesis 19 we learned about the men of Sodom, who asked Lot to give them the men that had come to him (the two angels). Lot also offered his virgin daughters to the wicked men, but the wicked men were not content with that offer. They pressed hard against Lot and drew near to break down the door, but the angels rescued Lot and struck the wicked men with blindness. The angels also urged Lot to take his family and flee Sodom, for the Lord was going to judge it with sulfur and fire from heaven. This was a microcosm of the greater and final judgment that would one day come. The Lord will not tolerate sin forever. There will be a day when his Son will come again, and it will not be in salvation, but in judgment. Will we be found as those of Sodom and Gibeah or will we be found clothed in the righteousness of our King, Jesus Christ?

Except for the grace of God, we too would be like the wicked men in Sodom and Gibeah. Let us give thanks that the Holy Spirit is sanctifying our hearts, leading us in paths of holiness and righteousness for the sake of Christ. Let us remember in times of darkness, when the Lord has seemingly turned his face away and is not delivering us, that he is revealing his justice and our desperate need for salvation.

II. The Lord Judges Israel and the Benjamites (20)

Ironically, the division of the concubine's body (into twelve parts) brings unity to the people of Israel, for we read, "The congregation assembled as one man to the LORD at Mizpah" (20:1). Four hundred thousand of the chiefs presented themselves in the assembly. We also learn that the Benjamites were aware of this great assembly against them (20:3). The people of Israel inquired of the Levite in order to find out how the "evil" happened. This is an amazing question in light of all the times we have read in the book that "the people of Israel did what was evil in the sight of the LORD." Here we see that they actually recognized evil in their midst.

The Levite recounted the story to them. But first the narrator inserts a note about the Levite that is telling. He says that he is "the husband of the woman who was murdered" (20:4). Here we clearly see that the sixth commandment has been broken. More than that, the commandment that sums up the second tablet of the law, "Love your neighbor as yourself" (Mark 12:31), has been broken. The Levite now tells the reason for his division of the concubine, "for they have committed abomination and outrage in Israel. Behold, you people of Israel, all of you, give your advice and counsel here" (20:6–7).

Again they all arose as one man to exercise judgment on the sin of Gibeah. In fact, this is stated twice in verses 8–11. The author of Judges is emphasizing this unity against Gibeah. The first thing that the tribes of Israel did was to send men through all the tribes of Benjamin, asking them to give up the worthless fellows in Gibeah so that they could put them to death and purge evil from Israel. But the tribe of Benjamin was more concerned with protecting their own men than they were with purging Israel of evil. They would not listen to the rest of Israel; instead, they sided with sin. So they brought judgment on themselves as well.

The battle was a bit uneven; Benjamin was represented by twenty-six thousand men plus seven hundred "supermen" of Gibeah who never missed a shot, but the men of Israel who came against them were 400,000 in number. It seems easy to determine who would win, but we will see that the situation is more complicated than that.

The people arose and went up to Bethel (the ark had been taken from Shiloh to Bethel at this point) to inquire of God. We are reminded here of 1:1–2 where the Israelites inquired of the Lord concerning who should go up first against the Canaanites. His answer is the same in both cases; Judah was to go first.

The first time the men of Israel went up against Gibeah, they lost twenty-two thousand men. But the people of Israel took courage, and again formed the battle line. They wept before the Lord and inquired of the Lord, and he again told them to go up against Gibeah. But nowhere do we see the people of Israel repent of their own sin, nor do we see them go through the proper channel of the high priest to inquire of the Lord's will. So the second day they went against Gibeah and eighteen thousand men of Israel were destroyed. Through these two times of failure, the Lord brought them to repentance. First, they went up to Bethel and wept. Second, they sat before the Lord and fasted until evening. Third, they offered sacrifices before the Lord. Fourth, they inquired of the Lord through the proper channel of the high priest Phinehas as to whether they should continue to battle their brothers the Benjamites. And the Lord made them a promise at this point. He would give them into their hand the next day.

How we can relate to the Israelites! How often do we get angry over sin and judge it without ever looking at the sin in our own hearts? We are all sinners saved by grace, but we are often blinded to this. Somehow we think that we are saints while everyone else is a sinner. But the Lord wants us to remove the log from our own eye first. We cannot exercise judgment in the name of the Lord with self-righteous hearts. The Lord desires humble and dependent people, and he works in our lives to bring us to humility and dependence on him alone. It is only then that we are ready for service for him.

So the Israelites were ready for service in the name of the Lord. Their hearts had been humbled, and they recognized that they were simply agents of judgment in God's hand because of this grievous sin in Gibeah. They knew that they were no better than their brothers. The men of Israel set up a surprise attack, and the Lord defeated Benjamin before Israel; there were 25,100 Benjamites destroyed that third day. Benjamin saw that they were defeated, but the men of Israel were not satisfied to let the battle end.

Vengeance was taken up by the men of Israel, and they pursued the Benjamites hard, striking down their city, men, beasts, and all that they found, as well as setting their towns on fire. They were relentless in their pursuit. Only six hundred men were left, and these were left because they had fled toward the wilderness to the rock of Rimmon and remained there four months. Otherwise they would have been destroyed too. This vengeance against their own kinsmen is both sad and ironic. Sadly, the Benjamites had for all practical purposes become Canaanites. So Israel was, for the first time, engaging in holy war, as they should have against Canaan, except ironically it was with their own brothers.[2]

III. The Lord Graciously Spares the Tribe of Benjamin in Spite of Israel's Sin (21)

The people of Israel were again humbled. They realized that because of their vow at Mizpah, no man would give his daughter in marriage to a Benjamite, so a tribe would be lost in Israel. The people went to Bethel again and wept, built an altar, and offered burnt and peace offerings. But they did not wait for the Lord's answer. Instead they came up with a plan of their own out of the compassion they felt for the tribe of Benjamin. What emotional swings! One moment there is all-out revenge, and the next moment there is compassion. This is a clear indicator that they were acting according to their ways rather than the Lord's. If they had been acting according to the Lord, they would have had his peace. But instead they were doing things in their own way.

Their solution lay in the tribe that had not gone up to Mizpah, and therefore had not made the oath not to give their daughters to the Benjamites. The tribe was Jabesh-gilead. Because Jabesh-gilead had not joined them against the Benjamites, they decided to judge them for this by destroying them, but they saved the four hundred virgins they found for the tribe of Benjamin. These virgins were brought to Shiloh.

The men of Israel sent word to the six hundred Benjamites who had fled to Rimmon and declared peace. The six hundred Benjamites returned and were given the four hundred virgins. But two hundred men still needed wives. Again the Israelites had compassion on the Benjamites. Why? The narrator says that the Lord had made a breach in the tribes of Israel. This should be of great encouragement to us. In spite of sinful man, the Sovereign Lord is still in control. He is working out his plan of redemption in the midst of a messy people.

But again the people did not seek the Lord. Instead they devised another plan of their own. They did not trust the Lord to preserve his

2. Daniel I. Block, *The New American Commentary*, vol. 6, *Judges, Ruth* (Nashville: Broadman & Holman, 1999), 567–68.

own, even though he was really the One doing the preserving all along. Their plan involved the annual feast of the Lord at Shiloh, north of Bethel. They commanded the Benjamites to catch wives, literally! They were to lie in ambush in the vineyards and watch for the daughters of Shiloh to come out and dance. Then they were to quickly snatch them and take them home to the land of Benjamin, which, if you remember, had been destroyed by fire. Not exactly where a new bride who had already experienced snatching would want to be! They anticipated that the men of these snatched women would have something to say about this. But they figured that they could appease them by saying snatching was better than war or breaking their vow. So the men of Benjamin in need of wives followed the plan and, after succeeding in snatching, returned to their inheritance and rebuilt their towns.

Every man then went to his inheritance, to his tribe and his family. But the author does not end on that note. He adds his own commentary on the situation. "In those days there was no king in Israel. Everyone did what was right in his own eyes" (21:25).

By God's grace, he preserved his people. He did this because of Jesus Christ. He was going to raise up Christ through his people. Therefore he must preserve them. And he did, and he does, and he will. In the history of redemption, the Davidic line came. King David was only a type of the greater King to come. Although Israel enjoyed blessing under King David, and the promises of God found a microcosmic fulfillment under King Solomon, the greater blessing was to come, and the fulfillment of the promises was to come in Christ Jesus.

You and I live in the age in which Christ has already come. What the book of Judges anticipated has come to fruition. And yet Christ's reign has only been inaugurated; it has not yet been consummated. We still struggle in our sin and selfish motives. We too, like Israel, often make man-made plans with little or no regard for the Lord. But in his grace he preserves us. We are sealed for salvation by the Spirit and sanctified by him. Jesus Christ is the one who has borne our sin, and because he has, we can now approach the throne of grace with confidence. We have a Savior who is great enough to save us from all our sins. And he has. Let us rest in his work on the cross on our behalf today, praising him and thanking him for salvation.

CONCLUSION

What pictures are missing from your scrapbook? Sexual immorality? Idolatry? Adultery? Homosexuality? Theft? Greed? Addictions? Abusive behavior? All these are listed in 1 Corinthians 6:9–10. But Paul goes on to say in 6:11 some of the most beautiful words in Scripture: "And such *were* some of you. But you were washed, you were sanctified, you were justified in the name of the Lord Jesus Christ and by the Spirit of our God." I love the word "were." It does not say "are." The label does not stick forever. The grace of Jesus Christ has washed the sin and the label away. But the portrait is still there. Paul still names what they were. Why? Because against the darkness of our sin shines the brightness of God's salvation through Jesus Christ his Son. The book of Judges does the same. And that is what our scrapbooks should be all about too.

LESSON 14

Introduction to Ruth

I HAVE ALWAYS LOVED TO JOURNAL. My favorite thing about journaling is that I can go back and read about (1) God's faithfulness in my life, (2) his hand of providence as I've looked back on events, and (3) his acts of redeeming me from Satan's snares, worldly ways, and my sinful self. There are days penned when I am weary of the mundane, and soon after the Lord shows me his faithfulness through the monotonous circumstances of life. There are days that record my running away from God toward another person or place that I think will provide what I need, only to end in disappointment, frustration, and more hunger. There are days when I have been so full that I am about to burst and days that I've been so empty I'm about to crack but the Lord fills me with his life-giving water. There are days recorded when the Lord has used me in the life of another person to display his covenantal love and kindness, leading the other person back to faithful living. There are lots of days recorded of waiting, waiting for the Lord to see how he will resolve a matter. And of course, my wedding day is recorded and the births of my children. One thread runs through all of it—my need for a Redeemer and a King, and the Lord's faithfulness to be that Redeemer and King.

215

When I come to the book of Ruth in Scripture, I feel that I am open-ing up a journal. Not just any journal, it is God's journal. It is a journal that displays God's mighty acts through the mundane circumstances of one family's life. It is a journal that displays a prodigal daughter returning to the Lord and a woman outside the covenant community being brought to saving faith. It is a journal that displays God's hand of providence in the lives of three main people—Naomi, Ruth, and Boaz—in order to bring about redemption and kingship. It is a journal that displays the faithful God bringing Naomi from empty to full. It is a journal that displays God's covenantal lovingkindness to his people in the midst of difficult circumstances. It is a journal that displays Naomi and Ruth learning how to wait for God's timing. It is a journal that displays God's faithfulness to ordain a marriage and to bless a couple with a child. It is a journal that displays God's faithfulness to preserve his chosen family line in order to bring forth King David and King Jesus Christ. But most importantly, a journal that displays that in this King, Jesus Christ, there is a Redeemer who preserves the name of those who belong to God's family and buys back their inheritance that they lost in the garden of Eden.

PURPOSE

The purpose of Ruth can be seen throughout the book: "In the days when the judges ruled there was a famine in the land. . . . and Jesse fathered David" (1:1; 4:22). At the beginning of the book we are reminded that the events of the book took place during the time of the judges, which was when "there was no king in Israel. Everyone did what was right in his own eyes" (Judg. 21:25). Thus the book of Ruth is the story of God's providential working to usher in his chosen king for Israel, King David, which in turn points to the final and perfect Davidic king, Jesus Christ.

We also see repeatedly in chapter 1 the Hebrew word for "return," which we meet again in chapter 4 (4:15; translated as "restorer of life" in the ESV[1]). The book of Ruth is in part a story of how God returns

---

1. The Hebrew verb, *shub*, translated in the ESV in Ruth 1 as "return," "turn back," "go," "bring back," "gone back," "brought me back," is found twelve times (vv. 6, 7, 8, 10, 11, 12, 15

a prodigal woman to himself, which is part of the larger story of the entire Bible of how God returns a prodigal people to himself through his Son, Jesus Christ.

We also see in chapter 1 a Gentile conversion. Ruth's words, "Your people shall be my people, and your God my God" (1:16), reflect God's own covenantal language in Scripture, "I will be your God and you will be my people." The book of Ruth displays God's plan to reconcile a people to himself from every tribe, tongue, and nation.

We see in chapter 2 God's providence displayed. The book of Ruth reveals that, though largely hidden to us, God is orchestrating every detail of our lives. The book of Ruth teaches us that God's hand of providence is working in our lives as well and leads us to deeper faith and trust in the Providential God.

We see in chapter 3 that even when we run ahead of God's timing and try to accomplish his plan in our own ways, we still cannot thwart his ultimate plan. We see that there is a Redeemer. Not just the nearer relative, not just Boaz, but Jesus Christ. He is the final and perfect Redeemer. We no longer have to wait to see how the matter will turn out, for the matter has already been settled on the cross of Calvary. Jesus Christ bought us with his precious blood. We have been redeemed; we have been reconciled to God. We see in chapter 4 that just as Boaz, Ruth and Naomi's redeemer, preserved the name of Elimelech's family and bought back their inheritance, so too our Redeemer, Jesus Christ, has preserved the name of those who belong to his family by fulfilling God's commands perfectly during his life on earth and by being obedient unto death; he has bought back our inheritance by his precious blood. Thus he was crowned as King of Kings and Lord of Lords after he ascended to the Father, being given a name that is above every other name. He is the final and perfect Davidic king.

The book of Ruth is the gospel story. God the Father sent his Son into the world to return a prodigal people to himself, to preserve the

---

[twice], 16, 21, 22 [twice]). In 4:15 it is the Hiphil participle in the Hebrew translated "restorer of life." Robert L. Hubbard Jr., *The Book of Ruth*, The New International Commentary on the Old Testament (Grand Rapids: Eerdmans, 1988), 128, 271–72.

name of those who belong to his family and buy back their inheritance. There is a Redeemer!

AUTHOR

Though the human author of the book is unknown, the divine author is not.

> All Scripture is breathed out by God and profitable for teaching, for reproof, for correction, and for training in righteousness, that the man of God may be complete, equipped for every good work. (2 Tim. 3:16–17)

Whoever the human author was, the Lord mightily used their skill in masterful storytelling, their knowledge of the Abrahamic covenant, and their recognition of God's hand of providence in order to display the truth of Romans 8:28, "For those who love God all things work together for good, for those who are called according to his purpose"; the truth of Ephesians 1:7–8, 11,

> In [Christ] we have redemption through his blood, the forgiveness of our trespasses, according to the riches of his grace, which he lavished upon us, in all wisdom and insight. . . . In [Christ] we have obtained an inheritance, having been predestined according to the purpose of him who works all things according to the counsel of his will[;]

and the truth of Genesis 12:3, "And in [Abraham] all the families of the earth shall be blessed."

DATE

Like the author, the date is also unknown, but since the genealogy of David is included in the book, it would have to be after the time of David's enthronement as king. Also, because the author looks back on the day of the judges (1:1) and finds it necessary to explain the former custom in Israel of attestation (4:7), he is evidently writing some time after this period. Scholars have noted that the classical Hebrew used in the book seems to point to a preexilic date, which would not be any later than the seventh century B.C.[2]

HISTORICAL BACKGROUND OF RUTH

In order to understand the book of Ruth, we need to first go back to the book of Genesis. When God created Adam and Eve, he placed them in the garden of Eden and told them to "be fruitful and multiply and fill the earth and subdue it" (Gen. 1:28). But before the first man and woman accomplished this task, they sinned. And with sin came exile from the garden and curses pronounced on the serpent, Eve, and Adam. Within the exile and curses, though, we see God's grace. First, he told Satan that he would put enmity between him and the woman, and between his seed and her seed; her seed would bruise his head, but Satan would bruise his heel (Gen. 3:15). Second, God could have immediately killed Adam and Eve for their disobedience, but instead he clothed them with garments of skins and sent them out from the garden (Gen. 3:21, 24). But the command to be fruitful and multiply and fill the earth and subdue it was still in effect, as is clearly seen from the reiteration of it in the Noahic covenant (Gen. 9:1). Here we already see the key themes of land and seed that become so prominent in the Abrahamic covenant and in the plan of redemption.

In Genesis 12 we learn of the call of Abraham and that God's plan of redemption is going to come through a family line. God tells Abraham that he is going to make of him a great nation, that he is going to bless him and make his name great so that he will be a blessing, that he will bless those who bless him and curse those who dishonor him, and that in him all the families of the earth will be blessed (Gen. 12:2–3). "The promise that Abraham will become a great nation, implying both numerous seed and land, must be understood as being subservient to God's principal desire to bless all the families of the earth."[3]

2. Joyce Baldwin, "Ruth," in *New Bible Commentary*, 4th ed., ed. G. J. Wenham et al. (1994; repr., Downers Grove, IL: IVP Academic, 2008), 287.

3. T. D. Alexander, *From Paradise to the Promised Land: An Introduction to the Pentateuch* (Grand Rapids: Baker Academic, 2002), 146.

In Genesis 15 God makes a covenant with Abraham, and we see for the first time the key words "land" and "offspring" (seed) used in God's promises to Abraham. God promised to give Abraham numerous offspring and promised to give him the land of Canaan for his possession. When Abraham asked how he would know that he would possess it, the Lord God responded by making a covenant with Abraham; God alone passed between the cut pieces of the heifer, goat, and ram, guaranteeing the covenant himself.

In Genesis 17 God institutes an official seal of the covenant, circumcision, in order to confirm the covenant. Again we see the key words "land" and "offspring" (seed). The difference between this phase of the covenant and the previous one is that this one is conditioned on Abraham's walking in blamelessness before the Lord (17:1–2). Second, circumcision is an everlasting sign that emphasizes a special relationship between Abraham's seed and God (17:7, 10–14). Third, the focus is primarily on Abraham as the father of many nations; God is going to make Abraham and his descendants a light to the nations.

In Genesis 22 God swears to his covenant promises in order to make his unchanging nature of purpose clear to the heirs of what was promised in the Abrahamic covenant. Since Abraham was willing to sacrifice his only son, Isaac, he displayed that he was willing to walk before the Lord in blamelessness and obedience, the requirements of the covenant of circumcision. Thus God gives his divine oath, which includes many descendants, the possession of land, and that all nations would be blessed through his seed (singular), Jesus Christ (22:16–18).

These key themes of land, seed, and God's principal desire to bless all the families of the earth are also key themes in the book of Ruth, as we will clearly see as we move through this study. The book of Ruth moves God's plan of redemption through Abraham's family line forward, as God uses Ruth and Boaz to continue the line of seed, leading to king David, and then to *the seed* and *the King*, Jesus Christ.

Under the leadership of Moses and the giving of the law at Mount Sinai, Israel became a theocratic nation. They were to be a kingdom of priests and a holy nation (Ex. 19:6). And God clearly told them that if they disobeyed, they would experience curses (Deut. 28:15–68). After Moses died, God raised up Joshua to lead his people into the Promised Land, the land that the Lord was giving them in fulfillment of the Abrahamic promise (Gen. 12:1, 5–7; 15:18). But there were certain instructions that the Lord gave the people. First and foremost, they were to be careful to do according to all the law that Moses, God's servant, had commanded them (Josh. 1:7). They were to meditate on the book of the law day and night, to be careful to do according to all that was written in it so that they would have good success (Josh. 1:8). Second, they were to be strong and courageous as they subdued the land, just as the Lord had commanded them (Josh. 1:9). And the people told Joshua, "All that you have commanded us we will do, and wherever you send us we will go. Just as we obeyed Moses in all things, so we will obey you" (Josh. 1:16–17).

After Joshua died, the land was still not completely subdued of Israel's enemies. So the people asked the Lord who should go up first against the Canaanites to fight against them (Judg. 1:1). He told them that Judah should go up and he would give the land into his hand. Judah did this, but not all the tribes drove out the Canaanites, so there was a failure by Israel to conquer the land. They failed to obey God's words: "You shall make no covenant with the inhabitants of this land; you shall break down their altars" (Judg. 2:2). So the Lord said, "I will not drive them out before you, but they shall become thorns in your sides, and their gods shall be a snare to you" (Judg. 2:3). The generation that arose after Joshua and his generation did not know the Lord or the work that he had done for Israel (Judg. 2:10), so they did evil in the sight of the Lord, served the Baals, and abandoned the Lord who had delivered them from Egypt (Judg. 2:11–12). So the Lord gave them over to plunderers who plundered them, and he sold them into the hand of their surrounding enemies, so that they could no longer withstand their enemies (Judg. 2:14). They were in terrible distress (Judg. 2:15).

So God, in his grace, "raised up judges, who saved them out of the hand of those who plundered them. Yet they did not listen to their judges, for they whored after other gods and bowed down to them"

(Judg. 2:16–17). Repeatedly throughout the book of Judges, the words appear, "and the people of Israel did what was evil in the sight of the Lord" (2:11; 3:7; 3:12; 4:1; 6:1; 13:1) and "in those days there was no king in Israel" (18:1; 19:1; 21:25). The latter reference adds, "Everyone did what was right in his own eyes."

It is during this dark time that the story of Ruth takes place. This is extremely significant on several accounts. First, the book displays that the Lord has not completely abandoned his people. He is blessing those who look to him in faith. Second, the Lord is faithful to his promise to Abraham. He is still fulfilling his promise of seed (offspring), of land, of the blessing of a covenantal relationship with him, and of the blessing of all the families of the earth through his people. Third, the Lord is accomplishing his plan of bringing forth a king for his people, not just King David, but also and ultimately the King of Kings, his Son, Jesus Christ. Fourth, the Lord is displaying his plan of redemption and reconciliation for his prodigal people through the lives of Naomi, Ruth, and Boaz. Fifth, the Lord is displaying his *hesed*, his covenant faithfulness and mercy through the lives of this small family in Bethlehem, not only for their benefit, but for the benefit of generations to come, that they might know the Covenant God and trust him, serve him, and bring glory and honor to his name.

STRUCTURE AND GENRE OF RUTH

Conservative scholars usually call the book of Ruth a historical short story. Some have identified it with pastoral literature since so much of it centers around home and family life, faith, the harvests, love, and community. The repetition of certain words throughout the book serves to emphasize key themes the author is pointing out to the audience that would have heard the book of Ruth read. Overall, the structure is one in which the plot line leads us from seeming tragedy to resolutions of obstacles, especially climaxing in chapter 4 with the resolution of the kinsman-redeemer, and ending on a happy note, followed by a significant genealogy emphasizing the key to the book.

THEOLOGY

As we study the theology of Ruth . . .

1. We need to remember to read it with a covenantal perspective in mind.
2. We need to seek to understand what the book is teaching us about God.
3. We need to seek to understand what the book is teaching us about his Son, Jesus Christ.
4. We need to seek to understand what the book is teaching us about God's covenant with his people.
5. We need to seek to understand how the book helps to further reveal God's covenantal story of redemption and restoration.
6. We need to seek to understand how the Holy Spirit would have us apply what we have learned to our own lives.

First, God is fulfilling his covenant promises. The central aspect of God's covenant is, "I will be their God and they shall be my people." Certainly God's people need to be reminded of this most when they are in the time of the judges. The book of Ruth reminds God's people that they are still his and encourages them that God had a plan to redeem them from their waywardness and bring them a king, ultimately the Redeemer and King, Jesus Christ.

- *The Covenant of Creation.* God made a covenant with Adam to be fruitful and multiply and fill the earth and subdue it and have dominion over the fish, the birds, and every living thing that moves on the earth. The fall did not annul our responsibility to multiply, subdue, and offer our work to the glory of God. The book of Ruth displays the covenant of creation as God's people work the land during the harvest, as Ruth and Boaz marry and bring forth a child, and as the townspeople and elders give them a strong blessing to do so.
- *God's Covenant with Adam.* At the same time that God pronounced a curse on the serpent for deceiving Eve, on Eve for

eating of the fruit, and on Adam for taking the fruit from Eve and eating it, God also promised that he would redeem a people for himself. This finds complete fulfillment in Christ, who at the same time he took on the curses of the old covenant also inaugurated the new covenant. Though Satan would bruise Christ's heel by his suffering on the cross, Christ would bruise his head by complete victory on the cross. God both initiated the enmity between the offspring of the woman (the redeemed line) and the serpent (the unredeemed line), and assured the victory of the seed of the woman (Jesus Christ). The book of Ruth displays this struggle between the godly and ungodly lines (Ruth and Orpah respectively; Boaz and Mr. So-and-So respectively), and God's preservation and victory of the redeemed, as seen most clearly and comprehensively in the book's closing genealogy.

- *God's Covenant with Noah.* In God's covenant with Noah, he both displays his judgment against sinful humanity and his grace on his children. By preserving the world, the stage is set for the Redeemer to come and God's presence among his people to be fully realized. The book of Ruth displays God's preservation of the world and his common grace among all peoples. We also see from the harvests God's promise: "While the earth remains, seedtime and harvest, cold and heat, summer and winter, day and night, shall not cease" (Gen. 8:22).

- *God's Covenant with Abraham.* The Lord promised Abraham land, offspring, blessing, blessings on all nations through him, and a curse on those who cursed Abraham. The book of Ruth displays God's promise to bless all the families of the earth through Abraham. Indeed he even used a family that was not looking to him solely for provision to bring a Moabite into the people of God. We also see the blessing of being in covenantal relationship with the Lord in the book. As Ruth and Boaz displayed covenant faithfulness and love to the Lord and to their neighbor, they were blessed. We also see the promise of offspring/ seed in (1) the continuation of Elimelech's line by way of Boaz redeeming Ruth, (2) carrying on Elimelech's line with the birth of their first son, Obed, (3) the genealogy of David, and (4) the fact that David's genealogy points forward toward the birth of Jesus Christ.

- *God's Covenant with Moses.* The law was added to govern a theocratic nation to be a kingdom and priests in the land. In the days of the judges, we see the need of the people (who failed to function as a theocratic nation and failed to obey God's laws) to have a king and a redeemer. With the failure of the people and the judges, the stage was set for King David to step onto the scene, to assemble the chosen people of God as a nation under his kingly rule, ultimately pointing to Jesus Christ as the final and perfect Davidic king. Most likely, the famine that we read about in Ruth 1 is a curse for the people's disobedience during the days of the judges (Deut. 28:15–68), but evidently many in Bethlehem turned back to the Lord in faith, for "the LORD had visited his people and given them food" (Ruth 1:6).

- *God's Covenant with David.* God promised an eternal kingdom and king on the throne, which are both fulfilled in Jesus Christ as King of Kings and Lord of Lords. The redeemed make up the kingdom of God, which is inaugurated in the present age, but will not be consummated until Christ's second coming. The book of Ruth points forward to the Davidic king, as it tells the story of King David's great-grandmother and great-grandfather. Ultimately the book points forward to the final and perfect Davidic king, Jesus Christ.

- *The New Covenant.* God promised the indwelling of the Holy Spirit within his people, forgiveness of sins, the law written on the heart and mind, and personal knowledge of God. The book of Ruth points to the need of redemption and the need of a final and perfect King, which culminates in the new covenant, where all the promises of God find their yes in Christ (2 Cor. 1:20).

225

Second, the book teaches us that God is providentially working in the lives of his people in order to accomplish his redemptive-historical plan. The book also teaches us about God's *hesed*, his covenantal faithfulness, love, and mercy toward his people.

Third, Jesus Christ is the Redeemer of redeemers. He is the King of Kings. He has preserved the name of those who belong to God's family, and has bought back their inheritance.

Fourth, God is faithful to fulfill his covenant promises to his people in that he preserved his people through the time of the judges and was bringing them a king, ultimately *the* King. He blessed his people with his *hesed*. He blessed his people with harvests in the land of Bethlehem. He blessed Ruth and Boaz with offspring in the birth of Obed.

Fifth, the book of Ruth displays another step in redemptive-historical history that culminates in Jesus Christ. This is part of the background of Christ's family line. Ruth and Boaz are found in the genealogy of Jesus Christ (Matt. 1:1–17). The book of Ruth also points forward to redemption in Jesus Christ. It points toward Christ's work on the cross, in which he preserved the name of those who belong to God's family and bought back their inheritance. It also points forward to the Davidic king, ultimately fulfilled in Jesus Christ. It also points forward to the dividing wall between Jew and Gentile being removed through the cross, as Ruth the Moabite is included in the people of God.

Sixth, the Holy Spirit wants us to apply this to our lives in many ways that will be discussed throughout this study. But I think the ones that come to the forefront are to remember that (1) God is providentially at work in the lives of his people, (2) he causes all things to work together for good for those who love him, (3) he preserves a people for himself through family lines, and (4) he displays his *hesed* through his people in order to bring people from every tribe, tongue, and nation to himself.

CONCLUSION

As you open up the book of Ruth over the next few weeks, remember that this is not just anyone's journal. This is God's book, the voice of the living God speaking to you. Don't miss what he is saying through the

book of Ruth. Don't miss his invitation to a life of fullness from emptiness. Don't miss his compassionate and faithful arms outstretched to a
prodigal daughter, inviting her to return to him. Don't miss the mighty
act of regeneration that he accomplishes in the life of a Gentile. Don't
miss the providential hand of God orchestrating events of his children's
lives. Don't miss the provision and protection of what could have been
disastrous, but wasn't. Don't miss the faithfulness of God to provide
a redeemer and a child. But ultimately, don't miss the covenantal love
and faithfulness of God to provide a Redeemer in Jesus, his own Son,
and not just a Redeemer, but also a king, the King of Kings and Lord
of Lords, Jesus Christ. May the book of Ruth lead us on to know the
only true and triune God more so that we can worship him and glorify
him for his mighty acts of redemption and deliverance in the lives of
his people, including ours.

Ruth 1

Please use the question paradigm from pages 301–2 as you work through the following. See the introductory comments there that explain each part of the process below in more detail.

- **Pray.**
- **Ponder the Passage.** Read Ruth 1 once a day from different translations for the entire week, looking for its:
  - Point
  - Persons
  - Problem
  - Patterns
  - Persons of the Trinity
  - Puzzling Parts
- **Put It in Perspective.**
  - Place in Scripture. Skim Judges 1:1–3:6.
  - Passages from Other Parts of Scripture

1. Based on your observations of the text, what is the basic content of this passage? Try to summarize it in your own words, using a sentence or two.

2. What was it like in the days when the judges ruled? Read Judges 2:11–3:6; 18:1; 19:1; 21:25. What need does this reveal for Israel? How does this relate to the closing verses of the book of Ruth? How does this in turn relate to Matthew 1:1–17?

3. In view of the historical context of the book of Ruth, why might there be famine in the land? Skim Deuteronomy 28:15–68.

4. Why should Elimelech have remained in the Promised Land rather than going to Moab? Read Joshua 1:10–16. What is the history between Israel and Moab that gives even further reason for not going to Moab? Read Genesis 19:30–38; Numbers 22–24; 25:1–9; Deuteronomy 23:3–6; Judges 3:15–30.

5. Using a study Bible or Bible dictionary, what are the meanings or possible meanings of the names Elimelech, Naomi, Mahlon, Chilion, Orpah, and Ruth?

6. Look up "Ephrathites" in a Bible concordance. What do you learn? What do you learn about the significance of Bethlehem in Scripture? Look up 1 Samuel 16:1, 18; Matthew 2:1. Using a study Bible or Bible dictionary, what does Bethlehem mean? How does this relate to the book of Ruth?

7. Why should Mahlon and Chilion not have taken Moabite wives? Read Deuteronomy 7:3; 23:3–6.

8. What is the irony between Naomi's situation in 1:1 and at least ten years later in 1:5? Has the journey to Moab accomplished what this family thought it would?

9. Why does Naomi return to Bethlehem? What does this signify happened in that city? Read Deuteronomy 30:2–3, 9. What does this reveal about God's character?

10. Look up the word "return" in a concordance or study Bible. How many times is it used in this chapter? What is its meaning? How else is it used in the Old Testament? How does it relate to the theme of this chapter?

11. Look at the location of Moab and Bethlehem on a map of the Bible lands. How far a journey would this have been for these women?

12. How many times does Naomi tell Orpah and Ruth to return to Moab? How many more times does she tell just Ruth after Orpah has turned back? What is her reasoning for urging them to return (1:8–9)? How does she want the Lord to deal with them? Look up "kindly" in a Bible concordance or dictionary. What do you learn? What does she want them to find? Where is this ultimately found (Heb. 4)?

13. How do Ruth and Orpah respond the first time to Naomi's request? How do they respond the second time? What is Ruth's reason for staying with Naomi? Compare her words to the Lord's words in Genesis 17:7–8; Exodus 6:7; Leviticus 26:12. How is the covenant displayed in these verses? Also read Matthew 19:29. How does Ruth embody this?

14. What is Naomi's response after these beautiful words of covenant commitment grounded in a conversion to the Covenant God of Israel?

15. Compare 1:19 with Matthew 21:10. In light of Matthew 1:1–7 and the closing verses of the book of Ruth, how are these events connected?

16. How does the town respond to Naomi and Ruth's arrival? How does Naomi respond to the women's question, "Is this Naomi?"

17. Compare 1:1 with 1:22. How do the circumstances of the land portray God's graciousness (Deut. 30:2–3, 9) and his covenant of preservation made with Noah (Gen. 8:22)?

- **Principles and Points of Application.**
  1. We can all identify with Elimelech and Naomi at some point or another in our lives. We bear the name Christian, but do we really live with Christ as the Lord of our lives? In what "famine" does the Lord have you right now that you need to run toward him rather than away from him?
  2. From where are you seeking rest right now in your circumstances? Read Hebrews 4; Matthew 11:28–29. Where should

you find rest? Lay your circumstances before the Lord today and rest in him.

3. Who are the "Moabites" that God has brought into our lives? Are we seizing the opportunity to share the gospel with them? Pray and ask God this week to reveal to you whom he wants you to share the gospel with, and then follow him in obedience.

4. All of us are faced with the same choice as Orpah and Ruth. We can either live in the land of faithfulness to the true and living God or we can follow the ways of the world's wisdom and never enter eternal rest with Jesus Christ. Have you ever made the choice to cling to the true and living God? If so, how do your actions testify to your faith?

5. What relationship in your life do you need to ground in Christ? Who is hard for you to love right now? Ask God to give you the grace to cling to him first so that you are able to cling to them, displaying his lovingkindness toward them.

6. How does your life reflect the cost of discipleship (Matt. 16:24; 19:29)? If not, why not?

7. How do we respond to famines in our own lives, to times where it seems as if the Lord is totally emptying us of everything? Do we display bitterness? Or do we pour out our hearts in honest emotion before the Lord? Do we recognize that the way to eternal glory is through suffering, just as it was for our Lord and Savior Jesus Christ? Do we offer our suffering to him as a sacrifice of praise and worship? Take your emptiness to the Lord today and cry out to him, asking him to fill you with the joy of his presence and to use your emptiness to show his fullness to those around you.

NOTES FOR RUTH 1

Ponder the aim of this lesson concerning our:

Mind: What do we need to know from this passage in Scripture?

God often uses suffering in order to move his redemptive purposes forward, return people to faithfulness toward him, and bring the fullness of blessings to his people.

Heart: How does what we learn from this passage affect our internal relationship with the Lord?

It prepares us to be kingdom disciples who turn to God in every circumstance of our lives, especially times of suffering, in order to display his glory of bringing fullness from famine.

Hands: How does what we learn from this passage translate into action for God's kingdom?

It enables us to:

1. Turn to God during times of famine and barrenness in our lives and trust his lovingkindness in the midst of suffering.
2. Give thanks when God reverses our times of famine to times of fullness.
3. Find rest in the house of the Lord rather than in the things of this world.
4. Respond to suffering in our lives by recognizing God's hand of sovereignty along with his hand of grace, and to help others do the same.
5. Ground our relationships with our spouses, children, parents, in-laws, etc., in the Lord so that we can embody God's loving-kindness to them.
6. Lay any hardships before the Lord, asking him to redeem them for his glory and our good.
7. Uphold those in our lives with fledgling faith by sharing the love of Christ with them and the promises of his covenant.
8. Share Christ with the "Moabites" in our lives who have never heard the name of Jesus or called on him in saving faith.

INTRODUCTION

My first ministry position out of seminary brought me from Dallas back to the Atlanta area where I bought my first home. I was single and missing the elderly whom I had lived with and ministered to in a retirement home while going to seminary, but the Lord graciously provided me with another older woman to befriend and to befriend me in my new neighborhood. Widowed relatively early in life, she still had four children who were taking care of her, but none of them were as close as I was to her for a visit. Thus I became one of her "daughters." And after I did marry and have children, my children became her "grandchildren."

I loved to regularly visit my older friend. I loved to see the response on her face when she opened the door after a long, lonely day within four walls where there was nothing but the sound of the television to keep her company. I loved to hear the stories of her family, those memories that were distant but kept her going each and every day. I was able to put my life circumstances in better perspective after leaving her, but one thing that I had that she didn't was a strong faith.

Though at one time my friend had been an active member of a church that preached the Word of God faithfully, the Jehovah's Witnesses had attracted her attention by their love for one another in their communities, and she had become involved with them, even opening up her home on a weekly basis to have a Bible study with them. This distressed me, so I began praying for my friend and engaging in discussions with her about the Christian faith and about Jehovah's Witnesses. I was able to share my concern for her, let her know that I disagreed with the beliefs of Jehovah's Witnesses, and tell her that I was praying for her. She would not have accepted my words except that I had a relationship with her that I was faithful to continue on a regular basis, and the Holy Spirit was working through it. I knew that the Lord had placed me in her life to embody his call for her to return to him.

We see a similar pattern in Ruth 1. God uses Ruth to strengthen Naomi's fledgling faith. He uses her to embody his call for her to return to him. He uses Ruth to display his covenantal love and grace in Naomi's life.

We can divide the lesson into three sections:

I. Turning from Bethlehem to Moab (1:1–5)
II. The Return Journey from Moab to Bethlehem (1:6–18)
III. The Return Arrival in Bethlehem (1:19–22)

I. Turning from Bethlehem to Moab (1:1–5)

The opening phrase, "In the days when the judges ruled there was a famine in the land" (1:1), is crucial not just for the chronological and political context, but also and most importantly for the theological context of the book of Ruth. First, this is the first time in the book that "land" is mentioned. We looked at the significance of this in the introduction with regard to how it relates to the Abrahamic covenant. Second, the book of Judges begins by recounting the fact that during the days of Joshua, Israel, who had seen all the work that the Lord had done for them, served the Lord. But after Joshua and his generation died, there arose another generation who didn't know the Lord or the work that he had done for Israel. Thus the people did evil and served the Baals, abandoned the Lord, and provoked the Lord to anger. So he gave them over to plunderers and sold them into the hand of their enemies. Then the Lord raised up judges who saved them out of the hand of those who plundered them, displaying his grace and mercy even during a time of rebelliousness. For the Lord was moved to pity by Israel's groaning. We see a cycle in the book of Judges of Israel's disobedience, their crying out to the Lord, and the Lord's raising up deliverers by way of judges (Judg. 2:8–3:15). The book of Judges ends with the phrase, "In those days there was no king in Israel. Everyone did what was right in his own eyes" (21:25). This same phrase (or parts of it) is seen in Judges 17:6; 18:1; 19:1, in order to emphasize the ungodliness in Israel at the time. So the time of the judges clearly points to the need for a king in Israel. And the book of Ruth reveals how one family is used to bring this king into being.

But the time of the judges being one of rebellion and disobedience, also possibly and probably points to the reason why there was a famine

235

in Bethlehem (literally, "House of bread"), one of the most fertile regions of the land. Bethlehem is most closely associated with the life of King David and then with the life of our King, Jesus Christ, in Scripture. It served as the birthplace for both of them. When God made a covenant with Israel at Mount Sinai (the Mosaic covenant), he made it very clear that obedience would result in blessing in the Promised Land, but disobedience would result in curses and eventually exile from the land. Deuteronomy 28:15–52 clearly includes famine as one form of the curses.

It was during this time of rebellion and disobedience that a man of Bethlehem in Judah, of the clan of Ephrath, went to sojourn in the country of Moab. Elimelech was living in the time after God had brought his people into the Promised Land and given each tribe an inheritance of the land. He was living after the time of the Mosaic covenant when Israel knew disobedience would bring the curse of famine. Thus, when Elimelech left for Moab he was turning his back on the inheritance that the Lord had given him. He was turning his back on the chastening hand of the Lord. He was turning his back on the Lord's timing for provision. And he was turning toward his own plan of provision in a land of ungodliness. Elimelech, whose very name meant "My God is king," was forsaking his role of servant of the King and placing himself on the throne instead.[1]

We can all identify with Elimelech and Naomi at some point or another in our lives. We bear the name Christian, but do we really live with Christ as the Lord of our lives? So often we want what we want when we want it and take the best action that will seem to get our desired result. Waiting for the Lord's timing is difficult, enduring the chastening hand of the Lord can be painful, and so we run away from the very shelter of his wings. We run to our own "Moab." What are you running away from today? Where are you running? Return to the shelter of the Lord today, submitting to his timing to provide you with what you need.

Moab was not the place for a God-fearing Jew to take his family. The history of Moab begins with the incestuous relationship between

---

1. Iain M. Duguid, *Esther and Ruth*, Reformed Expository Commentary (Phillipsburg, NJ: P&R Publishing, 2005), 132–33.

Lot and his firstborn daughter in a cave after the destruction of Sodom. It was out of fear that there was no offspring to preserve the family line that Lot's daughters came up with the plan to get their father drunk so that they could lie with him (Gen. 19:30–38). The Moabites were also the people who did not meet the Israelites with bread and water when they came out of Egypt (Deut. 23:4), and Balak, king of Moab, hired Balaam to pronounce a curse on them (Num. 22–24). So God forbid them to seek a treaty of friendship with them as long as they lived (Deut. 23:3–6). Also, while Israel lived at Shittim, they began to "whore with the daughters of Moab." These women invited the Israelites to the sacrifices of their gods, and Israel joined with Baal of Peor, bringing great judgment from God in the form of a plague (Num. 25:1–9). Finally, there had been recent enslavement to the king of Moab for eighteen years as a judgment from the Lord for the evil that Israel had done (Judg. 3:12–14), but when the people cried out to the Lord he delivered them by way of Ehud (Judg. 3:15). As we can see, then, taking one's family to Moab was not leading them to paths of righteousness! And, as we will see, it had serious ramifications.

We have no way of knowing how Naomi felt about her husband's leading them to Moab, but the fact that she stayed there about ten years after he passed away most likely indicates that she was in support of his decision. Her sons' marriages to two Moabite women, Orpah and Ruth, was not within God's will, for they were not to intermarry with those who served other gods (Deut. 7:3; 23:3–6). Although the text does not explicitly say it, we cannot help but wonder if the deaths of Elimelech, Mahlon, and Chilion are a judgment for their unfaithfulness to God. Because they were living during the time of the theocratic nation of Israel, Elimelech was supposed to stay in Bethlehem. And God very clearly brought judgment on those who disobeyed his law (Deut. 28:15–68). Regardless, God chose to spare Naomi and her two daughters-in-law. He preserved the lives of these three women, and in doing so he displayed his grace. He was preserving these women for the purpose of his glorious plan to save a people for himself. For as we will see, God used Naomi and Ruth as instruments in bringing both King David and the King of Kings, Jesus Christ, into the world.

Before leaving this section, let us reflect for a moment on Naomi's lot in life. She, along with her husband and two sons, had turned away from the land of God's favor to a pagan land. And for ten years she had lived in the midst of a pagan people. We have no way of knowing how this affected her, but we can be certain that it did not strengthen her faith. She had removed herself from the people of God and the Promised Land of God. But during these ten years she had also experienced tremendous grief. Not only had she turned away from the Lord, but also she felt that the Lord had turned away from her (1:21). She not only buried a husband, but buried two sons as well. Think about that for a moment: this woman had wept over the gravesides of three men who were nearest and dearest to her. Now she was left alone as a foreigner in a pagan land. Not unlike the Prodigal Son (Luke 15:11–32), Naomi was alone in a far country without anything. But wait, the stage is set for the arms of the compassionate Father to reach out and welcome her home.

Can you relate to Naomi today? Or do you know a loved one who could? The compassionate Father still reaches out his arms to welcome us home. Run to him and return to him today. Pray for your loved ones who are far from him to do the same.

II. The Return Journey from Moab to Bethlehem (1:6–18)

Verse 6 introduces us to the key theme of the chapter by the first of twelve uses in chapter 1 of the Hebrew verb *shub*, meaning "return, turn back, gone back, brought back" in Ruth 1 and in Jeremiah 15:19, where the Covenant Lord promises to restore his people if they repent, and in Ezekiel 14:6; 18:30, 32, where the Covenant God commands his people to repent. Whenever an author uses a verb that many times, especially in Old Testament narrative, we should take notice. What does this have to do with the story? As we will see, God is turning the heart of his prodigal daughter, Naomi, back to him, while at the same time turning the heart of Ruth from a different tribe, tongue, and nation to himself for saving faith.[2] And in the process he uses an unnamed person who proclaimed within earshot of Naomi that the Lord had visited his people and given them food. This is the first of two times in the entire book that the narrator explicitly states God has acted (see also 4:13). Given the context of Ruth, we can conclude that God's people must have turned their hearts back to the Lord in order for the famine to be lifted. Thus Naomi is headed back to a city that has already displayed for her what she also needs to do: repent and return to the land of blessing.

Evidently during the ten years that Naomi was in Moab, she had not turned her back totally on the Lord and embraced the Moabite god of Chemosh, for she set out on the way to the land of Judah to return to the Promised Land. This was a significant trip, for it would have been seventy to one hundred miles and would have taken at least a week. This is the second time that the word "land" is used in the book, again reminding us of the key theme of land that finds its roots in God's covenant with Adam and God's covenant with Abraham.

Somewhere along the way, Naomi urges her daughters-in-law to return to their mothers' houses. Those of us thinking from an evangelistic perspective may be cringing at this point. Here Naomi has an incredible opportunity to be a witness to two foreign women who were raised in a land that worshiped other gods, and she blows it. She urges them to go back to their paganism! But it is evident from the text that Naomi is not in this frame of mind. Instead, she speaks with love and compassion out of a desire for her two daughters-in-law to feel the kindness of the Lord that she no longer feels. This word "kindness" is extremely significant. It is the word *hesed* in the Hebrew, and it recurs throughout the book (1:8; 2:20; 3:10). This word is used in the Old Testament to describe God's covenant love. It refers to his promise to preserve a people for himself despite their sinfulness and rebelliousness. Ultimately it is displayed in the gracious gift of his Son, Jesus Christ, in order to reconcile his people to himself. It is his utmost loyalty to his own people even when they are not loyal. It is his display of longsuffering for a wayward people.

2. Sinclair B. Ferguson, *Faithful God: An Exposition of the Book of Ruth* (2005; repr., Bryntirion, UK: Bryntirion, 2009), 25–26.

Naomi also wants her daughters-in-law to find the rest that she no longer has or feels that she can provide for them. Indeed we see this same language on the lips of Rahab when she speaks with the Israelite spies (Josh. 2:12) and on the lips of the spies when they agree to treat Rahab with faithfulness and kindness (Josh. 2:14). We will also see this same language later in the book (2:20) on the lips of Naomi to bless Boaz.

It is possible that because she could not see God's hand of goodness toward her, Naomi did not believe that he could provide rest for these Moabite women either. One could read the text as if she seemed to give the gods of Moab more credit than Yahweh to provide rest for them, and in this she would be wrong.[3] But she may also be holding out a challenge to them of the cost of discipleship, especially in light of her own circumstances of suffering.[4]

The theme of "rest" that is introduced here is a key theme of the book. It will be picked up again in 3:1 when Naomi continues to feel the burden to find rest for Ruth in a husband for her. Ultimately this search for rest can only be resolved by the Sabbath rest that God holds out to each one of his children (Heb. 4). Where are we seeking rest right now in our circumstances? Do we think we will find it in a location? Do we think we will find it in a relationship? God's Word is clear that true rest is found in Christ alone.

Who are the "Moabites" that God has brought into our lives? Are we seizing the opportunity to share the gospel with them? Pray and ask God this week to reveal to you whom he wants you to share the gospel with, and then follow him in obedience.

Either Naomi really wants Orpah and Ruth to count the cost of leaving their homeland and following her to Bethlehem or she really cannot see how God would provide for their needs in Bethlehem. For she urges them again to turn back since she is empty and feels that she has no rest to offer them, neither does she have any husband to produce any more sons for them. Perhaps Naomi remembered the story of Tamar

---

3. Dean R. Ulrich, *From Famine to Fullness: The Gospel According to Ruth*, The Gospel According to the Old Testament (Phillipsburg, NJ: P&R Publishing, 2007), 32.

4. Ferguson, *Faithful God*, 36.

who remained in her father's house as a widow, waiting until Shelah grew up. However, Tamar grew tired of waiting for Judah to make good on his promise, and so dressed as a prostitute and met him on the road. The result of this was twin boys, Perez and Zerah (Gen. 38). Naomi's only hope for her daughters-in-law at this time lies back in the land of Moab. Listen to her words: "It is exceedingly bitter to me *for your sake* that the hand of the LORD has gone out against me" (1:13). Naomi is not completely self-focused; she is grieved for her daughters-in-law as well. But her words speak of the time of the judges also, for we read in Judges 2:15 that "whenever [Israel] marched out, the hand of the LORD was against them for harm, as the LORD had warned, and as the LORD had sworn to them. And they were in terrible distress."

So Orpah chooses to go back. She chooses to turn away from the land of the Lord to the land of idolatry. And with such a choice she walks off the pages of Scripture, and remains on the outside of the Promised Land for all eternity. But Ruth, by God's grace, chooses differently. Ruth clung (the same word used in Gen. 2:24 and translated "hold fast" in the ESV for the marriage relationship) to Naomi. But she did not just cling to Naomi, as we will later see. She clings to the true and living God. This same word is also used in Deuteronomy 10:20; 13:4; and Joshua 23:8 in relation to Israel holding fast to the Lord in covenant faithfulness.

All of us are faced with the same choice as Orpah and Ruth. We can either live in the land of faithfulness with the true and living God as our Redeemer and King or we can follow the ways of the world's wisdom and never enter eternal rest with Jesus Christ. Have you ever made the choice to cling to the true and living God? If so, how do your actions testify to your faith?

The fourth time that Naomi urges Ruth to turn back brings a profession of faith by Ruth, making public to Naomi what God had already wrought in her heart—saving faith. The key to Ruth's words is found in the center of them with the phrase, "Your people shall be my people, and your God my God" (1:16). This is covenant language. If there is one way to sum up all the covenants in Scripture, it is with the phrase, "I will be your God, and you shall be my people" (Gen. 17:7–8; Ex. 6:7; Lev. 26:12). Here we see that God, in his grace, has used one of his wayward children to bring one from another nation into a covenant relationship with him. Ruth the Moabite has become part of the family of God! And in doing so, God has portrayed the mission that was first given to Adam and then to Israel and now to the New Testament church to be witnesses and ambassadors in bringing people from every tribe, tongue, and nation to him. Even Naomi recognized that she could not argue with what God had done! Or was her silence because she was not favorable toward this decision?[5] Ruth had just spoken one of the most beautiful commitments in all Scripture, and it seemed to fall on deaf and ungrateful ears. We will see how the Lord uses this new convert to display his grace and covenant love to his wavering daughter Naomi in order to strengthen her faith. Indeed the commitment that Ruth had toward the Lord was the foundation of the commitment she had to Naomi.

How different our relationships look when Christ is the foundation of them. We are only able to love our husbands and in-laws and parents and siblings well when Jesus Christ is the foundation of our commitment toward them. We are only able to love those who seem silent and ungrateful toward our commitment when we know the love of our Father in his gift of the Son. What relationship in your life do you need to ground in Christ? Who is hard for you to love right now? Ask God to give you the grace to cling to him first so that you are able to cling to them, displaying his lovingkindness toward them.

Is Ruth's commitment to the Lord without cost? Let's take a closer look at her words. First, she leaves her land. While God called Abraham out of Ur of the Chaldeans and gave him a promise, Ruth had not received a promise from God before she left Moab. Yet she was willing to leave her homeland for the Promised Land of God that she had heard about by way of Naomi's family. Certainly the Moabites had heard about the God who had delivered his people from Egypt and had most recently delivered his people from the king of Moab after eighteen years

5. Duguid, *Esther and Ruth*, 143.

of servitude (Judg. 3:12–14). Second, Ruth leaves her people. She leaves her family. Those of us who know of Muslims who have left their families to embrace the Christian faith know how costly this might have been for Ruth. Third, Ruth left her religion that she had known all her life. If her world was anything like some of the persecuted countries today, this could have cost her life. Fourth, she left any heritage of being buried in her own land behind her. Ruth exemplified what Jesus later spoke of in Matthew 19:29, "Everyone who has left houses or brothers or sisters or father or mother or children or lands, for my name's sake, will receive a hundredfold and will inherit eternal life."

How does your life reflect the cost of discipleship (Matt. 16:24; 19:29)? Whom or what have you left behind for the sake of Christ?

III. The Return Arrival in Bethlehem (1:19–22)

Except for the narrator, we would not know whether Ruth had made the entire journey with Naomi. Upon her arrival in Bethlehem, the focus is clearly on Naomi. Indeed, even Naomi's focus is on herself in her words, "The LORD has brought me back empty" (1:21). Nevertheless the text tells us that the whole town was stirred because of *them*. And it is evident from later chapters (2:6, 11–12; 3:11) that Ruth's commitment and conversion had been the talk of the town.[6]

Apparently Naomi had changed quite a bit since she had left. Ten years of grief and living outside the Promised Land had etched itself on her externally as well as internally. In fact, she won't even accept the name Naomi ("Pleasant"), because she feels that the Lord has dealt bitterly ("Mara") with her. It is important to recognize that the text does not say that Naomi was bitter, but that she felt that the Lord had been bitter toward her. Some commentators portray Naomi as shaking her fist in the face of God, lonely and angry and estranged from him. In light of the Israelites' experience at Marah, where they grumbled because of the bitter water and yet God displayed his grace to them by

6. Jerram Barrs, *Through His Eyes: God's Perspective on Women in the Bible* (Wheaton, IL: Crossway, 2009), 134.

turning it sweet (Ex. 15:25), perhaps this is the case. If so, we should be encouraged that if the Lord did that for Israel, he will graciously do that with Naomi also.

But it seems instead that Naomi has honest emotions before the Lord. Yes, she has wandered and is in need of returning to him, but her faith is still alive, however small. This is evident even from the prayers that she prayed in this chapter for her daughters-in-law. Even if they were more of habitual or polite prayers, she still prayed. It is also evident from the fact that she came back to Bethlehem, even if she thought it was the only choice she had. Why would she have returned if she didn't believe in the faithfulness of God? No, she has a similar view of her circumstances as Job's friends did of his. The Lord had testified against her going to Moab and had brought calamity on her. While it is certainly true that God judged Israel for their disobedience according to the blessings and curses of the Mosaic covenant, he has always dealt with his children by way of gracious discipline. Naomi could not yet see this. She could not yet see the Redeemer who would testify on her behalf and release her of her sentence. She could not yet see that she had really gone away from Bethlehem empty of faith and the Lord had brought her back to fill her with faith in his promises again. She could not yet see that "pleasant" was exactly what the Lord had in store for her.

How do we respond to famines in our own lives, to times when it seems as if the Lord is totally emptying us of everything? Do we accuse the Lord of dealing bitterly with us? Or do we pour out our hearts in honest emotion before him? Do we recognize that the way to eternal glory is through suffering, just as it was for our Lord and Savior Jesus Christ? Do we offer our suffering to him as a sacrifice of praise and worship? Take your emptiness to the Lord today and cry out to him, asking him to fill you with the joy of his presence and to use your emptiness to show his fullness to those around you.

Again the narrator includes Ruth the Moabite to inform us that she has indeed returned with her mother-in-law. And he gives us some very significant information concerning the timing of their return. God has brought them back not at the end, but at the beginning of the barley harvest. This was the time of the Feast of Passover, the beginning of the year on the Jewish calendar. It was one of three times a year that the Lord had commanded Israel to keep a feast to him. They were to keep the Feast of Unleavened Bread (part of Passover), the Feast of Harvest (also known as Feast of Weeks and Pentecost), which celebrated the firstfruits of their labor, and the Feast of Ingathering at the end of the year when they gathered the fruit of their labor (Ex. 23:14–16).

The Feast of Passover derived its name from what it celebrated, the Lord's act of passing over the houses of the firstborn sons of the Israelites during the tenth plague of Egypt that killed all the Egyptians' firstborn sons. The Israelites were commanded to smear the blood of the lamb on their doorposts so that the Lord would know which houses to pass over. This pointed forward to the true Lamb of God, who would take away the sin of the world by the sacrifice of his own body. His blood of redemption delivers us from death; God will pass over us on the final day of judgment because we are covered with his blood.

In the context of the chapter, the time of Passover is significant. Naomi and Ruth have just been through their own exodus from the land of Moab to the Promised Land of Bethlehem. The time of Passover, the beginning of the year, provided them with a new beginning.[7] In 1:1 we saw that Naomi left Bethlehem at the time of a famine, and it coincided with a time of famine, both spiritual and physical, in her own life as well. But now she returns to Bethlehem at the beginning of barley harvest. Will this also coincide with a harvest in her spiritual and physical life? We'll have to study on to see!

But before moving on, let us pause for a moment and reflect on how this chapter connects to the gospel. We see that Israel is in desperate need of a king and that Ruth and Naomi are in desperate need of a redeemer. With the location set in Bethlehem ("House of bread"), we are reminded of the Bread of Life who came as a baby to the humble beginnings in Bethlehem, the Redeemer and the true and final Davidic King.

We also see that Elimelech led his family away from God's will for their lives into a land of exile and emptiness in order to build their own

7. Duguid, *Esther and Ruth*, 165.

house by their own ways. But Jesus Christ followed God's will to the land of exile, away from heavenly glory, in order to experience emptiness on our behalf in order to build God's house, the church.

The covenantal language of "Your people shall be my people, and your God my God" (1:16) also points us to the gospel. For the only reason that God is our God and we are his people is because of the reconciliation that Jesus Christ has brought between the Father and us by his life, death, resurrection, and ascension.

We also see the cost of discipleship. We see that death leads to life. This is the pattern set before us by our Lord and Savior Jesus Christ. We also see that our deaths are often used in the lives of others to bring them to a saving knowledge of faith in Jesus Christ. While God is concerned about us, his plan does not revolve around us. He is weaving our paths into a larger plan that often entails suffering and challenges, not just for our sake but also for the sake of those around us.

CONCLUSION

Over time my older friend seemed to grow more and more unhappy with the Jehovah's Witnesses. As I prayed and visited, I was able to witness God's Holy Spirit at work in this woman's life, drawing her away from "other gods" and back to him, but I don't know the end of the story. Our family moved away from the neighborhood to another state, and I lost contact with my friend. But I trust that God is faithful to use men and women to embody his lovingkindness in prodigals' lives, and I trust the Lord's will for my friend's salvation. Who has God placed in your life whom you need to uphold and strengthen through prayer, love, and the sharing of the gospel? Turn toward these people in love and compassion so that they might see the love of Christ turned toward them and come to be strengthened in their faith or to believe for the very first time.

Ruth 2

Please use the question paradigm from pages 301–2 as you work through the following. See the introductory comments there that explain each part of the process below in more detail.

- **Pray.**
- **Ponder the Passage.** Read Ruth 2 once a day from different translations for the entire week, looking for its:
  - Point
  - Persons
  - Problem
  - Patterns
  - Persons of the Trinity
  - Puzzling Parts
- **Put It in Perspective.**
  - Place in Scripture. Skim Judges 1:1–3:6.
  - Passages from Other Parts of Scripture

1. Based on your observations of the text, what is the basic content of this passage? Try to summarize it in your own words, using a sentence or two.

2. Why is the statement by the narrator in 2:1 important? How does it relate to chapter 2 as a whole? Look up Deuteronomy 25:5–10. How does this relate to Ruth 2?

3. Who initiates making provision for the two widows in 2:2? In light of Ruth's commitment in 1:16–17, how does this put action to previous commitment?

4. Look up the word "gleaning" in a concordance or Bible dictionary. How does God make provision for the poor through this process?

5. How is the narrator using the phrase, "and she happened to come," in this verse (2:3)? What is really happening here? How does this relate to what we just learned in 2:1?

6. What do Boaz's words to the reapers, and their response, indicate about Boaz's faith? Look up Psalm 129:7–8.

7. Why would Boaz ask, "Whose young woman is this?" (2:5) instead of "Who is this young woman?" What might this signify?

8. How is Ruth's work ethic displayed in 2:7?

9. How does Boaz address Ruth in 2:8 (compare this also with 2:5)? How does he display both his protection and provision of her in 2:8–9?

10. How does Naomi respond to Boaz (2:10)? What terminology does she use to describe herself? How does this compare with Boaz's terminology?

11. How does Boaz answer Ruth's question in 2:11–12? Compare his prayer with Naomi's in 1:8–9. Look up Exodus 19:4. How does this prayer relate to one of God's redemptive-historical acts in history?

12. How does Ruth answer her own question in 2:13?

13. How does Boaz display his provision for Ruth in 2:14? What future meal does this point toward (see Luke 22:14–23)?

14. How does Boaz go beyond what the law requires in 2:15 (see Lev. 19:9–10)?

15. Putting the time phrase in 2:17 together with 2:7, how long has Ruth gleaned in the field? How much barley has she collected?

Look up "ephah" in a Bible dictionary or study Bible. How much barley would this have been?

16. How is Naomi's response in 2:19 telling of how much barley Ruth brought home (2:18)? What is her response toward the owner of the field (2:19)?

17. How does Naomi's prayer in 2:20 compare with what she said in 1:8? Whose kindness does Naomi say has not forsaken the living or the dead, the Lord's or Boaz's? What further information does Naomi reveal in this verse? Is this the first time the word "redeemer" is mentioned in the book? Look up the word "redeemer" in a Bible dictionary. What do you learn? To whom does this ultimately point?

18. What is Naomi's response to Boaz's protection of Ruth (staying in his field close to the young women)? What does this suggest about the nature of gleaning in Bethlehem during the time of the judges?

19. Look up "barley" and "wheat harvest" (or feast/festival) in a Bible dictionary or study Bible. What do you learn about these harvests and the time of year during which they occurred?

- **Principles and Points of Application.**

1. What field has God providentially directed you toward to provide for your needs? Spend time thanking him today for his providential grace in bringing you there, and ask him to show you how he wants you to serve him and glorify him there.

2. How are you displaying through your interactions with others that you love the Lord? How are you "addressing one another in psalms and hymns and spiritual songs, singing and making melody to the Lord with your heart, giving thanks always and for everything to God the Father in the name of our Lord Jesus Christ" (Eph. 5:19–20)?

3. In what ways are you displaying God's love and care for the foreigners, the poor, and widows in your community? If you're not, ask the Lord to show you this week someone in need of provision, and then take action to provide for their spiritual and/or physical needs.

4. Meditate on 2:10 in light of Christ's favor toward you. Spend time today facedown before your Redeemer, thanking him for taking notice of a sinner like you.

5. Under whose wings do you take refuge during the storms of life? Under whose wings should you? Confess this to the Lord today and begin taking shelter under his wings.

6. In whom do you find your satisfaction? Meditate on Psalm 103:5; 105:40; 107:9; 147:14; Proverbs 13:4; Luke 6:21a today. Spend time confessing any idols from which you're trying to gain satisfaction, and ask God to help you find satisfaction in him alone.

7. How are you displaying God's lovingkindness toward others through your actions and attitudes toward them? God sent his Son, Jesus Christ, in order to reveal his love and character to us and in order to accomplish redemption of his chosen people. But he now sends us into the world to tangibly show the world his love through the lives of his people and to tell the people of his work of redemption on the cross. How are we doing as individuals and as the church? Are we outwardly focused? Are we reaching out to display God's lovingkindness to the world around us and speaking to them of Christ's work on the cross?

NOTES FOR RUTH 2

Ponder the aim of this lesson concerning our:

Mind: What do we need to know from this passage in Scripture?

God displays his covenantal love through the lives of Ruth and Boaz.

Heart: How does what we learn from this passage affect our internal relationship with the Lord?

It prepares us to be kingdom disciples who display God's covenantal love from our hearts to our actions.

Hands: How does what we learn from this passage translate into action for God's kingdom?

It enables us to:

1. Spend time thanking the Lord today for his providential grace in bringing us to our present "field" and asking him to show us how he wants us to serve him and glorify him there.
2. Display through our interactions with others that we love the Lord, "addressing one another in psalms and hymns and spiritual songs, singing and making melody to the Lord with [our hearts], giving thanks always and for everything to God the Father in the name of our Lord Jesus Christ" (Eph. 5:19–20).
3. Display God's love and care for the foreigners, the poor, and the widows in our community by asking the Lord to show you this week someone in need of provision, and then taking action to provide for his or her spiritual and/or physical needs.
4. Meditate on 2:10 in light of Christ's favor toward us and then spend time today facedown before your Redeemer, thanking him for taking notice of a sinner like you.
5. Take refuge under the Lord's wings during the storms of life.
6. Spend time confessing any idols we're trying to gain satisfaction from, and to ask God to help us find satisfaction in him alone.
7. Display God's lovingkindness toward others through our actions and attitudes toward them.
8. Reach out to those around us, displaying God's lovingkindness and speaking to them of Christ's work on the cross.

INTRODUCTION

Somewhere along the way in my evangelical upbringing, I came to believe that although God had a plan for my life, I could miss it, that if I didn't discern God's plan for my life correctly, then I had missed his perfect will for my life. This thinking was detrimental to someone like me who wanted to please my heavenly Father and get his plan for my life "right." Making decisions about which man to marry, which place to live, which job to accept, which college major to choose, which seminary to attend, and numerous other decisions were agonizing for me. If only I had a bright, flashing light in the sky to tell me, I would know that I wasn't making a mistake and that I wasn't stepping outside God's "perfect will" for my life. There were many times when I wished that I didn't have freedom to choose, so that I wouldn't mess up and so that I would please God. It was not until I learned and embraced Reformed theology that I came to rest in the providential hand of God. I came to realize that I could not miss God's plan for my life. I came to learn about God's revealed will in his Word (that I was responsible to follow) and his hidden will that I could not discern and should not try to discern, but that I could trust. I came to learn that his sovereignty and providence grounds my trust in him. I came to embrace the truth that nothing happens by chance; God has ordained all things for his purposes and for his children's good.

That doesn't mean that it has always been easy. There have certainly been relationships, events, and circumstances in my life that I believe were ordained by God but were extremely difficult for me to walk through. But, while I walk through them, the truth of God's providence and covenantal love acts as a guardrail to keep me from despair and disillusionment.

One of the many purposes of the book of Ruth is to display God's hand of providence in order that we might trust and recognize his providence in our own lives. As we see God's hand of providence leading Ruth to the right field at the right time to meet the right redeemer, our own faith is strengthened that God will do the same in our lives.

We can divide the lesson into four sections:

   I. God Guides Ruth to Boaz's Field (2:1–7)
  II. God Displays His Favor toward Ruth through Boaz (2:8–13)
 III. God Displays His Fullness through Boaz (2:14–16)
  IV. God Displays His Protection and Provision through Boaz (2:17–23)

I. God Guides Ruth to Boaz's Field (2:1–7)

The narrator continues the break in the story line here to give us some important information to keep in mind as we read chapter 2. Why is it important that Naomi had a relative of her husband's? These women had come back to Bethlehem for food, but they had no land and no food and no way to get it. But God had graciously made provision for people like Naomi and Ruth in his law. All three of the following provisions are critical ways that God displays his *hesed* in the book of Ruth, and as all three are introduced in this chapter, it is appropriate to discuss them here.

First, he had made provision through the process of gleaning. In keeping with the commandment to "love your neighbor as yourself" (Lev. 19:18), Israel was not to reap their field right up to its edge nor gather the gleaning after their harvest. They were not to strip their vineyard bare, nor gather the fallen grapes of their vineyard. They were to leave them for the poor and the sojourner, because the Lord was their God who had brought them out of the land of slavery in Egypt (Lev. 19:9–10; 23:22). So in the same way they were to display his deliverance and provision for them by leaving their gleanings for the poor and the stranger. This was also connected to Exodus 19:6, which says that Israel was to be a kingdom of priests and a holy nation. Missions began among themselves, but it was not to end there. As others outside the covenant community saw them display the provision of gleaning for their own people, it would attract them to the lovingkindness of God that they were exemplifying. Unfortunately, as many of the prophets testify, Israel did not do a good job of this (Isa. 10:1–2; Mal. 3:5). But as we will see, there was at least one in Bethlehem who not only followed the law but also went beyond the law's requirements out of love for God.

Second, the Lord had made provision through levirate marriage. The Latin word for "brother-in-law" is *levir*, thus the designation "levirate marriage" for this marriage designated by the law of Moses. Under this law, if a brother died and did not have a son, his wife was not to be married outside the family to a stranger, but rather to her brother-in-law in order for him to care for her. The firstborn son would carry on the name of the dead brother in order to preserve his name in Israel. If the brother-in-law refused, the wife was to go to the elders of the city who would then speak with him. If he still refused, the wife was to take his sandal off his foot and spit in his face, and he would live with that reputation for the rest of his life. So he was shamed severely (Deut. 25:5–10), but the wife was protected from a marriage in which the husband didn't want her.

Third, the Lord had made provision through a kinsman-redeemer. The kinsman-redeemer was obligated under the law to help relatives who were under financial distress and had mortgaged property by buying the property back (Lev. 25:25–34). If they had become enslaved, he would buy them out of slavery (Lev. 25:47–52). Thus he would restore not only the family to a unified whole, but also the land, both of which were extremely important in Israel. This is extremely significant theologically. The reason for these laws is based on the Lord's redemption of his people from Egypt. His people were to follow in his footsteps. Rather than act as Pharaoh did and cruelly oppress God's people, they were to exemplify his redemption and the freedom that they had received when they had come out of Egypt. God's grace in this aspect of the provision of the law ensures that Israel's freedom embodies his own and that they embody the equality and unity that is to be found among God's people. Another aspect of this law that we see clearly in Ruth is the fact that the redeemer would marry the widow in order to produce an heir so that the clan would remain strong. Each clan had received an allotment of the Promised Land, and it was important for them to maintain it, as the Lord's promise was inextricably bound up with the land.[1] It is here that Boaz, the third main character, and I would suggest the most important character, steps onto the scene.

It bears repeating that God had graciously provided a way of provision for widows in his law. Deuteronomy 24:19 says, "When you reap your harvest in your field and forget a sheaf in the field, you shall not go back to get it. It shall be for the sojourner, the fatherless, and the widow, that the LORD your God may bless you in all the work of your hands."

1. Robert L. Hubbard Jr., "Redemption," in *New Dictionary of Biblical Theology*, ed. T. Desmond Alexander et al. (Downers Grove, IL: InterVarsity Press, 2000), 717.

Certainly Naomi knew about this law, but it is Ruth who takes the initiative. The text does not tell us why Naomi does not go with her. It is not likely that she was too old, but for whatever reason it is Ruth who bears the responsibility and, indeed, graciously offers to do so. Again we see her displaying God's *hesed* (covenantal lovingkindness) to Naomi.

We should take note of the fact that although we are not under the Law as the theocratic nation of Israel was, the principles that lie behind the laws remain the same. Christ did not come to abolish the Law, but to fulfill it (Matt. 5:17). We are to care for orphans and widows and the poor, as James makes abundantly clear in his letter (James 1:27; 2:15–16). It is not always materialistic needs that must be met, but emotional ones and spiritual ones as well, as the following story from my own life displays.

I spent my early twenties living in a retirement community. I lived on the fourth floor across from a retired doctor in his eighties who was in poor health but loved the Lord. Next to me was an elderly woman in her nineties who was bedridden and required constant care. And adjacent from me was a couple—the wife was in her late nineties, a sweet woman, but poor health and unable to get around well, and the husband was in his early hundreds and was on so many medications that he had turned grouchy and hard to live with.

All the residents, for the most part, found themselves removed from life as they had once known it, enclosed into a small room with four walls that breathed little of outside news and deflated their hope. I imagine they were surprised when I moved into one of the rooms. Young and full of energy, hopes, and dreams, I brought something that they did not have. I was a window to the outside world for them.

The retirement community had implemented a program to put two seminary students at their location to tend to the maintenance needs of the building. In exchange for labor, they would receive free lodging. When I found out about the program, I immediately applied. I had always loved older people. They were so full of wisdom and knowledge about life; I sought their company. And if you have ever been in or met someone in seminary, you know that money is tight, so a free place to live was just what I needed. However, I was not very good at maintenance work. I painted walls well, changed lightbulbs quickly, and scrubbed elevator tracks hard, but it wasn't long before I was asking the director to change my job description. It ended up that I played the piano for the residents during their lunch and dinner times, conducted a Bible study for them in the chapel, and made individual visitations to pray and encourage the residents. This in fact proved to be more of what they needed than painted walls. As I engaged in conversation with these sweet people, I came to realize that I was interacting with people who used to be "somebodies" in their communities. But now forgotten by the world, they felt trapped in their rooms and were hurting. Some were full of faith and knew the Lord had not forgotten them and were continuing to read or listen to the Bible, attend church, and participate in fellowship. Others were struggling in their walk with the Lord. They knew God, but they were struggling at the plan he had for their lives. And some had never truly accepted Christ as their personal Lord and Savior, but played the part of being a social Christian and a morally good person.

The retirement home was filled with "Naomis," people who had come to escape famine in their lives. Embittered by their circumstances, they remained closed into their four walls, lonely, angry, and hopeless. They had lost loved ones, they had endured hardships, and they had lost purpose and faith. They were in need of "Ruths," devoted, kind, loving, hopeful people who would come alongside them to encourage their hearts and give them hope for the future. The places that were supposed to be supplying "bread" (such as good health) had failed them, and they had come to "Moab," a place of escape that might meet their needs. But in Moab they found what Naomi found to be true. Their needs were still unfulfilled and unmet. Circumstances still devastated them. They needed true bread. They needed Christ. They needed a reason to live and hold on until they walked through the gates of glory. They needed someone to express God's love to them. They needed it embodied so they could tangibly see his faithfulness.

God has placed "Naomis" all around us who feel the hand of God is against them and need to be shown true love and faith. The question is, will we be bold enough to live this kind of faith out before their eyes? Will we be women of faith who present God's *hesed* (covenantal lovingkindness) to a world in need?

Evidently Ruth gleans in a field that belongs to more than one person, because "she happened to come to the part of the field belonging to Boaz" (2:3). The narrator, knowing full well that it is God's providence that brings her, uses the language of chance in order to arouse our attention. In fact, this is a good place for us to pause and reflect on God's providence.

Providence is God's hidden hand at work in our lives. Our gracious heavenly Father orders everyday events that seem mundane. Unexpected events and unordinary occurrences are sovereignly ordained. Our seeming mistakes, luck of the draw, and chance happenings are not that at all. The hand of the Master who works all things for his glory and our good orchestrates them. Ruth's heavenly Father was providentially involved in her life to bring her to the field of her redeemer. He divinely decreed what looked like chance to her, and it was done so out of his lovingkindness toward his daughter. Yet it was also part of a larger plan in the redemptive-historical scheme of things. The Lord was bringing an even greater Redeemer through this family's line. But we will wait to say more on that until later.

What field has God providentially directed you toward to provide for your needs? Spend time thanking him today for his providential grace in bringing you there, and ask him to show you how he wants you to serve him and glorify him in that field.

The word "behold" in 2:4 should give us pause. Someone important has arrived on the scene. Indeed, when we compare it with other uses of "behold" in Scripture, we see this is true. It is used in Isaiah 65:17 to refer to the Lord's creating the new heavens and a new earth. It is used in Luke 1:38 when Mary refers to herself as the servant of the Lord. It is used in John 1:29 by John the Baptist to refer to the Lamb of God who takes away the sin of the world. It is used in John 19:5 by Pilate when he tells the crowd to "behold the man!" It is used by Jesus in John 19:26 when he tells Mary to behold her son John. It is used in the book of Revelation to refer to the dwelling place of God being with man, and all things being new, and Jesus' second coming (Rev. 21:3, 5; 22:12).

Just as King David and King Jesus Christ came from Bethlehem, so too Boaz comes from Bethlehem, not to be a king (though he is part of a royal line) but to be a redeemer who points to the final and perfect Redeemer, Jesus Christ. The words that he speaks are telling. They are not empty words, but full of faith grounded in the God of Israel. Psalm 129:5–8 tells us that, contrary to those who hate Zion and do not pass by and say, "The blessing of the LORD be upon you! We bless you in the name of the LORD!" and thus will be put to shame, Boaz and his workers love Zion and will not be put to shame.

How are you displaying through your interactions with others that you love the Lord? How are you "addressing one another in psalms and hymns and spiritual songs, singing and making melody to the Lord with your heart, giving thanks always and for everything to God the Father in the name of our Lord Jesus Christ" (Eph. 5:19–20; Col. 3:16)? How are you using your "field" as a place where God's name is proclaimed?

Boaz's question is interesting. He doesn't ask who the woman is or what her name is, but whose she is. The text does not tell us, but we can't help but wonder if he already knows that this is Ruth whom he has heard about and he wants to confirm it.

In verses 6–7 we find out what happened before Ruth began gleaning. She revealed her identity and asked permission to glean. She didn't have to ask permission for what the Law required, but out of a humble and respectful heart she did so. The text also reveals what a hard worker she is. She has gleaned from early morning until the time that Boaz got there with only a short rest. She certainly exemplifies the Proverbs 31 woman who "works with willing hands" and "rises while it is yet night and provides food for her household" (31:13, 15). No wonder that the Hebrew Bible places the book of Ruth immediately after the book of Proverbs, which ends with the woman who fears the Lord!

In what ways are you displaying God's love and care for the foreigners, poor, and widows in your community? If you're not, ask the Lord to show you this week someone in need of provision, and then take action to provide for his or her spiritual and/or physical needs.

II. God Displays His Favor toward Ruth through Boaz (2:8–13)

For the first time in the book, two of the three main characters—and definitely the two main characters of this chapter (Ruth and Boaz)—meet each other. These are the two characters in the book through whom God portrays his covenant love. Boaz's language is filled with lovingkindness, compassion, protection, and provision. Rather than refer to her as a foreigner or as Naomi's, he claims Ruth as his "daughter" (2:8). This is the same way that Naomi has referred to Ruth (1:11–13; 2:2), so we already see here a foreshadowing of Boaz's desire to protect and provide for Ruth.

First, his field is for her. There is no need for her to look anywhere else for provision; she is welcome to gaze on and gather all the provision on his land. Second, he tells her to literally "cling to" his young women. This is the same word used to describe Ruth clinging to Naomi in 1:14. Third, Boaz is particularly concerned that she be kept sexually pure from the young men. Indeed he has already spoken with them and charged them not to touch her! Finally, he provides for her thirst. Not only does he grant her access to water, but he also has it drawn for her!

How do we welcome new converts into the covenant community, especially those who may be different from us? Do we look at the poor, widowed, and foreigners around us as potential converts to the kingdom who need to be loved and need to hear the gospel? Boaz exemplified James' later words in James 2:1–10. He told the poor woman to sit in a good place in his field. He treated his neighbor as himself. He honored the poor woman that God had chosen to be rich in faith and an heir of the kingdom. We are to do the same.

Ruth is understandably overwhelmed. She literally "fell on her face, bowing to the ground" (2:10). She places herself as an inferior at a superior's feet, bowing in humble submission and respect. Her question exposes that she well knows who she is. She is a foreigner. She did not expect to be noticed or treated with such favor. She most likely came to Bethlehem not even knowing if anyone would uphold the provisions in the Mosaic law, much less surpass them!

Meditate on this verse (2:10) in light of Christ's favor toward you. Spend time today facedown before your Redeemer, thanking him for taking notice of a sinner like you.

Boaz has a ready answer for Ruth's question. He has been fully told of her attitude and her actions toward Naomi after the death of her husband. More importantly, he recognizes her conversion in the phrase, "under whose wings you have come to take refuge!" (2:12). Throughout the Old Testament this imagery is used to describe God's compassionate and covenantal protection of his people (Ex. 19:4; Ps. 17:8; 36:7; 57:1; 61:4; 63:7; 91:4; Matt. 23:37). Exodus 19:4 especially speaks of God's deliverance of Israel from Egypt: "You yourselves have seen what I did to the Egyptians, and how I bore you on eagles' wings and brought you to myself."

Boaz was reminding Ruth that her faith was grounded in the God who had acted in history to display his lovingkindness, and this same God would act in her history to deliver her from her distress as well. In fact, this is part of a prayer that Boaz prays for Ruth, which consists of three elements. First, he asks that the Lord would repay Ruth for what she has done. Second, he asks that the Lord would give her a full reward. And third, he thanks the Lord that she had placed herself under the authority and protection of the God of Israel. This prayer is reminiscent of Naomi's prayer for Ruth in 1:8–9. We will find later that Boaz will have the divine opportunity to be an answer to his own prayer!

We should also note the third use in the book of the word "land" in verse 11. Like Abraham, Ruth was willing to leave her land for the Land of Promise, but unlike Abraham, she had not received a promise from God. Again we see the theme of land, so prominent in the Abrahamic covenant, in the book of Ruth.

In whose wings do you take refuge during the storms of life? In whose wings should you? If you do not hide under the Almighty's wings, confess this to the Lord today and begin taking shelter under his wings.

Ruth adds her own answer to her question after asking Boaz for his (2:13). It is not because of her actions and attitude, but because of

Boaz's attitude and actions as a man of God, from which he conducts his life, that she has found favor in his eyes. In other words, while Boaz is recognizing Ruth's actions and attitudes as his reason for favoring her, Ruth is recognizing his attitude and actions as the reason. Because God had taken hold of Boaz's heart, he was able to speak to Ruth's heart (literally, "spoken to the heart of your servant"), displaying God's lovingkindness. Though Boaz has recognized her as his "daughter," Ruth still places herself on the level of a servant with restricted rights.

III. God Displays His Fullness through Boaz (2:14–16)

Not only does Boaz open up his field for Ruth, but he also opens up his food to her. He invites her to join him and his reapers for mealtime, an extraordinary gesture of kindness that elevates her far beyond the servant that she sees herself as in the previous verse. Boaz does not just offer her dry bread, but bread dipped in wine (the word in the Hebrew that the ESV translates "wine" most likely refers to a sour sauce or condiment used to moisten and spice up bread).[2] Furthermore, there was no limit as to what she could have. She ate until she was satisfied and still had some left over. What a meal this must have been for Ruth! Not only was her heart satisfied (2:13), but her stomach was satisfied as well.

There would be another Redeemer who would invite his disciples to join him for mealtime before accomplishing salvation for the people of God. But far beyond meeting their physical needs, he met their spiritual needs through his body and blood that was crushed and poured out for the iniquity of God's people. Today we are invited to participate in the Lord's Supper, one of the means of grace given to the church, in order to be strengthened in our faith as we feed on Christ.

In whom do you find your satisfaction? Meditate on Psalms 103:5; 105:40; 107:9; 147:14; Proverbs 13:4; Luke 6:21 today. Spend time confessing any idols from which you're trying to gain satisfaction and ask God to help you find satisfaction in him alone.

---

2. Daniel I. Block, *The New American Commentary*, vol. 6, *Judges, Ruth* (Nashville: Broadman & Holman, 1999), 667.

Boaz continues to give provision that goes far beyond the require-ments of the Mosaic law (2:15–16). First, Ruth is to be allowed to glean among the sheaves, evidently in contrast to just staying around the outer borders of the field. Second, she is not to be shamed for having to do this, nor is she to be insulted for her status. Third, the reapers are even told to pull out some from the bundles for her and leave it on the ground for her to glean!

IV. God Displays His Protection and Provision through Boaz (2:17–23)

If you remember, Ruth has been at Boaz's field since early morn-ing (2:7), and it is now evening (2:17). Ruth has put in a very long day of gleaning out of lovingkindness to provide for her mother-in-law. The Lord has already rewarded her by displaying his lovingkindness through Boaz. Indeed she has a whole ephah of barley. To put this in perspective for us, this would have been between thirty and fifty pounds of barley, enough food to last for several weeks.[3] And Ruth had to carry this home!

No wonder Naomi inquires of where Ruth has gleaned when she sees thirty to fifty pounds of barley as well as a leftover bag from Ruth's meal! Naomi blesses the man who took notice of Ruth before she even knows who he is. She extends her prayer (2:20) when she learns from Ruth that it is Boaz, which is the same prayer that she had used for Ruth and Orpah in 1:8. Both prayers use the word *hesed*, which we have already seen is mostly used in the Old Testament for God's covenant love for his people. Ruth and Boaz are both exempli-fying God's covenantal love. The context makes it clear that it is the Lord whom Naomi ascribes with the kindness that has not forsaken the living or the dead.[4] This is significant as it displays Naomi's own recognition of the Lord at work, a step forward for her in her own faith. But in light of the entire book, we can also say that the

---

3. Iain M. Duguid, *Esther and Ruth*, Reformed Expository Commentary (Phillipsburg, NJ: P&R Publishing, 2005), 161.

4. Ibid., 162.

Lord has used Boaz to display his kindness to Naomi and Ruth. So both the Lord and Boaz have displayed covenantal lovingkindness to these two widows.

How are we displaying God's lovingkindness toward others through our actions and attitudes toward them? God the Father sent his Son, Jesus Christ, in order to reveal his love and character to us. But he now sends us into the world to tangibly show the world his love through the lives of his people and to speak of Christ's life, death, resurrection, and ascension. How are we doing as individuals and as the church? Are we outwardly focused? Are we reaching out to display God's lovingkindness to the world around us? Are we proclaiming the life, death, resurrection, and ascension of Jesus Christ?

We learn in verse 20, from one of the main characters in the story, Naomi, what we had already learned from the narrator in 2:1. Boaz is a close relative of theirs, one of their redeemers. This is the first time in the book that the word "redeemer" is introduced (though we have already explained it at the beginning of this lesson). Ruth obviously does not realize the importance of this statement, for she continues to tell Naomi the rest of what Boaz has said. Naomi agrees that what Boaz has instructed her to do is wise for the same reasons. She too is familiar with the sexual harassment and shame that Ruth could face in the fields.

The word "redeemer" in this verse points us toward another Redeemer that God would send to display his love to us, to satisfy his justice, and to reconcile a sinful people to himself, our Lord and Savior Jesus Christ.

Ruth literally "clung" (see 1:14) to the young women of Boaz (2:23), gleaning until the end of the barley and wheat harvests, probably a seven-week period (late April to early June). Before we skip past this reference too quickly, let us reflect for a moment on the meaning behind these time references in 1:22 and 2:23. Ruth and Naomi returned to Bethlehem at the beginning of the barley harvest, which was the time that the Jews celebrated the Feast of Passover. This was a feast that reminded them of God's deliverance from their oppression in Egypt, the first exodus, the new beginning for God's people. It was the beginning of the year for the Jews. Like our New Year's Day, it was a time when people felt that they had a new beginning, a new start, not unlike when we make New Year's resolutions to have a new start in our own lives for specific things. Ruth and Naomi needed a fresh start after returning from Moab, and they were just in time.

The end of the barley and wheat harvests was the time that the Jews celebrated the Festival of Pentecost, also known as the Feast of Weeks or Festival of Firstfruits. Ruth and Naomi have certainly experienced the firstfruits of God's blessings in the fact that he has provided food for them through Boaz. But there is further blessing to come! Pentecost was the day that God chose, in his redemptive-historical plan, to pour out his Spirit, as recorded in Acts 2. This brought the people of God, both Jews and Gentiles, into one new people of God, the New Testament church. Thus Ruth herself, a Gentile among the Jews, was a "firstfruit" of what God would do in his perfect timing in the redemptive-historical calendar.[5] We too have been given the firstfruits of our inheritance. "And not only the creation, but we ourselves, who have the firstfruits of the Spirit, groan inwardly as we wait eagerly for adoption as sons, the redemption of our bodies" (Rom. 8:23). Jesus Christ has gone before us, the firstfruits of the resurrection, and we will follow when he returns.

The chapter ends by telling us that Ruth is living with her mother-in-law. As the curtain goes down on chapter 2, we already see how the Lord has provided for Naomi and Ruth's physical needs. But there are still two significant outstanding issues. How will the Lord preserve the name of Elimelech's family since there is no heir? And how will Ruth and Naomi receive back their inheritance of the land? We now know that there are "redeemers," but we do not know which one, if even one, will step forward. We do know, though, that God's hand of providence has brought Ruth to Boaz's field, and with Naomi's and the narrator's information, our sense of anticipation is heightened that Boaz just might

5. Ibid., 165.

be the one God will use as his instrument to display his *hesed* toward Ruth and Naomi.

We too have come to the field of grace, the covenant community of believers. We have been given the means of grace in the Lord's Supper to feed on Christ by faith. We have been offered a feast, invited to the marriage supper of the Lamb. We have been fully satisfied in Christ, the true bread that came down from heaven, the living bread, the bread of life (John 6:41, 48, 50–51). "Christ has been raised from the dead, the firstfruits of those who have fallen asleep" (1 Cor. 15:20). Glory be to the Father, who has given us a Redeemer in his Son, Jesus Christ! His lovingkindness will never forsake us. Indeed Christ was willingly forsaken by the Father on the cross of Calvary so that we never would be (Matt. 27:46). Have you forsaken your first love (Rev. 2:4)? Run into his loving arms today, bowing before him in adoration and worship; he is calling you home to glean in his fields of mercy. Have you ever believed in the name of the Lord Jesus Christ as your Lord and Savior? His arms are open wide for you today.

CONCLUSION

God's providence must ground our trust in him. There is nothing that happens by chance; God has ordained all things for his sovereign purposes and for the good of his children. We can cry out with David, "Your eyes saw my unformed substance; in your book were written every one of them, the days that were formed for me, when as yet there was none of them" (Ps. 139:16). We can trust God's providential hand in our relationships, careers, ministries, marriages, parenting, and every other area of our lives. He has revealed his moral and saving will to us in his Word, and we must make decisions accordingly. But what my major should be, whom I should marry, what ministry position I should take, what house I should live at, are not listed in Scripture. However, there are certain principles that must govern these decisions, such as 2 Corinthians 6:14, which tells us we must marry a believer. Otherwise, our own judgment, counsel from godly mentors, and the desires of our hearts are valid means in decision making. Although we do not have access to God's hidden will, we know that Acts 17:26 is true: God has "determined allotted periods and the boundaries of [our] dwelling place." Thus we can rest in God, knowing that we can't miss God's will for our lives, but that he orders all things according to his purposes and our good.

Ruth 3

PLEASE USE THE QUESTION paradigm from pages 301–2 as you work through the following. See the introductory comments there that explain each part of the process below in more detail.

- **Pray.**
- **Ponder the Passage.** Read Ruth 3 once a day from different translations for the entire week, looking for its:
  - Point
  - Persons
  - Problem
  - Patterns
  - Persons of the Trinity
  - Puzzling Parts
- **Put It in Perspective.**
  - Place in Scripture. Skim Judges 1:1–3:6.
  - Passages from Other Parts of Scripture

1. Based on your observations of the text, what is the basic content of this passage? Try to summarize it in your own words, using a sentence or two. Pay close attention to 3:1, 18 in connection with 3:9.

2. Where else have we seen this concern to find rest (3:1) in the book? Is this rest just so that it may be well for Ruth, or is it for Naomi's benefit too (see 4:14)?

3. Where have we already learned the information in 3:2a?

4. Compare 3:3 with 2 Samuel 12:20 and its surrounding context. What do you learn? How does this shed light on Ruth's dress?

5. List the step-by-step instructions that Naomi gives to Ruth (3:3–4). What is Ruth's response (3:5)?

6. How does the narrator portray Ruth's response in 3:6? Why is this important in light of Ruth's request in 3:9? Why would Ruth have added these words?

7. Compare 3:9 with Ezekiel 16:8. What do you learn?

8. What is Boaz's first question when he wakes up at midnight? How does he respond to Ruth lying at his feet? What is Ruth's first kindness? What is her last kindness?

9. Compare 3:10 with 1:8. What do you learn?

10. How does Ruth describe herself (3:9), and how does Boaz address her (3:11)?

11. Compare "for all my fellow townsmen know that you are a worthy woman" (3:11) with Proverbs 31:10–31. How does Ruth exemplify the Proverbs 31 woman?

12. What is the seeming "obstacle" in 3:12 (see Deut. 25:5–10)? Why is it significant that Boaz reveals this? What does that tell us about Boaz's character? What promise does Boaz make to Ruth in 3:13?

13. Why does Boaz have Ruth stay the night but leave before it is daylight? What is his motivation(s) behind this?

14. What does the giving of six measures of barley signify for Ruth and Naomi?

15. What are Naomi's instructions to Ruth in 3:18? How does this compare with her instructions at the beginning of the chapter?

- **Principles and Points of Application.**

1. From where or whom do you seek rest? Read Exodus 35:2; Psalm 62:5; Matthew 11:28; Hebrews 4:3. Spend time today thanking

God for Sabbath rest in Christ, which was inaugurated at the cross and will be consummated at Christ's return.

2. In what ways are you running ahead of God right now in your own life circumstances? Confess this to him today and then wait for his plan and timing to unfold.

3. Meditate on Ezekiel 16:8 along with Revelation 19:7; 21:2, 9. Marinate in the truth that you have a Redeemer and you are a part of the church, his bride. How are you reflecting this union in your life, and how are you sharing Christ with others?

4. Read Proverbs 31:10–31 today. How is God using you to display acts of kindness toward your spouse, family, neighbors, etc., in order to exemplify his lovingkindness? Ask God to give you the opportunity to do so this week.

5. In what situation has the Lord asked you to wait? Are you waiting well for the Lord to bring about his plan or are you trying to accomplish it in your own power? While you wait, commit to worshiping God, accepting his plan and timing, inviting him to be Lord over your circumstances, and trusting him with the outcome.

NOTES FOR RUTH 3

Ponder the aim of this lesson concerning our:

Mind: What do we need to know from this passage in Scripture?

God reveals his lovingkindness, graciousness, protection, and provision through Boaz's response to Ruth and Naomi.

Heart: How does what we learn from this passage affect our internal relationship with the Lord?

It prepares us to be kingdom disciples who reflect God's grace, protection, and provision in our responses to others in need.

Hands: How does what we learn from this passage translate into action for God's kingdom?

It enables us to:

1. Spend time thanking God today for Sabbath rest in Christ, which was inaugurated at the cross and will be consummated when Christ returns.
2. Meditate on the truth that we have a Redeemer and are part of the church, his bride, and to reflect this union in our lives, sharing Christ's love with others and inviting them to church with us.
3. Exemplify God's lovingkindness to our husband, children, neighbors, etc., in light of Proverbs 31:10–31, asking God to draw others to himself.
4. Wait well in our present situations (rather than trying to bring about our desired outcome), by worshiping God, accepting his plan and timing, inviting him to be Lord of our lives, and trusting him with the outcome.

INTRODUCTION

I have always had a hard time waiting. When I was in high school, I wanted to be in college. When I was in college, I wanted to be in seminary. When I was in seminary, I wanted to be in full-time ministry. When I was single, I wanted to be married. When I was married, I wanted to have children. Well, you get the picture. I have definitely been guilty of running ahead of God's timing, but God has always been faithful to his plan for my life, even when I make things really messy.

I find this is true for all of us. We don't wait well. Raised in a culture that is built around scheduled time, daily planners, drive-thrus, minute clinics, microwave meals, takeout restaurants, mobile devices, and the like, we have trained ourselves to have what we want when we want it. And it of course has influenced how we see the church and how we see

Christ as well. Many times Christ is viewed as a person we cry out to if we need help with a problem only after we've come to the desperate point of being at the end of our own resources. And the church is often viewed as a place where we go to enjoy Christian programs that will enhance our spirituality or to have a worship experience or to do things for God rather than receiving what he has already done for us through the preaching of the Word and the sacraments. But Scripture is clear that we are to wait for the Lord. The Psalms remind us of this: "Be still before the LORD and wait patiently for him" (Ps. 37:7). Proverbs reminds us of this: "Wait for the LORD, and he will deliver you" (Prov. 20:22). Isaiah reminds us of this: "Blessed are all those who wait for him" (Isa. 30:18). Jesus reminds us of this: "Wait for the promise of the Father" (Acts 1:4). Paul reminds us of this: "But if we hope for what we do not see, we wait for it with patience" (Rom. 8:25). And John reminds us of this: "And [the saints were] told to rest a little longer" (Rev. 6:11).

Ruth 3 also speaks about waiting. At the beginning of the chapter, Naomi runs ahead of God's timing. And by doing so, she puts Ruth in a dangerous position and Boaz in a compromising situation. But God is faithful to his plan, even when Naomi makes things messy. In marked contrast, by the end of the chapter Naomi tells Ruth to wait. And she does. They both do.

We can divide the lesson into three sections:

   I. Naomi's Plan (3:1–5)
  II. Ruth's Request for a Redeemer (3:6–13)
 III. Boaz's Protection and Provision (3:14–18)

I. Naomi's Plan (3:1–5)

Verse 1, along with the final verse of this chapter, gives us the main point of chapter 3: the need for rest. Naomi is seeking rest for Ruth in the form of marriage, but Naomi is also in need of rest by way of Ruth's marriage, because she too will find restoration and nourishment by way of it (4:15). We will also see that Boaz will lose rest on account of these two widows, both during the middle of the night and during the legal process of redemption. The legal process will not be resolved in this chapter, but the final verse concludes on the note that Boaz will not "rest" until he settles the matter that day.

In chapter 2 we saw that Ruth initiated providing food for Naomi, but here we see that Naomi initiates finding rest for Ruth. She is still burdened by what she has been concerned with for her daughters-in-law since chapter 1—rest for them in the way of a husband. It seems that Naomi is not following her own advice that she later gives Ruth, to wait (3:18). It does not seem that she is waiting for the Lord's timing in bringing Ruth and Boaz together, but is trying to accomplish matters in her own risky way. If it is true that she did run ahead of God's plan and timing (as many commentators believe), I can completely relate! There have certainly been times in my life when I have laid a situation before the Lord, grown tired of waiting, and taken matters into my own hands, only to be reminded that it's never a good idea to do that! Regardless, we see that God is faithful to his children even in the midst of far-from-favorable circumstances and in the midst of our running ahead of his timing and plan. As we will see, the redeemer (Boaz) proves instrumental in keeping this plan from disaster, pointing toward the faithful hand of God.

From where or whom do you seek rest? Read Exodus 35:2; Psalm 62:5; Matthew 11:28; Hebrews 4:3. Spend time today thanking God for Sabbath rest in Christ, which was inaugurated at the cross and will be consummated at Christ's return.

In what ways are you running ahead of God right now in your own life circumstances? Confess this to him today and then wait for his plan and timing to unfold.

In verse 2 Naomi restates what the narrator has already told us in 2:1 and what Naomi told Ruth in 2:20. Evidently she has given time and thought toward how to bring the two of them together, and she knows where Boaz will be that night.

Given Naomi's concern for Ruth's safety from assault (2:22), we are surprised that Naomi's plan involves putting Ruth in that very danger (3:3–4). Going down to the threshing floor at night was not exactly the safest thing to do. This would be the equivalent of telling your single daughter to get dressed and go walking down the streets of downtown in the dark of night where many of the prostitutes gather to offer their services. However, we must be careful to observe that Naomi is not telling Ruth to act like one! We see this same act of washing, anointing, and putting on a cloak in 2 Samuel 12:20 after David was done mourning for his son. Exodus 22:25–27 also uses the term here for "cloak" to refer to an outer garment that poor people used to keep warm. So Naomi's words are far removed from getting all dressed up in order to attract Boaz for a sexual encounter. Rather, it seems to point in a different direction of leaving the hard period of widowhood behind her and traveling through the chilly night with her coat on down to the threshing floor in order to privately ask Boaz to be her redeemer.

Ruth is to wait until Boaz has finished eating and drinking. This is not because Boaz will be drunk and easier to take advantage of, as in the case of Lot when his daughters got him drunk in order to preserve their father's line. (Lot's eldest daughter bore Moab, the father of the Moabites [Gen. 19:30–38].) But rather his heart would be merry (3:7) and he would be content to retire for the night. This would ensure that Ruth was meeting Boaz in private, not at a table with food and drink where others could observe them. She is to observe the place where he lies down, evidently from her place of hiding, and then she is to go and uncover his feet and lie down, waiting for him to tell her what to do. In other words, Ruth is to say nothing but instead to wait for Boaz to speak first. True to Ruth's character, she agrees to Naomi's plan.

II. Ruth's Request for a Redeemer (3:6–13)

The narrator tells us in verse 6 that Ruth did indeed follow through on her word and did just as Naomi had commanded her, so we should not take Ruth's speech in the following verses as deviating from her word, but rather answering Boaz's question and protecting her reputation by stating why she is lying at his feet.

Boaz acts just as Naomi has anticipated. And Ruth follows through with the plan by going softly to uncover his feet and lie down. The text does not tell us how long it was between the time that Boaz ate and drank and midnight, but we can be sure that it was at least a few hours. Also, the text does not say what startled the man, but some commentators think the night air would have grown cool by then and Boaz would have felt it across his uncovered legs and awakened. Whatever the case, he woke up to more than he expected! A woman was lying at his feet, and in the pitch-black night (there were no night-lights or city lights) he had no idea that it was Ruth. So he initiates the conversation by asking who she is. And Ruth, being the woman of integrity that she is, removes all ambiguity from the situation at this point by telling Boaz exactly why she is there.

First, she responds by telling Boaz her name and calling herself his servant (3:9). The Hebrew word for "servant" here is of higher rank than the word used for "servant" in 2:13. The latter would not have been eligible to marry someone of Boaz's status, but the former would. Thus she is placing herself on a social level where she is eligible for marriage. Second, she tells Boaz to spread his wings over her because he is a redeemer. We have already been introduced to this word (*go'el*) in 2:20, but we will now see it recur frequently in chapters 3 and 4, indicating a theme of this chapter directly linked to the main point of finding rest (3:1, 18). This language is used in Ezekiel 16:8 referring to what God did for Israel, so it is full of covenant language: "When I passed by you again and saw you, behold, you were at the age for love, and I spread the corner of my garment over you and covered your nakedness; I made my vow to you and entered into a covenant with you, declares the Lord GOD, and you became mine." Thus, this verse points us beyond Boaz as the redeemer, to Jesus Christ as the perfect and final Redeemer, who is the final yes to all the covenant promises (2 Cor. 1:20), spreading his wings over his church because he is her Redeemer.

Don't miss the significance of the setting here. We have noted previously that the book of Ruth continues the themes of land, seed, and the blessing of all nations of the earth in the Abrahamic promise. Here at the threshing floor, full of the seed of the harvest,[1] Ruth proposes that Boaz be the provider of another kind of seed, the seed of carrying on the chosen family line, which ultimately leads to Christ.

Meditate on Ezekiel 16:8 along with Revelation 19:7; 21:2, 9. Marinate in the truth that you have a Redeemer and you are a part of the church, his bride. How are you reflecting this union in your life, and how are you sharing Christ with others?

Though Boaz realizes the dangerous situation Ruth has put herself in, or, perhaps more accurately, the danger Naomi has put Ruth in (3:14), he does not respond by reprimanding her. In his response, he exemplifies the graciousness of God; he first responds with a blessing! Naomi uttered these words for Boaz in 2:20 because of his kindness, and now Boaz is uttering them for Ruth because of hers (3:10)! The two are well matched in godly character! He invites God's blessing on her because she has made this last kindness greater than the first. The word for "kindness" here is again *hesed* (God's covenantal loving-kindness, loyalty, and compassion) that we've already seen in 1:8 and 2:20. This is the last time that it is used in the book. What was Ruth's first kindness? Her first kindness was all that she had done for her mother-in-law since the death of her husband, how she left her father and mother and her native land and came to a people that she did not know before (2:11). What is her last kindness? Boaz says it is that she has not gone after young men, but has come to him, a proper redeemer for her since he is one of Elimelech's relatives. In other words, Ruth is following the law. And she is seeking an heir for Naomi. While Naomi is concerned to find rest for Ruth in a redeemer, Ruth is concerned with finding rest for Naomi in an heir.

Second, Boaz responds with a promise. He tells her not to fear, because he will do for her all that she asks. Why? He will have the full support from the townsmen because they know that she is a worthy woman. The word here is the same word used for "excellent wife" in

---

1. Mark J. Boda, *After God's Own Heart: The Gospel According to David*, The Gospel According to the Old Testament (Phillipsburg, NJ: P&R Publishing, 2007), 22.

the book of Proverbs (31:10), which the book of Ruth follows in the Hebrew Bible! But this is not the only reason that he will do for her all that she asks. Boaz is not a man who sticks to the letter of the law; Boaz is a man who goes above and beyond the law, displaying the *hesed* of God that he already knows so well. Third, Boaz responds in honesty, as a man of integrity. Despite the fact that he must be at this point strongly attracted to Ruth and longing to take her as his own, he does what is proper according to God's law. There is another redeemer who has first rights, and he must make sure that he is allowed the opportunity for redemption. He even goes so far as to say that this is good. In other words, Boaz has Ruth's best interest at heart, not his own. His main concern is for her to have a redeemer, even if it cannot be him. But if it can be him, then he promises to redeem her. Fourth, he protects her by telling her to lie down until morning, keeping her from night's harm.

Read Proverbs 31:10–31 today. How is God using you to display acts of kindness toward your husband, family, neighbors, etc., in order to exemplify his lovingkindness? Ask God to give you the opportunity to do so this week.

III. Boaz's Protection and Provision (3:14–18)

Just as Ruth complied with Naomi's plan, now she obeys Boaz and lies down until morning (3:14). But continuing his protective role, Boaz tells her to leave before morning's light so that no one will know Ruth came to the threshing floor. It could not be for the reason of keeping Boaz from disgrace if he decided not to redeem Ruth, for he had already promised that and the matter would become public that day. No, it was for the sake of Ruth's reputation. As we have already seen, the threshing floor was not the place that good girls presented themselves at night, and Boaz wanted nothing to be said against Ruth who had not done anything wrong.

Not only did Boaz protect Ruth, he provided for her (3:15). He poured six measures of barley into her cloak. This would have been a hefty amount of grain (some commentators think it could have been eighty pounds)! It was so much that Boaz had to help by putting it on her. And it certainly would have spoken volumes to Naomi, who was waiting for Ruth's return at home. The six scoops, one less than seven (a number of completeness in Scripture), may even signify that this is a down payment for an intended complete fulfillment of redemption.[2]

On Ruth's return to Naomi in the city, she is able to answer Naomi's question favorably but not absolutely (3:16–18). The question in the Hebrew is literally, "Who are you?" This is the same question that Boaz asked Ruth when he discovered her at his feet. In other words, Naomi was asking if she was going to be Boaz's new wife. However, in light of the context of the entire book, this question takes on even deeper significance. Who are you, daughter of Moabites, yet married into a covenant family and now a covenant child yourself? What role does God have for you to play in redemption? But the answer to these questions will have to wait. Naomi understands the six measures of barley as Boaz's promise to settle the matter that day for a redeemer for Ruth. And she has confidence in Boaz's character, for she knows that he will immediately settle the matter. Because she knows that he will not keep them waiting any longer than is necessary, she is able to tell Ruth to wait until she learns how the matter turns out. There is nothing more that Ruth needs to do except rest in the redeemer, and ultimately in the final Redeemer, Jesus Christ. What a vast contrast there is in Naomi's advice between the beginning of this chapter and the end! Naomi has gone from anxiously devising her own scheme and running ahead of God, to waiting for the redeemer's timing, ultimately the final Redeemer's timing.

Waiting is difficult, especially when it is not just for a day, but also for a week, or month, or year, or years. In what present situation has the Lord asked you to wait? Are you waiting well for the Lord to bring about his plan, or are you trying to accomplish it in your own power?

---

2. Iain M. Duguid, *Esther and Ruth*, Reformed Expository Commentary (Phillipsburg, NJ: P&R Publishing, 2005), 175.

As the love story develops between Ruth and Boaz in this chapter, we are pointed beyond human love to divine love. In the context of the book of Ruth, the loving God stands beyond Boaz, reaching out his arms, calling his prodigal daughter, Naomi, home, and calling one from another tribe, tongue, and nation—Ruth—to himself. There is a Redeemer indeed. And it is not just Mr. So-and-So, neither is it just Boaz, but it is our Lord and Savior Jesus Christ. The loving Father sent him to this earth in order to reconcile us to himself. And our Redeemer willingly obeyed and lived a life of active obedience and died a death of passive obedience in order that we might exchange our sin-filled rags for his sinless ones. Do you know this Redeemer? Have you met with him on your darkest night when you feel like you are being threshed and torn asunder? His arms are outstretched for you. He is not just willing to be your Redeemer. You do not have to wait to see how the matter will turn out today. It is already finished. The legal transaction has already occurred. Jesus Christ justified you on the cross and won his place as your Redeemer. Indeed he has purchased his bride, the church, and he is returning for her one day. Have you given yourself to him? And if so, have you shared his love with those around you?

CONCLUSION

The Lord has been faithful to bring many circumstances into my life to teach me to wait. During my first ministry position, the Lord laid a definition for waiting on my heart that has stuck with me for years and has been helpful for me in many different situations when my desire has been to run ahead of God's timing rather than wait for his perfect timing and his perfect plan. While we wait, let us *Worship* God. By doing so we will remember who he is and why he is worthy of our trust. Let us *Accept* his plan and timing. By doing so, we are submitting ourselves to him, acknowledging that he is Lord of our lives. Let us *Invite* him to be Lord of our lives. By doing so we are placing ourselves in a servant position and displaying our willingness to lay our lives down for him. Finally, let us *Trust* him with the outcome of the circumstances. By doing so, we are relinquishing our will to his, trusting that it will bring him far greater glory and will bring us even more good than we ever could have imagined. "Wait, my daughter, until you learn how the matter turns out, for [the LORD] will settle the matter [in his perfect time]" (3:18).

LESSON 18

Ruth 4

PLEASE USE THE QUESTION paradigm from pages 301–2 as you work through the following. See the introductory comments there that explain each part of the process below in more detail.

- **Pray.**
- **Ponder the Passage.** Read Ruth 4 once a day from different translations for the entire week, looking for its:
  - Point
  - Persons
  - Problem
  - Patterns
  - Persons of the Trinity
  - Puzzling Parts
- **Put It in Perspective.**
  - Place in Scripture. Skim Judges 1:1–3:6.
  - Passages from Other Parts of Scripture

1. Based on your observations of Ruth 4, what is the basic content of this passage? Try to summarize it in your own words, using a sentence or two.

2. Compare 2:3 with 4:1. How do you see God's hand of providence orchestrating people being at the right place at the
   right time?

3. If you have access to a literal translation, a study Bible, commentary, or other reference tool, what is the literal term for the
   nearer redeemer's name that the ESV translates "friend" in 4:1?
   What does this signify?

4. Why are the elders of the city gathered? What is their role? See
   Ruth 4:9–11.

5. What information does Boaz give to the nearer kinsman at first?
   What information does he withhold? What is the first answer
   that the nearer relative gives?

6. What information does Boaz add after the nearer redeemer's
   first answer? How does the nearer redeemer respond? Why?

7. Joshua 1:3 may shed some light on the custom in Israel to confirm a transaction with a sandal. If so, how does it?

8. What role does Boaz tell the elders and all the people they have
   played (4:9)? Why does Boaz say that he has bought Ruth? Why
   is this important in the larger historical-redemptive context of
   the meaning of the land (see Josh. 1:1–9)?

9. To better understand the blessing that the people and the elders
   bestow on Boaz, we need to look up some Scripture passages.
   First, with regard to Rachel and Leah, read Genesis 29:31–30:24;
   35:16–18. Second, to see how God fulfills the promise of Boaz
   to be renowned in Bethlehem in the future, read 1 Samuel 16:1,
   18; Matthew 2:1. Third, with regard to Tamar and Judah and
   their son Perez, read Genesis 38. How do these passages increase
   your understanding of this blessing and how it fits into God's
   larger historical-redemptive plan?

10. To whom does the narrator attribute Ruth's conception? Where
    is the only other time in the book that the Lord is the subject of
    the verse (think back to chapter 1)? Using a concordance, look
    up the word "barren." Who else in Scripture was barren (or a
    virgin!) that the Lord enabled to conceive?

11. How has 4:14 been fulfilled in the context of the book of Ruth? How has it been perfectly and finally fulfilled in the context of the entire Bible (look up the words "redeemer," "redeemed," "redemption," etc., in a concordance)?

12. Compare 4:15, which literally reads, "he who causes life to *return*," with 1:21, which literally reads, "the Lord has *returned* me empty." In light of the emphasis on the word "return" in chapter 1, how does this verse in chapter 4 connect?

13. Compare 4:15, "your daughter-in-law who loves you, who is more to you than seven sons," with 1:5, "the woman was left without her two sons and her husband." How do you see God's covenant faithfulness and mercy displayed through Ruth?

14. How do we see Naomi's situation redeemed in 4:16–17 (again, compare with 1:5)? Using a study Bible, commentary, or Bible dictionary, what does "Obed" mean? Look up "servant" in a concordance. Who else do we see is named a servant in Scripture? Why is this significant? To whom does Obed ultimately point?

15. Why is it significant that the book closes with a genealogy? From what you know of Perez from 4:12, what line is this? Though the line ends with David in the book of Ruth, what other king comes from this line later (see Matt. 1:1–17)?

- **Principles and Points of Application.**
  1. How do you respond to opportunities that the Lord brings into your life to display his lovingkindness to others? Are you more concerned about what it will cost you? Do you evaluate ministry opportunities based on how it will fit into your schedule, or are you willing to make the sacrifice of money, time, and energy in order to be obedient to God?
  2. If you are married, spend time today thanking the Lord for bringing you and your husband together. Thank the Lord for all the wonderful attributes that your husband has. Pray for those areas of his life in which he needs to grow. Pray that you will fulfill your God-given design to be his helper. If you are single

283

and desire to be married, spend time today in prayer for God's will to be done in your life concerning marriage. If you are single and believe you are called to remain single, spend time praying that you will glorify God as a single woman.

3. What of your past is still standing in the way of your relationship with the Lord? Scripture speaks very clearly of the fact that Jesus came to save sinners. We are not fooling God when we get all cleaned up and put on our facades. He knows that we are messy, sin-filled people in need of a Savior. That is why he sent his Son. There is a Redeemer for you and for me. He takes away our emptiness and fills us with

> every spiritual blessing in the heavenly places, even as he chose us in him before the foundation of the world, that we should be holy and blameless before him. In love he predestined us for adoption as sons through Jesus Christ, according to the purpose of his will, to the praise of his glorious grace, with which he has blessed us in the Beloved. In him we have redemption through his blood, the forgiveness of our trespasses, according to the riches of his grace, which he lavished upon us, in all wisdom and insight making known to us the mystery of his will, according to his purpose, which he set forth in Christ as a plan for the fullness of time, to unite all things in him, things in heaven and things on earth.

> In him we have obtained an inheritance, having been predestined according to the purpose of him who works all things according to the counsel of his will, so that we who were the first to hope in Christ might be to the praise of his glory. In him you also, when you heard the word of truth, the gospel of your salvation, and believed in him, were sealed with the promised Holy Spirit, who is the guarantee of our inheritance until we acquire possession of it, to the praise of his glory. (Eph. 1:3–14)

Spend time in confession and thanksgiving today.

4. Our days of advanced technology have not made it any easier to experience singleness, infertility, miscarriages, stillbirths, or the

loss of older children. Many women long to be married and are not, many long to conceive and cannot, many experience the heartache of miscarriage or stillbirth, and some are asked to bury their own child. Though it is extremely difficult, if we know and understand that God sovereignly gives and takes away, we will be better prepared to handle these circumstances in our lives when they do occur. Perhaps you are single today and longing for a husband, perhaps you long for a baby, or maybe you are grieving the loss of a child. Take your grief to the Lord today; pour out your heart before him in thanksgiving and prayer; accept his plan and timing; invite him to be Lord over your infertility, singleness, or other circumstances; and trust in his lovingkindness even when it may not seem like love or kindness at all.

5. Stop and ponder the words, "Blessed be the LORD, who has not left you this day without a redeemer" (Ruth 4:14). Spend time today thanking God that he has given us his Son, Jesus Christ, to redeem us from our sin and reconcile us to him. Look up Romans 3:24; Galatians 3:13–14; Ephesians 1:7, 14; Colossians 1:14; Hebrews 9:12.

6. Where is your name preserved today? Is it in the Book of Life? Is Jesus Christ Lord and Savior of your life? Have you ever spoken the words, "Here I am. I will be a part of your people. You will be my God"? Your Elder Brother extended his arms wide open for you so that he could lead you home to the Father. The way is open before you today to run into those arms, laying aside your will for his will, your way for his way, and your life for his life.

NOTES FOR RUTH 4

Ponder the aim of this lesson concerning our:

Mind: What do we need to know from this passage in Scripture?

> Boaz acts as a redeemer, preserving the name of Elimelech's family and buying back their inheritance, pointing forward to the final

Redeemer, Jesus Christ, who as the Elder Brother preserves the name of those belonging to God's family and buys back their inheritance of the eternal land of rest by way of his life, death, resurrection, and ascension.

Heart: How does what we learn from this passage affect our internal relationship with the Lord?

It prepares us to be kingdom disciples who rest in our Redeemer, Jesus Christ, the one who has preserved our names in the Book of Life and given us an eternal inheritance.

Hands: How does what we learn from this passage translate into action for God's kingdom?

It enables us to:

1. Respond in obedience to demonstrate God's love and kindness to others, even at great cost to us with regard to our time and finances.
2. Rest in the Lord's timing and the Lord's will today if we (or someone we love) are struggling with singleness, infertility, miscarriage, or the death of a child.
3. Spend time thanking God for sending us his Son, our Redeemer, and to share his acts of redemption with others.
4. Set about the mundane tasks in our lives with godly fervor, knowing that God accomplishes great things through the lives of ordinary people.

INTRODUCTION

Being a mom has given me another opportunity to learn the doctrine of total depravity on a practical level. From the day that my precious children were given to me from the Lord as a gift, they displayed for me what I already knew so well from myself; namely, we are self-centered creatures. We want what we want when we want it, and if we don't get it, we either go about our own way of getting it through our own means, or we throw a tantrum about it so that everyone knows how miserable we are.

Marriage has also taught me many things, not the least of which has been the truth that there is a war raging within me that is between my kingdom and God's kingdom; our "quarrels" and "fights" as James calls them (4:1) can always be traced back to our kingdom of self. But just as a parent slowly teaches the child that the world does not revolve around him or her, and just as spouses remind each other of the same, God's Word clearly teaches us that God's plan does not revolve around us. He loves us and he cares for us, but we are not the focal point of his plan—redemption through Christ is. The triune God made an eternal covenant of redemption in order to reconcile a fallen people to God through the life, death, resurrection, and ascension of Jesus Christ. Jesus Christ, our Redeemer and King, is the focal point of God's plan. All the Old Testament and the Gospels lead up to the climax in the work of Christ for our redemption.

We see a miniature view of this in the book of Ruth. Certainly God is interested in and loves Naomi, Boaz, and Ruth, but we see very clearly in the last chapter that God is weaving together a greater plan, the plan to bring his Son into the world as a baby so that he could save the people that God had chosen for himself. All Naomi and Ruth's pain, all their labor, all their waiting, all their praying, was part of a bigger picture. Their lives were not all about them. Their lives were about Christ.

We can divide the lesson into four sections:

  I. Boaz Takes the Right of Redemption (4:1–6)
 II. The Confirmation and Blessing of the Transaction (4:7–12)
III. The Marriage of Boaz and Ruth (4:13–17)
IV. The Genealogy of King David (4:18–22)

I. Boaz Takes the Right of Redemption (4:1–6)

Boaz, being the man of integrity that he is, does not waste any time settling the legal matter of redemption. At this point the reader knows that Naomi and Ruth will have a redeemer one way or another, but which one it will be is not yet clear. Evidently Boaz knew that the other redeemer would be passing by the town gate that morning. The town gate was the place where "court" was held, the place where important decisions were discussed among the town elders. The phrase that he uses to address him in the Hebrew is best likened to the idiom, "so-and-so." So instead of addressing him as a friend, he is addressing him as "Mr. So-and-So." This name serves to foreshadow that this man's actions will not be worthy for him to have his name recorded in Scripture. Obviously this man either respects Boaz or is subordinate to him, because he follows his directions immediately. Boaz truly exemplifies Proverbs 31:23: "Her husband is known in the gates when he sits among the elders of the land."

Boaz begins the legal matter with no mention of Ruth or Naomi at all. Instead he focuses on the asset of land for sale that belonged to their relative Elimelech (4:3). As we have previously studied, according to Leviticus 25:23–25, the land was not to be sold in perpetuity, for it was the Lord's. This was to remind the people that they were strangers and sojourners with the Lord. So, in all the country that they possessed, they were to allow redemption of the land. If a brother became poor and sold part of his property, then the nearest redeemer was to come and redeem what his brother had sold.

Again, this reminds us of the important theme of land that we first saw in the book of Genesis and that has run through all the Old Testament books leading up to the book of Ruth. The theme is connected with God's promise to Abraham, and we have already seen the word in 1:1 (*eretz*). Although the word is different here (*sadeh*), because it is specifically talking about a field within Bethlehem, the concept is still the same. God had promised his people land, and Elimelech's clan was in danger of losing it.

"So I thought I would tell you of it" (4:4) highlights Boaz's integrity even further. Evidently he could have sidestepped this legal transaction and bought the land without consulting with the nearer redeemer, but that would not have honored God's law. Here he makes it very clear that if the nearer redeemer does not want it, he will redeem it, reiterating the promise that he made to Ruth at the threshing floor (3:13). The first response of the nearer redeemer gives the reader pause. The direction we thought that the story was headed just took a devastating turn. Everything earlier in the story seemed to point to Boaz as the redeemer, and what reader wouldn't want Boaz instead of Mr. So-and-So!

Boaz remains calm though; it seems that he knows this man's character and how things will ultimately end. He has waited until now to reveal the fact that along with the purchase of the land comes Ruth the Moabite, the widow of the dead, in order to perpetuate the name of the dead in his inheritance. As we have already studied, levirate marriage was one of the provisions that God had made for his people in the law (Deut. 25:5–6). The nearer redeemer would be responsible to provide an heir, whom he would have to raise and who would also be a beneficiary of his inheritance. This was something Mr. So-and-So was not willing to do. Just like Orpah, who chose the faithless road and walked off the pages of Scripture, so this man chooses the road that serves self and never even gets a name in Scripture! Why was he not willing to buy the land and acquire Ruth? He was not willing because it would impair his own inheritance. Here is the striking difference between Mr. So-and-So and Boaz. Mr. So-and-So was concerned for himself and his own children for material needs, while Boaz was concerned about others and their spiritual and material needs. Because of this, Boaz now has the opportunity to redeem Ruth and Naomi; he has gone through all the proper steps as a man of integrity, and he is free to act as kinsman-redeemer.

How do you respond to opportunities that the Lord brings into your life to display his lovingkindness to others? Are you more concerned about what it will cost you? Do you evaluate ministry opportunities based on how they will fit into your schedule, or are you willing to make the sacrifice of money, time, and energy in order to be obedient to God?

II. The Confirmation and Blessing of the Transaction (4:7–12)

The narrator now gives us a historical-cultural note on the manner of attesting in Israel (4:7). Evidently it is a different, but related, custom to that described in Deuteronomy 25:7–10. Some readers may think

Mr. So-and-So is worthy of the latter treatment at this point! Ruth would have been able to go up to him, pull off his sandal, and spit in his face, saying, "So shall it be done to the man who does not build up his brother's house." Then his house would be called, "The house of him who had his sandal pulled off." But at the same time, we are grateful that Boaz is the one who will protect and care for Ruth, for he is a godly man. We are thankful that the law did not force the marriage, for that would have been a difficult marriage for Ruth. Again we see God's hand of providence on his daughter and son's lives, bringing them together, just as he brought the first man and woman together.

If you are married, spend time today thanking the Lord for bringing you and your husband together. Thank the Lord for all the wonderful attributes that your husband has. Pray for those areas of his life in which he needs to grow. Pray that you will fulfill your God-given design to be his helper. If you are single and desire to be married, spend time today in prayer for God's will to be done in your life concerning marriage. If you are single and believe you are called to remain single, spend time praying that you will glorify God as a single woman.

The exchange in 4:8–10 is much less shameful than the custom in Deuteronomy 25:7–10, as the nearer redeemer simply pulled off his sandal (the symbol of the exchange) and told Boaz to buy it for himself. Thus the elders and all the people witnessed the transaction that Boaz had bought from the hand of Naomi all that belonged to Elimelech, Mahlon, and Chilion, as well as Ruth the Moabite in order to perpetuate the name of the dead in his inheritance, so that it would not be cut off from among his brothers and from the gate of his native place. Notice that Boaz had no shame in calling Ruth "the Moabite." Neither does your heavenly Father have any shame when he redeems you from your past, your origins, and your family. Though there can be little doubt that Boaz loved and wanted Ruth at this point, the story emphasizes his obedience to God's law first and foremost.

Let us stop for a moment and reflect on what God has just accomplished through Boaz. We have spoken at length in the introduction about God's promise to Abraham of land, seed, and the blessing of all the families of the earth. We saw at the beginning of the book how Elimelech's disobedience to leave the land threatened the fulfillment of that promise. But here we are reminded that God's plan of redemption cannot be thwarted. Despite several seeming obstacles, God preserves Elimelech's land and his name through Boaz, the redeemer. And by doing so, he continues the line that will bring the ultimate and final promised seed, land, and blessing of all families on earth—Jesus Christ.

What is the response of the people? They agree to their witnessing role and speak a prayer of blessing on Boaz (4:11–12). The prayer was directed toward Ruth to be like Rachel and Leah who together built up the house of Israel. Indeed they did; the twelve sons of Israel were the heads of the twelve tribes of Israel, which advanced the historical-redemptive plan of God (Gen. 29:31–30:24; 35:16–18; 49:2–27). Leah was the mother of Judah, the very line through which Jesus Christ came. The witnesses did not have any idea how their prayer would be answered in future years in such a mighty way. Ruth would indeed help to build up the house of Israel! She was the great-grandmother of King David, the very line from which our King of Kings was descended! Boaz certainly would be renowned in Bethlehem, for it would be the very city where King David was born (1 Sam. 16:1, 18), and later the King of Kings, Jesus Christ (Matt. 2:1).

The second part of the prayer focuses on the family of Perez. First, it is significant that this is the first and only time in the book of Ruth that the word *zera* ("offspring"), the same word that is used in the Abrahamic promise, is used. Again we see how God is using the lives of Naomi, Ruth, and Boaz to accomplish his larger redemptive-historical plan. Second, Boaz's house was indeed like the house of Perez, whom Tamar bore to Judah (Gen. 38), for God had again brought a Gentile into his family in order to ultimately be a part of the means he would use for the incarnation of his Son, Jesus Christ.

It would be worth our time to stop for a moment and look more closely at the story of Judah and Tamar, and their firstborn son, Perez. The story comes as somewhat of a surprise to readers of the book of Genesis. It is placed in the middle of the Joseph narrative, seemingly interrupting it, which tells us that it is of great importance. Why?

While Joseph's position as the firstborn is assumed in the Genesis narrative, a subtle development occurs involving Judah. This centers chiefly around Genesis 38, which interrupts the Joseph story in order to focus attention on the seed of Judah. The account of Judah's relationship with Tamar concludes by describing the birth of twins during which the younger boy, Perez, "breaks out" in front of the "first-born" Zerah. The significance of this event should not be overlooked in the light of the larger story, which unfolds in the books of Genesis to Kings [of which Ruth is a part!]. Whereas the tribe of Ephraim is initially presented as the one from which Israel's leader will come, as reflected for example in the important role played by Joshua, the "first-born" line of Ephraim is rejected in the time of Samuel and replaced by the line of David, from the tribe of Judah.[1]

We suggest that [the consummation-child, Jesus Christ] might well be named Perez. For he breaks through [Perez means "to break through" or "breach"] beforehand, making a breach for himself. That is, the Covenant of Redemption all along the line of its administration, more profoundly in the New Testament but already in the Old Testament, is a coming of the Spirit, and intrusion of the power, principles, and reality of the consummation into the period of the delay. Breaking through first of all in the Old Testament period, the Intrusion finds itself in an age which is by the divine disposition of history, or, more specifically, by the divine administration of the Covenant of Redemption, and age of preparation for a later age of fulfillment and finality. Its appearing, therefore, is amid earthly forms which at once suggest, yet veil the ultimate glory.[2]

The women that we find in the line of Christ should greatly encourage us as women that struggle daily with sin in our own lives. First, Tamar deceived her father-in-law by dressing up as a prostitute so that she might have a child. Though Judah applauded her as being "more righteous" and "did not know her again," Tamar's deception was still wrong, but she too

1. T. D. Alexander, *From Paradise to the Promised Land: An Introduction to the Pentateuch* (Grand Rapids: Baker Academic, 2002), 106.
2. Meredith G. Kline, *The Structure of Biblical Authority*, 2nd ed. (Eugene, OR: Wipf & Stock, 1997), 156.

found redemption in the God of Israel. Second, Rahab was a prostitute, not just dressed like one, but the Lord redeemed her and brought her into the covenant family. Third, Ruth, though she displayed incredible character, still had the mark of a foreigner, but she was welcomed into God's family. And finally Bathsheba, seduced by David and bearing a child who was not her husband's, also found grace before the Lord. What of your past is still standing in the way of your relationship with the Lord? Scripture speaks very clearly of the fact that Jesus came to save sinners. We are not fooling God when we get all cleaned up and put on our facades. He knows that we are messy, sin-filled people in need of a Savior. That is why he sent his Son. There is a Redeemer for you and for me. He takes away our emptiness and fills us with

> every spiritual blessing in the heavenly places, even as he chose us in him before the foundation of the world, that we should be holy and blameless before him. In love he predestined us for adoption as sons through Jesus Christ, according to the purpose of his will, to the praise of his glorious grace, with which he has blessed us in the Beloved. In him we have redemption through his blood, the forgiveness of our trespasses, according to the riches of his grace, which he lavished upon us, in all wisdom and insight making known to us the mystery of his will, according to his purpose, which he set forth in Christ as a plan for the fullness of time, to unite all things in him, things in heaven and things on earth.
>
> In him we have obtained an inheritance, having been predestined according to the purpose of him who works all things according to the counsel of his will, so that we who were the first to hope in Christ might be to the praise of his glory. In him you also, when you heard the word of truth, the gospel of your salvation, and believed in him, were sealed with the promised Holy Spirit, who is the guarantee of our inheritance until we acquire possession of it, to the praise of his glory. (Eph. 1:3–14)

III. The Marriage of Boaz and Ruth (4:13–17)

"So Boaz took Ruth, and she became his wife" (4:13). Before we move past that phrase too quickly, let us meditate on it for a moment.

At the beginning of the book we learned that Ruth had been married for about ten years and then lost her husband. In her own widowhood, she assumed the utmost commitment of caring for her widowed mother-in-law. Her primary focus was providing food for Naomi, but when she realized Naomi's desire for her to find rest, she took the initiative in that as well (3:9). All throughout the book we have seen the faithful providential hand of God orchestrating events to bring his son and daughter together as one flesh. They have honored him and exemplified his character to one another and to others, and he blesses them with one another in marriage. What a faithful God we serve! They had delighted themselves in the Lord, and he had given them the desires of their heart (Ps. 37:4). They had committed their way to the Lord and trusted in him, and he had acted (Ps. 37:5). The Lord had brought forth their righteousness and their justice before the whole town (Ps. 37:6). They had waited patiently for the Lord, and the Lord had blessed them (Ps. 37:7). But it was not just for Ruth and Boaz that the Lord was concerned. He was concerned with blessing all the nations of the earth. And he used Ruth and Boaz to continue the line that would bring forth his Son, Jesus Christ, into this world to accomplish redemption through his life, death, resurrection, and ascension.

Likewise, our marriages are not just for our own blessing. If we are married, the Lord has placed us with our husbands for the purpose of his kingdom. How are we kingdom-minded in our marriages? How are we displaying God's *hesed* through our marriages to the world around us? How are we advancing the purpose of God's kingdom by way of our marriage?

We also learned in chapter 1 that Ruth had no children. Like Sarah, Rachel, Leah, and Tamar before her and Hannah, Elizabeth, and Mary after her, those whose wombs the Lord had to open, the Lord too gives Ruth conception. It is important to note here the larger historical-redemptive picture. Barrenness has been a threat to the line of Christ previously (Sarah, Rachel, and Leah), but God always takes the initiative to overcome this and secure his plan of redemption by orchestrating conception in his perfect timing. This is only the second time in the entire book that the Lord is said to take direct action. The other time is in 1:6 when the Lord had visited his people and given them food. But he has been taking action all along through his hidden hand of providence. Though we live in a day and age in which medical advancement has made many more options available for those who struggle with infertility, we must not forget that it is the Lord who works through those means. It is always the Lord who gives or withholds conception for his glory and our good.

Our days of advanced technology have not made it any easier to experience singleness, infertility, miscarriages, stillbirths, or the loss of older children. Many women long to be married and are not, or to conceive and cannot, or experience the heartache of miscarriage or stillbirth, and some are even asked to bury their own child. Though it is extremely difficult, if we know and understand that God sovereignly gives and takes away, we will be better prepared to handle these circumstances in our lives when they do occur.

Perhaps you are single today and longing for a husband, perhaps you long for a baby, or maybe you are grieving the loss of a child. Take your grief to the Lord today, and pour out your heart before him in thanksgiving and prayer, accepting his plan and timing, inviting him to be Lord over your infertility, singleness, or other circumstances, and trusting in his lovingkindness even when it may not seem like love or kindness at all.

Though Naomi has used the phrase "our redeemer" in the book (2:20), the focus up to this point has largely been on Ruth's need of rest in a redeemer. In 4:14–15 we see the culmination of the faithful Father who opened his arms for his prodigal daughter, Naomi, and gave her a redeemer, ultimately pointing to the true Redeemer, Jesus Christ. It is not Boaz, but Obed, Ruth and Boaz's firstborn son, who is her redeemer. He would be a restorer of life and a nourisher of her old age. The phrase in the Hebrew for "restorer of life" literally reads, "he who causes life to *return*." We saw this word "return" repeatedly in chapter 1. Ruth 1:21 literally says, "I went away full, but the Lord has *returned* me empty."

So we see how the women use Naomi's very words to remind her of God's faithfulness.

Jesus Christ instituted the Lord's Supper the night before he was betrayed, inaugurating the new covenant. The church continues to partake of the Lord's Supper regularly, for it is a 'means of grace. It points us to our Redeemer, who has restored our life with God and continually nourishes us. "It is a perpetual remembrance of the sacrifice of Christ in his death, the sealing all benefits thereof unto true believers, their spiritual nourishment and growth in him, their further engagement in, and to all duties which they owe unto him; and to be a bond and pledge of their communion with him and with each other, as members of his mystical body" (Westminster Confession of Faith 24.1).

The women are quick to point Naomi to the blessing that Ruth has been to her. This daughter-in-law of hers that she urged so strongly to go back to Moab in chapter 1 has faithfully loved her and has been more to her than not only the two sons that Naomi had lost, but more than seven sons, a number of fullness in Scripture. The same women who heard Naomi say that the Lord had brought her back empty in 1:21, now tell her that the Lord had not brought her back empty at all! He brought her back with fullness; he brought her back with Ruth, who has now provided a redeemer for her as well, ultimately leading to the final Redeemer in Christ Jesus.

Stop and ponder the words, "Blessed be the LORD, who has not left you this day without a redeemer" (4:14). Spend time today thanking God that he has given us his Son, Jesus Christ, to redeem us from our sin and reconcile us to him. Look up Romans 3:24; Galatians 3:13–14; Ephesians 1:7, 14; Colossians 1:14; Hebrews 9:12.

Now Naomi, who had been emptied of food, emptied of a husband, and emptied of her sons in chapter 1, has a full lap of blessing, a grandson to place near to her heart to remind her of God's loving provision and protection of her (4:16). The Lord had brought her back to fullness of faith in him by means of his lovingkindness embodied in his servants, Ruth and Boaz.

Again the women emphasize the fullness that the Lord has given Naomi, by saying that a son has been born to her (4:17). The name that the women gave him was Obed, meaning "Servant." He is both a servant of God and a servant of Naomi. He serves God's purposes in Naomi's life by being to her a restorer of life and a nourisher of her old age. He also points to the final and perfect servant who would follow later in his line, Jesus Christ, the one who would serve the Father and serve his people by bringing full reconciliation to the people of God that had been emptied in the garden of Eden. Obed also plays a key role in bringing forth Israel's king, King David, a man after God's own heart. And if you remember from 1:1, the time of the judges pointed to the need of a king, and the book of Ruth portrays how God worked through one family's life during the time of the judges to bring this about. In other words, his lovingkindness was not just demonstrated for Ruth and Naomi, but also it was shown for all of Israel, indeed, for all the world, as he orchestrated events to bring about a king and, even more importantly, the final and perfect King, Jesus Christ.

IV. The Genealogy of King David (4:18–22)

In light of the fact that we have already learned that David was part of the family line in 4:17, we may wonder why this extended genealogy is included here. What purpose does it serve to bring these other men into the closing of the book? One reason is that it gives the answer to the people and the elders' prayer in 4:11–12. Long after they prayed their prayer and that generation had passed away, God answered their prayers in a mighty way. Ruth is only a partial fulfillment of the Abrahamic promise that in Abraham "all the families of the earth shall be blessed" (Gen. 12:3); she pointed forward to the ultimate fulfillment of the Abrahamic promise in Jesus Christ.

Second, there is a very important word found here for the first time in the book, *toledot* ("generations"). This word is extremely significant in the book of Genesis. It connects the genealogies together in the book of Genesis, either introducing a chapter or signifying a new phase in the development in the book. It also focuses the reader's attention on an important individual and his children, tracing the chosen family line of Christ.[3] So here the narrator reminds us that the book of Ruth is connected to the chosen family line of Christ.

Ten generations (just as the genealogies in Genesis) are identified here, more than making up for Ruth's ten years of barrenness. Some have wondered why Perez is listed first rather than Judah. But in light of our previous study in 4:11–12, it is appropriate that Perez is listed first, especially because of the meaning of his name, "to break through," pointing to what Jesus Christ does in the incarnation. Perez points forward to the Lion of Judah, Jesus Christ. When Jacob blessed Judah, he said,

> Judah, your brothers shall praise you;
>> your hand shall be on the neck of your enemies;
>> your father's sons shall bow down before you.
> Judah is a lion's cub;
>> from the prey, my son, you have gone up.
> He stooped down; he crouched as a lion
>> and as a lioness; who dares rouse him?
> The scepter shall not depart from Judah,
>> nor the ruler's staff from between his feet,
> until tribute comes to him;
>> and to him shall be the obedience of the peoples.
> Binding his foal to the vine
>> and his donkey's colt to the choice vine,
> he has washed his garments in wine
>> and his vesture in the blood of grapes.
> His eyes are darker than wine,
>> and his teeth whiter than milk. (Gen. 49:8–12)

Perez was also the result of Judah and Tamar's promiscuous relationship. Tamar, like Ruth, was a foreign woman God included in the line to bring forth his Son into the world as a baby. We also see that Salmon fathered Boaz, which was by way of Rahab, another Gentile whom God included in his Son's line. Of course, Boaz fathered Obed by Ruth, the third and final Gentile whom Jesus' genealogy includes

---

3. Alexander, *From Paradise*, 102.

(Matt. 1:3, 5). Obed fathered Jesse, of whom Jesus Christ is said to be "the root" (Isa. 11:10), and Jesse fathered David, of whom Jesus is said to be "the Root" (Rev. 5:5). As mentioned earlier, David, the exemplar king of Israel, pointed to the final and perfect Davidic King, Jesus Christ.

The names here at the end may seem redundant or unnecessary to some, but they point out a very important principle in Scripture. Those who choose the path of life have their names preserved in the Book of Life, but those, like Orpah and Mr. So-and-So, who choose the world's path, walk off the pages of Scripture, and walk away from eternal life. Where is your name preserved today? Is it in the Book of Life? Is Jesus Christ both Lord and Savior of your life? Have you ever spoken the words, "Here I am. I will be a part of your people. You will be my God?" Your Elder Brother opened his arms wide for you so that he could lead you home to the Father. The way is open before you today to run into those arms, laying aside your will for his will, your way for his way, and your life for his life.

It is this Jesus who suffered outside the city gate in order to settle the legal matter of our need for a redeemer to reconcile us to God. Rather than being concerned about his own inheritance, he "emptied himself, by taking the form of a servant, being born in the likeness of men. And being found in human form, he humbled himself by becoming obedient to the point of death, even death on a cross" (Phil. 2:7–8). He did this in order to perpetuate the name of the dead in trespasses and sins and give us a name and an inheritance that would last forever in eternity. He has bought the church to be his bride by his own blood, redeeming her so that she is not cut off from a relationship with God. And we are to be witnesses to the nations of what Christ has done, making disciples and baptizing them in the name of the triune God and teaching them all that God has commanded through his Word. Jesus Christ is the final and perfect Kinsman-Redeemer, the final and perfect Servant, and the final and perfect Davidic King who rules the kingdom of God in righteousness and justice, and he is coming again to consummate this rule.

CONCLUSION

It is difficult to be God-focused rather than self-focused in the midst of physical pain, infertility, unwanted singleness, a difficult marriage, deep grief over the death of loved ones, financial crisis, or other difficult times. But we must remember that God is doing something much greater with our lives than we can even imagine. He is using us in a far greater way than our lifetimes will ever display. Naomi and Ruth never saw baby David; they never knew that the great king of Israel would come from their line. And they certainly never could have imagined that the greatest King and the greatest Redeemer, Jesus Christ, would be part of their genealogy.

Let us give "thanks to the Father, who has qualified [us] to share in the inheritance of the saints in light. He has delivered us from the domain of darkness and transferred us to the kingdom of his beloved Son, in whom we have redemption, the forgiveness of sins" (Col. 1:12–14).

Question Paradigm for Judges and Ruth

THIS QUESTION PARADIGM should be kept close at hand for every lesson. Each lesson's questions will follow this paradigm, but only this master page includes the explanations under each of the P's.

- **Pray.** Ask that God will open up your heart and mind as you study his Word. This is his story of redemption that he has revealed to us, and the Holy Spirit is our teacher.
- **Ponder the Passage.** Read the passage once a day from different translations for the entire week.
  - *Point.* What is the point of this passage? What is the point of the entire book? What is the point of the entire Bible?
  - *Persons.* Who are the main people involved in this passage? What characterizes them?
  - *Patterns.* What are the patterns of the text? Is there any chiastic structure, prose, or poetry?[1]
  - *Problem.* What sin or suffering is the Lord addressing in this text?
  - *Persons of the Trinity.* Where do you see God the Father, God the Son, and God the Holy Spirit in this passage?
  - *Puzzling Parts.* Are there any parts of the passage that you don't quite understand or that seem interesting to you or confusing?

1. A chiasm is "a literary device in which the second half of a composition takes up the same words, themes, or motifs as in in the first half, but in reverse order (A B B' A' pattern)." Andreas J. Köstenberger and Richard D. Patterson, *Invitation to Biblical Interpretation: Exploring the Hermeneutical Triad of History, Literature, and Theology,* Invitation to Theological Studies Series (Grand Rapids: Kregel Publications, 2011), 836.

- **Put It in Perspective.**
  - *Place in Scripture.* Where does this passage fit contextually? What is the original context? What is the redemptive-historical context—what has happened or hasn't happened in redemptive history at this point in Scripture? Where do you see the covenant(s) of God with his people? How is the gospel presented in this passage? How does the climax of redemptive history—the life, death, resurrection, and ascension of Jesus Christ connect with this passage? See especially the following passages of Scripture: _____.
  - *Passages from Other Parts of Scripture.* Look up any cross-references listed. How do these help illuminate the text? How is the main truth of this passage seen in earlier parts of Scripture? How is it seen in later parts of Scripture? Based on your observations of the text, what is the basic content of this passage? Try to summarize it in your own words, using a sentence or two. Questions will continue here that are specific to each lesson's passage.

- **Principles and Points of Application.**
- What do I learn about God in this passage? How does this reshape how I view present circumstances?
- What do I learn about God's Son, Jesus Christ? How does this impact my relationship with God and my relationship with others?
- What do I learn about God's covenant with his people? How am I to live in light of this?
- What do I learn about man's fallenness in this passage and about my need for a Savior?
- In light of where I am in redemptive history, how will I apply this information to my life today and in the future? Because of what Christ has done for me (justification), and what he is now doing in me (sanctification), how do I need to grow in knowledge (Col. 3:10), righteousness, and holiness (Eph. 4:24)? How should we apply this in our churches?
- Questions will continue here that are applicable to each lesson's passage.

Poem: Redeeming Love

Redeeming Love that will not let me go,
I've been off to Moab, wandering to and fro.
Your blessing of bread upon the land prompted my return,
But only you knew how much more I had to learn.

Beaten by the storms of life
I'd lost so many loved ones and endured so much strife.
I wanted more for my daughters-in-law,
But you and Ruth envisioned more than what I saw.

Beautiful Ruth expressed your covenant love to me;
She wouldn't return to Moab, not even at my plea.
You knew that you'd use her to point me back
To you, O God, in whom there's never any lack.
In you there is no lack of seed
For you provided through Boaz and Ruth wonderfully.

How my mind raced when Ruth had found Boaz's field;
I knew the results I wanted, but I didn't know if they'd be fulfilled.
I raced ahead of your timing and told Ruth to go to the place of seed;
I knew she'd go, for my daughter has always agreed.
I'm sorry that I went ahead of you and put her in such danger;
Thank you that Boaz did not treat her as a stranger.
Where I failed to obey,
You gave grace along the way,
And Ruth and Boaz still had hopes of a pure wedding day.

Thank you that you used Boaz to redeem our family line,
For taking Mr. So-and-So out of the way and making all things fine.
Ruth and Boaz were radiant on their special day;
They'd both pleased you, walking in the right covenant way.
And what a blessing it's been for me to hold Obed,
Close to my breast where my two sons and husband had once laid
        their heads.

Oh the pain those years brought that are now submitted to you;
Though we sometimes don't understand, you know why you do what
        you do.
And now you've redeemed those lost years in Moab when I was on
        the roam
And have brought me back to your land, given me a family and a home.

Redeeming Love, how I worship thee,
And how I'd praise you even more if I could clearly see
That through this family the Christ child would one day be born,
The Redeemer, the King, who on the cross was torn,
Broken for our sins to reconcile us to God,
Raised again to hold the scepter and the rod.
Seated at the right hand of God, he lives to intercede
For all those who are part of Abraham's chosen seed.

                             Sarah Ivill

Bibliography

Alexander, T. D. *From Paradise to the Promised Land: An Introduction to the Pentateuch*. Grand Rapids: Baker Academic, 2002.

Armerding, C. E. "Judges." In *New Dictionary of Biblical Theology*, edited by T. Desmond Alexander, Brian S. Rosner, D. A. Carson, and Graeme Goldsworthy, 171–75. Downers Grove, IL: InterVarsity Press, 2000.

Baldwin, J. G. "Ruth." In *New Bible Commentary*, 4th ed., edited by G. J. Wenham, J. A. Motyer, D. A. Carson, and R. T. France, 287–95. 1994. Reprint, Downers Grove, IL: IVP Academic, 2008.

Barrs, Jerram. *Through His Eyes: God's Perspective on Women in the Bible*. Wheaton, IL: Crossway, 2009.

Block, Daniel I. *Judges, Ruth*. Vol. 6 of *The New American Commentary*. Nashville: Broadman & Holman, 1999.

Boda, Mark J. *After God's Own Heart: The Gospel According to David*. The Gospel According to the Old Testament. Phillipsburg, NJ: P&R Publishing, 2007.

Calvin, John. *Institutes of the Christian Religion*, vol. 1. Edited by John T. McNeill. Translated by Ford Lewis Battles. Louisville: Westminster John Knox, 1960.

Davis, Dale Ralph. *Judges: Such a Great Salvation*. Fearn, Great Britain: Christian Focus, 2000.

De Graaf, S. G. *Promise and Deliverance*. Vol. 2, *The Failure of Israel's Theocracy*. St. Catharines, Canada: Paideia, 1978.

Duguid, Iain M. *Esther and Ruth*. Reformed Expository Commentary. Phillipsburg, NJ: P&R Publishing, 2005.

Ferguson, Sinclair. *Faithful God: An Exposition of the Book of Ruth*. 2005. Reprint, Bryntirion, UK: Bryntirion, 2009.

Henry, Matthew. *Matthew Henry's Commentary on the Whole Bible: Complete and Unabridged in One Volume*. Peabody, MA: Hendrickson Publishers, 1991.

Horton, Michael. *The Christian Faith: A Systematic Theology for Pilgrims on the Way*. Grand Rapids: Zondervan, 2011.

Hubbard, Robert L., Jr., *The Book of Ruth*. The New International Commentary on the Old Testament. Grand Rapids: Eerdmans, 1988.

———. "Redemption." In *New Dictionary of Biblical Theology*, edited by T. Desmond Alexander, Brian S. Rosner, D. A. Carson, and Graeme Goldsworthy, 716–20. Downers Grove, IL: InterVarsity Press, 2000.

Johnson, Dennis E. *Him We Proclaim: Preaching Christ from All the Scriptures*. Phillipsburg, NJ: P&R Publishing, 2007.

Kline, Meredith G. *The Structure of Biblical Authority*, 2nd ed. Eugene, OR: Wipf & Stock, 1997.

Köstenberger, Andreas J., and Richard D. Patterson. *Invitation to Biblical Interpretation: Exploring the Biblical Triad of History, Literature, and Theology*, Invitation to Theological Studies Series. Grand Rapids: Kregel Publications, 2011.

Longman, Tremper, III, and Raymond Dillard. *An Introduction to the Old Testament*. Grand Rapids: Zondervan, 2006.

Luther, Martin. *Werke*. Vol. 5, *Psalmenvorlesungen 1519–21 (Ps. 1–22)*. Edited by J. F. K. Knaake et al. Weimar, Germany: 1892.

Packer, J. I. "Sola Fide: The Reformed Doctrine of Justification." *Ligonier Ministries*. Accessed June 20, 2013. http://www.ligonier.org/learn/articles/sola-fide-the-reformed-doctrine-of-justification/.

Payne, J. B. "Judges." In *New Bible Dictionary*, 3rd ed., edited by I. Howard Marshall, A. R. Millard, J. I. Packer, and D. J. Wiseman, 627–31. Downers Grove, IL: IVP Academic, 1996.

Robertson, O. Palmer. *The Christ of the Covenants*. Phillipsburg, NJ: P&R Publishing, 1980.

Sanders, J. Oswald. *Spiritual Leadership*. Chicago: Moody, 1994.

Ulrich, Dean R. *From Famine to Fullness: The Gospel According to Ruth*. The Gospel According to the Old Testament. Phillipsburg, NJ: P&R Publishing, 2007.

Waltke, Bruce K. *Genesis*. Grand Rapids: Zondervan, 2001.

Webb, Barry G. "Judges." In *New Bible Commentary*, 4th ed., edited by G. J. Wenham, J. A. Motyer, D. A. Carson, and R. T. France, 261–88. 1994. Reprint, Downers Grove, IL: IVP Academic, 2008.

Younger, K. Lawson, Jr. *Judges/Ruth*. The NIV Application Commentary. Grand Rapids: Zondervan, 2002.

Sarah Ivill (BA, University of Georgia; ThM, Dallas Theological Seminary) has been leading, teaching, or writing women's Bible studies since she was eighteen. She has served at the Howard G. Hendricks Center for Christian Leadership, in Bible Study Fellowship, and as Director of Women's Ministry in the church, among other leadership positions. Sarah is the author of *Hebrews: His Hope, An Anchor for Our Souls* and *Revelation: Let the One Who Is Thirsty Come.* Presently a stay-at-home mom, she continues writing and teaching Reformed Bible studies for women. A member of Christ Covenant Church (PCA), Sarah lives with her husband and children in a suburb of Charlotte, North Carolina.